For Eva, Iris and Sarah,
whose friendship was more therapeutic
than any professional counselling.

For 'Harriet', who made it all possible,
and often impossible.

CONSUMING
PSYCHOTHERAPY

Ann France

FA^B

*'an association in which the free development of each
is the condition of the free development of all'*

Free Association Books / London / 1988

First published in Great Britain 1988 by
Free Association Books
26 Freegrove Road
London N7 9RQ

British Library Cataloguing in Publication Data

France, Ann
Consuming psychotherapy.
1. Psychotherapy
I. Title
616.89′14   RC480

ISBN 1–85343–004–8
ISBN 1–85343–005–6 Pbk

Typeset by Columns of Reading

Printed and bound in Great Britain by
Short Run Press, Exeter

CONTENTS

ACKNOWLEDGEMENTS

Thanks are due to my three therapists, who were not only kind and brave enough to let me publish the material but also read the manuscript and offered helpful comments. Their names, and those of others, have been changed where it seemed appropriate. Other therapists or friends in therapy likewise helped with both criticism and encouragement, particularly Clara, Eva, Linda, Jane and Sarah. Dr Peter Lomas kindly read the first two drafts of the book and gave most useful advice and encouragement. Since my views are similar to his, and I quote him frequently, I would like to stress that he has not been one of my therapists and that I only read his books after I had written the first draft of the present work.

Ann Scott ironed out the inconsistencies in the manuscript, gave much useful advice and was a joy to work with. I would also like to thank Bob Young for having the courage to publish a work that other publishers might have thought too controversial or maverick, and for his challenging comments that made me rethink not only the text but also the therapies. The conclusions I reached are not necessarily shared by any of the editorial staff of Free Association Books.

Maybe I'm even grateful to my parents for making me sufficiently neurotic to need psychotherapy, but sufficiently tough to withstand it.

I would like to thank the following for permission to quote from published material:

Associated Book Publishers (U.K.) Ltd, for *The Collected Works of C.G. Jung*, edited by H. Read, M. Fordham, G. Adler and W. McGuire, *The Client Speaks*, by J.E. Mayer and N. Timms, and *The Second Sin*, by T. Szasz; William Heinemann Medical Books Ltd, for *The Art of Psychotherapy*, by A. Storr; the author's estate and The Hogarth Press for *Transference and Counter-Transference*, by H. Racker; Pergamon Books Ltd, for D. Brenner's *The Effective Psychotherapist*, 1982, and *Structuring the Therapeutic Process*, by M. Cox, 1978; and Tavistock Publications for *On Learning from the Patient*, by P. Casement, and *Forms of Feeling: The Heart of Psychotherapy*, by R.F. Hobson.

I would also like to thank the following authors for permission to quote from their published work:
P. Halmos for *The Faith of the Counsellors*, Constable, 1965; N. Herman for *My Kleinian Home*, Quartet, 1985; P. Lomas for *True and False Experience*, Allen Lane, 1973, and *The Case for a Personal Psychotherapy*, Oxford University Press, 1981; S. Oldfield for *The Counselling Relationship*, Routledge & Kegan Paul, 1983; C. Rycroft for his edited essays *Psychoanalysis Observed*, Constable and Pelican, 1966, and *Psychoanalysis and Beyond*, Chatto & Windus and Hogarth, 1985; S. Schneiderman for *Lacan: The Death of an Intellectual Hero*, Harvard University Press, 1983; and D.J. Smail for *Psychotherapy: A Personal Approach*, Dent, 1978, and *Taking Care: An Alternative to Therapy*, Dent, 1987.

INTRODUCTION

The forces that have moulded contemporary psychiatry and psychotherapy have, I believe, made it very difficult for two people to meet each other to discuss, in a natural and ordinary way, the problems of one of them.
Lomas, *True and False Experience*, p. 19

The experience of this difficulty and the urge to overcome it formed the initial impetus for this book. My reflections centre round a process and a relationship broadly termed psychotherapy but which not infrequently seems to achieve its therapeutic aims more in spite of its conceptual framework than because of it. The discussion does not feel natural a good deal of the time. It creates an artificial situation and relationship, which could lead to artificial solutions of problems and the artificial creation of others. It need not do so, or feel this way, and the aim here is to examine various ways in which this might be achieved.

The basic intention of the present book is, then, to examine the experience of the one-to-one relationship in psychotherapy critically, from the functional and affective angle, paying particular attention to the ways in which certain features of the transaction appear beneficial or frustrating to the consumer, and to see to what extent these are inherent in the exercise and to what extent the result of theories that could fruitfully be modified.

While I hope it may clarify some doubts for people in, or contemplating, therapy and dispel some of the ignorance and fear that can be the source of considerable distress at the beginning of the venture, and while I hope also that it might encourage therapists, analysts and counsellors to examine afresh the validity of their concepts and the flexibility of their practices, there is no wish to write a manual for either set of people. This book is the result of my attempt to structure some of the questions, misgivings and also convictions which years of reading and therapy have instigated, and possibly to stimulate future thought along these lines in anyone interested.

I am not trying either to advocate therapy or to attack it. Nor am I writing from any particular theoretical bias, although temperament and conviction draw me towards certain practices and attitudes more than others, and this will become apparent. While some critical observations may come across more forcibly than the more enthusiastic remarks, the mere fact of writing the book suggests an attitude far from hostile or sceptical, in spite of certain doubts about the efficacy of psychotherapy. Some of these doubts concern what I understand to be the common theory and practice of psychotherapy rather than my own experiences, which suggest that it can be effective without following traditional guidelines. Other, more serious doubts concern ways in which it can simply be untherapeutic. The experience in the second of my three therapies made me aware of the dangers as well as the benefits, and I wish to share both of these with other people in therapy as well as with therapists.

It is significant that the difficulties are faced, in different ways, by both types of people in question, but the vast mass of literature on the subject presents the problem only from the point of view of the analyst (therapist, counsellor). Most of the books by professionals present the underlying theory, using their experience to illustrate this theory, perhaps even inspire it, but they tell us little of what it feels like to be on the receiving end. Individuals appear as case histories, designed to support certain views about how people behave in certain conditions and will react to specific forms of treatment. However, there is rarely any attempt to complete our knowledge by telling us how the experience of therapy felt to the person undergoing it. Exceptions to this are Lomas (*The Case for a Personal Psychotherapy*, 1981), Casement (*On Learning from the Patient*, 1985) and Hobson (*Forms of Feeling:*

The Heart of Psychotherapy, 1985). The authors are, however, analysts and they are not writing in collaboration with their patients.

As Dr Murray Cox says: 'Books on psychotherapy tend to describe patients as either experimental objects, to be worked "on" and studied, or to describe them in experiential, almost religious terms, so that clinical grasp is elusive' (1978, p. 57). And he mentions the 'disturbing fact that social work researchers as well as psychiatrists and psychologists have rarely explored the treatment situation from the standpoint of the client' (p. 216).

We know, then, very little of what sort of transaction really takes place, from the subject's point of view. A strange omission, surely, in such a very personal exchange. Carl Rogers declares:

The centrality of the client's perception of the interviews has forced itself upon our recognition. It is the way it seems to the client which determines whether resolution of conflict, reorganization, growth, integration – all the elements which comprise therapy – will occur. Our knowledge of therapy would be far advanced if we knew the answers to these two questions: What does it mean that the client experiences a relationship as therapeutic? and, How may we facilitate the experiencing of a relationship as therapeutic? We do not have the answers to these questions, but we have at least learned to ask them.

The way in which the client perceives or experiences the interviews is a field of enquiry which is new and in which the data are very limited. There has been no research as yet completed in this area and relatively little consideration has been given to it. It is an area which appears to have great future significance, however. (1951, p. 65)

Thirty years later our information on the subject is still meagre.[1] Some research has been done, particularly in the USA, and often instigated by Carl Rogers, which tends to prove his hypothesis that his 'client-centred therapy' is far more effective than any other, as we learn in his book of this name (which devotes an informative chapter to the question of the client's experience of therapy) and in his later works, particularly *On Becoming a Person: A Therapist's View of Psychotherapy* (1961). One notes the viewpoint. But, aware as he is of the real problem, that of what it **feels** like, Rogers tends, like other researchers, to **quantify**: to assess what is an essentially qualitative experience in terms of surveys, questionnaires, batteries of tests, etc., designed to **measure** the amount of improvement in clients' feelings and attitudes, and to present this highly nebulous change in terms of percentages and points on a sliding scale. This tells you as much of what a person feels like as the yes/no/maybe answers to the Minnesota Multiphasic Personality Inventory (a self-rating questionnaire used to diagnose psychiatric disorders and personality problems).

The problem is emphasized by Mayer and Timms:

Researchers have tended to identify research exclusively with the techniques required to carry it out, especially those needed for rigorous quantitative studies. Thus, the research literature is replete with discussions of experimental design, measurement criteria of outlook, the reliability of judgements, the use of statistics and so forth . . . researchers are anxious to appear 'scientific' [and this] has drawn attention away from the study of clients. (1970, pp. 16–17)

These same authors point to the lack of evidence about the effectiveness of counselling methods in both social work and psychotherapy and the need to gather this so that services which are really needed can be provided. Otherwise clients may be required to adjust to a system that does not really meet their needs.

If . . . social work resources [are to be deployed effectively] people will need to know at least something about the responses and reactions of those they are trying to help. Information of this type . . . has not been collected . . . clients are rarely asked to appraise the effectiveness of the services received. When appraisals are made, it has consistently been the social worker, not the client, who has made the appropriate series of judgements. Judgements of the practitioner and those of the client [do not always] coincide . . . research in psychotherapy . . . reveals similar patterns. (1970, pp. 2–3)

This omission has to some extent been rectified, by Rogers' works and by Mayer and Timms, *The Client Speaks* (1970), a survey of client response to work in a social agency, quoted above. There is also a survey by Strupp, Fox and Lessler, *Patients View Their Psychotherapy* (1969). None of these are or claim to be personal accounts. This dimension is to some extent added by the more subjective evidence and arguments which inspire Michael Barnett's *People Not Psychiatry* (1973), written from the perspective of anti-psychiatry, as is *The Radical Therapist* (1974), which challenges current practice and includes some personal testimonies to animate the theory. Dominique Frischer's survey *Les Analysés parlent* (1977) presents an interesting discussion of how people viewed their analysis; they evaluate its gains and drawbacks and the effect it had on their lives. Her respondents talked fairly frankly about their feelings, but none gave a coherent account of the exchanges or sessions seen as a developing picture. There are many opinions but inevitably no consistent viewpoint. A similar comment could be made about Lindsay Knight's *Talking to a Stranger: A Consumer's Guide to Therapy* (1986). This provides a very useful introduction to therapy and guide to the therapies available. It gives some idea of people's motives for seeking help and of how they viewed the experience but, as befits a survey, is in the nature of brief statements connected only by the author's comments.

The only book in English that I know of which makes a systematic attempt to view the process from the receiving end is Susan Oldfield's valuable and interesting survey (1983) of the counselling work done in the Isis Centre[2] in Oxford. This too is a survey, compiled from responses to a questionnaire by about 200 people who had attended the centre. As such it presents a wide spectrum of views, from people of different backgrounds, ages and temperaments, but again no consistent viewpoint. Moreover, although some people were seen over a long period and the nature of help provided often seems to have resembled psychotherapy, the counsellors were not usually trained therapists and the context is not entirely comparable in all aspects with that of analytic psychotherapy, although the findings are relevant to all forms of counselling or therapeutic relationships. The questions asked by this study are, however, very similar to those I wish to pose and which, guided by much the same motives, I shall attempt to explore. Oldfield points out:

Among research studies designed to consider the process and outcome of counselling and therapy of various kinds, there are remarkably few instances of researchers directly asking the consumer about his experience. Therapists of the analytic school have tended to consider that patients' reports would be too partial and distorted to be very valuable, and those working within behavioural systems have been impatient for quantifiable findings. Research effort has, therefore, been heavily weighted towards factors which may be clear to study, but which may also be of doubtful relevance, since they are almost exclusively drawn from the preconceptions of the researcher rather than from the experience of the client. The undirected responses of people to open-ended questions about their experience promise to give rich but possibly unmanageable material.

Nevertheless, it is likely that here lie the most fruitful starting points for understanding the complex process of therapy. (1983, p. 23)

My intention is to examine issues similar to those aired in this survey, but to supplement them by a more personal discussion of the problems encountered, seen against the background of a developing relationship. Inevitably this book lacks the wide reference of surveys like Oldfield's or Frischer's, although the more continuous viewpoint it provides may compensate. I hope too that the disadvantages of basing arguments on a restricted experience (which can be supplemented by further reading) will be outweighed by the use of this experience to illustrate theory and give a personal note to the convictions. This book also lacks the broad foundation of works by professionals who are basing their views on many years' experience and a sounder theoretical knowledge of the subject than mine. Theoretical knowledge is not, however, what is at stake; and if I have misunderstood what it is all about, or what certain aspects of the exercise are designed to achieve, the error itself could be instructive.

My intention is to give a personal view, with all the partiality that that implies, because only by saying how the application of the theory works in practice can questions about its justification have any relevance. For this reason issues are discussed first for their general implications; these are then illustrated from particular experience where relevant. While conscious of the apparent contradiction implicit in adopting an objective approach, when the intention is to convey what it feels like to be in therapy (as opposed to what the professionals say happens or should happen), this is at times necessitated by my main wish, which is to look at the underlying assumptions governing psychotherapy. I am concerned with theory only in so far as it affects people; but I am not concerned solely with the idiosyncratic experience of one individual. I choose to focus, therefore, less on the specific and possibly atypical details of the experience, but rather on what seem to me to be typical problems related to it. The attempt throughout has been to consider both problems I have personally encountered and those that I am aware of as constituting stumbling blocks to other people, and to use my own experience selectively.

My approach has, however, been modified over the successive drafts of this manuscript, and I have moved from an attempt at distanced objectivity to a more personal account of my own therapies. When I embarked on writing I tried to look at the techniques and concepts of psychotherapy as dispassionately as possible. My aim was to help other people in therapy understand them, judge whether they were likely to be helpful and claim their own rights as consumers. It was also to make psychotherapists more critical of their own practices. It therefore seemed important to generalize as much as possible and to bring myself in sparingly. My academic training dictated that I should cite my sources scrupulously, backed up by copious quotation, refrain from using the pronoun 'I', and hide my identity behind well-authenticated sources. However, it gradually became clear that I had left myself out of my own therapy. This seemed a rather crucial omission even to me.

I came to realize that there was usually something in my own experience that had triggered off my responses to these issues. Moreover, although I have spent my entire professional life trying to be less personal and more objective, this is perhaps a trend that it would be therapeutic to reverse. Psychotherapy was obviously an emotional experience for me. My intellect was involved too, but in writing about the experience I had been presenting a rationalization of my emotional responses. I then revised the manuscript, trying more often to present the rationalization as part of my emotional reaction, and to sacrifice some of my arsenal of quotations. The gradual shift in style, moving towards a more subjective approach, is, then, deliberate. It is intended to reflect the progress of my therapy and its influence on my attitude.

It had felt very painful and difficult putting down some experiences and feelings on paper at all. Some of them I had never admitted to anyone; some I had talked about with friends but kept from my therapist. Sheltering behind generalizations had helped me find words for the private trauma; being forced to own them as mine seemed impossible. Maybe doing this was the real therapy which psychopractice did not achieve – or which it enabled me to achieve?

My main aim, however, is still to stimulate discussion about issues, rather than to exorcize private nightmares or descend into the purely anecdotal or confessional. It therefore seemed desirable to retain the main lines of the initial, more objective approach, while at the same time drawing more freely on personal experience.

This resolve was strengthened by the fact that there are already many autobiographical works of a fictionalized nature. They are often moving or instructive, but they dwell more on the feelings inspired by the analyst or the institution than on the therapy, as is the case with Sylvia Plath's *The Bell Jar*, Anaïs Nin's *Journals* or Sarah Ferguson's *A Guard Within*. The experience of psychosis, rather than that of milder and commoner neuroses, is the core of Hannah Green's *I Never Promised You a Rose Garden*, David Reed's *Anna* and *Mary Barnes:Two Accounts of a Journey into Madness* by Mary Barnes and Joseph Berke. None of these books provide a critical scrutiny of the therapy itself. Closer to this, yet still primarily novels, are Marie Cardinal's *Les Mots pour le dire* ('The words to say it') and François Weyergans's hilarious and fantastical novel *Le Pitre* ('The clown'), based on his analysis with Lacan. There are also Serge Doubrovsky's novels *Fils* (meaning both 'threads' and 'sons') and *Un Amour de soi* ('Self-love'), but these are literature inspired by the analytic discourse, rather than in any way an account of the experience.[3] Similarly, Jacqueline Rousseau-Dujardin presents the psychiatrist's own reflections in a poetic text, a sort of stream of consciousness, with the double-edged title *Couché par écrit* ('Couched in writing'). Judith Rossner's novel *August* depicts an analysis, but the characters and situation are fictional so it cannot be used as a basis for serious discussion of the analytic process.

Most accounts of a therapy, like Marion Milner's *The Hands of the Living God*, Virginia Axline's *Dibs: In Search of Self*, Françoise Dolto's *Le Cas Dominique*, Sèchehaye's *Journal d'une schizophrène*, Flora Schreiber's *Sybil* and Schatzmann's *The Story of Ruth*, are written by the psychiatrist, not the patient, even when they purport to narrate it from the patient's point of view. Aldo Carentuto's *The Spiral Way: A Woman's Healing Journey* is a Jungian analyst's account of a middle-aged woman's venture into the unconscious, through her dreams and his analysis. There is one book written in collaboration, based on John Cleese's experience in group therapy with his co-author Robin Skynner, under the self-explanatory title *Families and How to Survive Them* (1983). This book presents theory in a readable and entertaining fashion, as a question and answer book for lay people backed up by personal experience, but it is not intended to be an account of a therapy.

The nearest to this so far is Nini Herman's *My Kleinian Home* (1985), which presents a tantalizing glimpse of three therapies (Jungian, Freudian and Kleinian) but stops just short of saying what each therapy was really like, and just how the Kleinian therapist proved so much more helpful. (Her frank account of some of the sessions makes it sound unmitigated hell.) As autobiography with a psychiatric interest the book is, however, fascinating. Another autobiography which gives considerable insight into the analytic process is Ronald Fraser's *In Search of a Past: The Manor House at Amnersfield, 1933–45* (1984). This shows both how psychoanalysis feels and how it functions. The main aim of the book is, however, to recover the author's past and not to discuss psychoanalysis, which provides the framework rather than the substance of the narrative.

A much more rigorous examination of the psychiatric process is provided by Stuart Schneiderman's *Lacan: The Death of an Intellectual Hero* (1983). This presents an informed and readable discussion of Lacan's practice but remains impersonal, saying little of how it felt to be analysed by him. The book is intended less for analysands than for psychiatrists (it is written by one), although bound to be of interest to anyone contemplating or undergoing a Lacanian analysis. One book in which the personal account of trauma provides insights into the feelings undergone and information about various treatments attempted, written from the informed but sceptical standpoint of a psychologist, Stuart Sutherland's *Breakdown* (1976), dismisses psychotherapy with little discussion, although the account of the author's negative encounter in this domain is illuminating.

There is, then, a substantial literature inspired by psycho-analysis. However, the first person accounts mainly record states of mind, or stages in a purely personal relationship, usually in highly lyrical (or vituperative) terms. They are autobiography or biographical fiction. They do not examine the obstacles encountered in the attempt to communicate and solve problems, **from the patient's point of view**. Even in those books where this mutual problem solving **is** considered to be a crucial issue, books where it is acknowledged that the relationship is central to the process and that there is, or should be, a warm personal contact between the two people, the narrative is mainly in the third person. An omniscient, authorial voice relates to us what the patient thinks or feels, and the snatches of dialogue, dream sequences or letters, are structured by the analyst's overview, often with the intention of validating the theoretical stance, or demonstrating the skill of the analyst.

My aim is to examine the tenets and practice of psycho-therapy in the light of experience, from the consumer's end, in order to evaluate what could be helpful and what was less so. The starting point of this enquiry is almost identical to that outlined by Dr Peter Lomas in his book *The Case for a Personal Psychotherapy*, but seen from the receiving rather than the practising end. He states in his introduction that his aim is

to consider what might be the most useful circumstances in which two people can meet in order that one may help the other (and to suggest that the essence of what we call psychotherapy lies in the circumstances of this meeting and the attitudes of the partners rather than in any theory of psychopathology). (1981, p. 2)

I was all the more interested to encounter these views, expressed by a practising psychotherapist, in that they echoed exactly my own hesitations over the years spent thinking about the subject. They crystallized for me, after the first draft of this book had already been written, my own less structured thoughts. For that reason, I shall be quoting from Dr Lomas with some frequency. His views do not necessarily lend credence to mine, since many of them are not widely held in the orthodox Freudian analytic circles where he received his training; perhaps for this very reason I think they should be emphasized. I should, however, like to make it clear that he has never been my therapist, although he did supervise two of my therapists; those referred to as Harriet and Simon. Dr Lomas agreed, on reading an early draft of this manuscript, that I had reached my views quite independently of him. Similar attitudes also inform Casement (1985) and Hobson (1985), both published after I had completed the second draft of my own work, and again written from the analyst's point of view.

Because this book is not a survey, drawing on a wide variety of experiences, many forms of therapy do not come within its scope. There is no attempt to discuss group or behaviour therapy, child therapy, or treatment in the psychiatric ward of a hospital or penal institution; nor is there any discussion of the more way-out 'alternative' therapies which became popular particularly in the United States during the sixties, such as Gestalt, Primal Scream, Bio-energetics, T-groups, etc. For a useful and balanced evaluation of these, see Ernst and Goodison (1981).

The discussion here centres on a one-to-one relationship, based mainly on verbal exchanges, taking place either in private practice or in a hospital out-patients' clinic. I use the term psychotherapy and discuss a practice which is more flexible than orthodox analysis because this corresponds to my own experience. I have never been in full analysis or an in-patient in a psychiatric hospital. After an initial period of counselling at the student counselling service, I was referred to the local psychiatric out-patients' clinic, where I had a few interviews and underwent a battery of tests before being referred to a private psychotherapist. I saw her once a week for three and a half years, and subsequently saw another therapist twice a week for four and a half years. During the last year of this therapy I concurrently saw a third therapist once a week. In each case we sat facing each other unless I chose to lie on the couch which was there.

The term psychotherapy will also be used because it is the most all-embracing, covering something very close to an in-depth analysis on the one hand, and a counselling relationship on the other, where the stress is more on the here-and-now problems of the client and the provision of a certain amount of guidance. The dividing line between the various sorts of analytical therapy and counselling is often very hazy in practice, so a certain amount of flexibility in the terms used would seem to be justified. Much counselling verges on the analytical, and is receptive rather than interpretative. Some therapists are aloof and silent, like the classical analyst, whilst others take a much more active part in the proceedings, do enter into discussions or give advice, while remaining basically analytical in their approach. Schneiderman states the difference, as he sees it, very clearly, but I am not sure that in practice psychotherapy is so problem-oriented, nor always so close to counselling, though my feeling is that this could be beneficial to many.

Psychotherapy concerns the problems of living. The therapist directs his gaze at a specific problem and considers his therapy successful if that problem is eliminated . . . the difference [between psychotherapy and analysis] would appear to be that psychotherapy focuses on specific problems and that the therapist is not a silent enigmatic figure, but a living human being, at times almost a friend who will help patients through the difficult moments of their lives, arranging with them their social and work relations . . . psycho-

therapy is a practice which is oriented towards the consumer. (Schneiderman, 1983, p. 107)

The question of terminology also comes to the forefront regarding what we should call the person referred to in traditional literature as the 'patient', and as the 'client' by those pursuing a non-directive (Rogerian) approach, modelled more on social work or counselling than analysis and often based on a more radical stance. 'Client' is also used by the Women's Therapy Centre in London, which is in part psychodynamic in approach.

Neither term seems to me satisfactory. The word 'patient' refers us immediately to the medical model which I find unhelpful and likely to perpetuate the authoritarian and hierarchical approach inherent in the medical profession and the training it inflicts on psychiatrists. It implies that the problems of living, or emotional disturbances, relate to physiology or pathology, and that the person suffering from them is 'sick' (of a different order from the rest of the population, in particular, the 'physician'). It ignores the sociological or ontological factors in the disturbance, recognized by many psychotherapists and mentioned earlier by Jung.

About one third of my cases are not suffering from any clinically definable neurosis but from the senselessness and aimlessness of their lives . . . most of my patients are socially well-adapted individuals, often of outstanding ability, to whom normalization means nothing. (1929, p. 41)

This phenomenon is possibly on the increase as psychotherapy gains wider acceptance and personal growth is regarded as a generally desirable goal. The inadvisability of using the word 'patient' is also stated clearly by Brenner.

It is an understatement to say that this term fails to describe those involved in an effective, helping relationship. If you use the word 'patient', you should examine your motivation for doing so. For . . . encouragement is a necessary ingredient in effective therapy, and few will find it encouraging when you imply that they are sick.

. . . What you call a person who seeks your professional help will influence that person's self-perception. (1982, p. 35)

The use of the word 'patient' is not then acceptable, because it stresses the notion of illness and inadequacy, as well as underlining the inequality of the relationship. However, 'client' does not appeal to me either. It is true that it has the advantage of referring to a context in which one person consults another (not necessarily their social or professional superior) about specific problems, in the hope of getting specialist help or advice. There is a slight problem already, in that one does not usually get advice from a therapist, nor can you buy their skills to solve your problems for you, as with a solicitor, an architect or an accountant. The main drawback is that the roles of client and consultant inevitably stress the financial side of the transaction, to the detriment of the helping side. It might be over-idealistic to suppose that the medical profession is motivated by altruism more than hope of financial gain, but there is at least the possibility that both motives were present in the choice of career, and in the subsequent exercise of it.

Neither word seems, then, quite appropriate to the sort of relationship which appears to me optimal, although I will use both at times, when convenient. 'Seeker for truth/growth' would better imply my meaning, but it is too cumbersome. It also minimizes the sense of distress, even illness, which some people entering therapy may feel. The term 'analysand' is often used, but strictly speaking designates someone in analysis, rather than the more flexibly structured sort of therapy which is the subject here.

I am tempted by *therapsid* which, according to *Webster's Dictionary*, comes from the Greek *theraps*, appropriately meaning 'attendant' and is 'Any of an order (*therapsida*) of Permian and Triassic reptiles that walked upright rather than crawled and are held to be ancestral to mammals.' The word and the action seem apt, but might, alas, lead to confusion and risk being as obscurantist as the jargon I wish to avoid.

'The person-in-therapy', clumsy as it is, expresses most exactly what I want to convey, without overtones, and so it will often be used in preference to other, more loaded terms. There is unfortunately no such word as 'counsellee', to match counsellor (is this perhaps indicative of the lack of attention this aspect of the transaction has received?), but both 'consulter' and 'consultee' do exist. While consulting is only a small part of the activity, the sort of relationship implied is appropriate. So I propose to use 'consulter' instead of patient or client, where the meaning seems to warrant it, and a circumlocution would be cumbersome. It seems preferable to 'consultee', since it has more active and dynamic connotations (by analogy with seeker, or employer:employee).

The mere fact that a non-professional, a communicant rather than celebrant of the sacraments, should presume to give a long, cool look at the sacred cows of psychotherapy is bound to arouse cries of 'resistance' and 'defensive intellectualization'. There is doubtless some foundation for this. However, there would also be an element of resistance and heavily guarded defences in the refusal to take the views expressed seriously for this reason.

Significantly, this hypothetical response from the professionals (alluded to, moreover, by Lomas [1973, p. 141] and Mayer and Timms [1970, p. 15]) is indeed one which therapists, at least of the more traditional variety, tend to mete out to patients who question any of the conventions governing the therapeutic procedure. 'Of course you don't like it,' they agree blandly (briskly/apologetically/insouciantly), 'most people don't.' The implication being: 'But that is how it is, and how it is going to be. Who-do-you-think-you-are-to-query-it? The Groan-Ups (sic) Have Decided.' I find support for this view in Lomas:

Psychiatry has always undervalued the capacities of the patient,
has tended to regard his views as at worst, meaningless, or at best,
the unbalanced and exaggerated preoccupations of an over sensitive
soul – in any event, the views of an unreliable witness. In part . . .
the fact that the psychoanalyst is preoccupied with the patient's
distorted, as opposed to his valid, perceptions, leads him to take
such a view, but one suspects that a question of status is involved:
that the therapist is unconsciously betrayed into an assumption of
superiority of judgement, and the patient's capacity for accurate
perception is correspondingly marked down. If this prejudice were
to be overcome, the evidence gained from patients . . . might be
taken more seriously. (1967, p. 12)

Strange though it may seem, all (or almost all) the practitioners
of the often ungentle art of psychotherapy must themselves
have undergone at least a training analysis and probably a
personal therapy too; yet one would rarely guess this from their
books, or even the practice of many. In the same way that all
parents must have been children once, yet often seem to have
forgotten how it felt to be a child, psychiatrists frequently
suggest, by their attitude to patients, that the latter belong to a
different species (or perchance, that they know they do not,
and are anxious to conceal this knowledge). This was not,
however, the attitude of my therapists, and it is the experience
we shared or created together which strengthened my existing
views.

This book **has** to be written, then, by a non-professional,
with the bias and lack of wide experience that is implied, and at
the risk of seeming to encroach on other people's territory. It is
precisely with the bewilderment of the outsider, aware that
there is a gap between reason and custom, between ideal and
perception, that I approach the matter. My aim is to provide,
as coolly as someone involved in the process can (and bearing
in mind that a certain amount of passion may be necessary and
even desirable at times), a viewpoint which seems to me
lacking in the serious literature on the subject; and to

emphasize by doing so, as well as by the opinions expressed, that psychotherapy is not only a question of technique and theory. It is also, indeed principally, an encounter between two people, in which one of them at least risks a great deal, exposes his or her most vulnerable emotions, in the hope of attaining greater growth and integrity. Unlike the professionals, I have no vested interest in claiming that the system works, or is justifiable; only the strong motivation of hoping that it does work, and wondering whether its more questionable practices can be adjusted in some way, so that more freedom may be available to those who seek to grow.

Part I

BEGINNING PSYCHOTHERAPY

1   EXPECTATIONS

Psychotherapy, as I define it, is the art of alleviating
personal difficulties through the agency of words and a
personal, professional relationship.
Storr, *The Art of Psychotherapy*, p. vii

What do people expect from this relationship, and why do they enter it? What are the chances of improvement? Does it only heal, or can it also be harmful? The latter question I am still asking myself, after eight years of psychotherapy; the first is easier to answer.

Some people may not have expectations. They come because they have been referred by their general practitioners (GPs), persuaded by their friends, employers, or educators; others come of their own volition. All are, presumably, experiencing some difficulties in their lives, in adjusting to people or circumstances. Most feel that they are not adequately fulfilling their potential. Some may be acutely distressed or undergoing a form of crisis. Psychotherapy is not only sought by the sick or seriously disturbed but by those who want to function better, to feel more comfortable in themselves and with others.

I initially started psychotherapy because I felt that problems had got out of perspective; that the degree of distress they caused in me probably had less to do with their objective magnitude than with something inside me which found them intolerable. I wanted to understand my reactions and behaviour better, and felt that these were to some extent a repetitive pattern, so that understanding the mechanism might bring about change. This reasonable and conscious aim was largely met. At a less conscious level I also hoped for a magical metamorphosis that would turn me into a sane, invariably cheerful being, who would not let things or people depress her ever again, would trust others and even like herself. None of this came about, though there was a marked improvement in this direction for about six years after the first therapy – no mean achievement; although it is difficult to say with certainty how much was due to the therapy.

The question of whether most people would improve spontaneously, without psychotherapy, or with drugs or other treatment, has been the subject of much controversy. The attacks by Eysenck in the fifties and Gellner in the eighties on psychotherapy have been countered by the more positive evaluations of Rogers, Rapaport, the study of Strupp, Fox and Lessler (1969) and Nini Herman's *Why Psychotherapy?* (1987), which puts the case very convincingly for this sort of treatment, as opposed to the use of drugs or electroconvulsive therapy. Janet Malcolm (1980) gives a concise but balanced view of the uncertainties which hover around the question of how and whether people improve.

I am less concerned here with whether anyone should enter psychotherapy in the first place than with the pitfalls and benefits of the experience, once it is under way. Obviously, the questions are interrelated and a negative response to the experience might again raise the question of whether or not it should have been undertaken. This book sets out to explore just that. For the moment, however, I am addressing myself to the question of what I and other people expect from psychotherapy, when about to embark on it. A useful book for those who have not yet reached this stage is Karen Horney's *Are You Considering Psychoanalysis?* (1946). Although it is a bit out of date and distinctly over-optimistic, it does present detailed and sensitive discussions of most of the crucial questions. A more contemporary guide, although a more summary one, in which the issues are not argued through so thoroughly, is Sheila Ernst and Lucy Goodison's *In Our Own Hands* (1981). A comprehensive introductory book is Lindsay Knight's *Talking to a Stranger: A Consumer's Guide to Therapy*

(1986). This gives useful advice about people's motives for entering therapy, and how realistic it is to expect these desires to be met. It sells psychotherapy hard, but does have the advantage for British readers that, unlike Horney's book, it takes the climate of opinion and availability of treatment in Britain into account.

Expectations of the kind that I harboured would seem to be fairly typical. The section entitled 'Clients' hopes and expectations' in Susan Oldfield's survey (1983, pp. 46 ff.), borne out by Lindsay Knight's book, revealed that people hoped for change or achievement in four main areas. Firstly, in feelings: through relief from distressing emotional states and increase in self-esteem and confidence. Secondly, through gaining greater understanding, both of self and of the problems to be dealt with. Thirdly, through regaining an ability to cope with life and becoming able to work effectively again. And fourthly, through an improvement in relationships.

Clients ranged from those who were driven by despair to those who had more positive expectations. The desire for improved relationships was sometimes general and sometimes specific. Often the precipitating crisis was due to the failure of a particular relationship, but this was felt to be part of a repetitive pattern, or vicious circle.

Some people may come to therapy at a fairly early stage in their problems. They may be in a state of chronic rather than acute discomfort, and want rather to improve the quality of their life, to explore problems or to break out of a vicious circle by reformulating them. As Anthony Storr puts it:

In psychotherapy, many of the things which the patient discovers about himself are things which he may say that he had known all along but never clearly recognized. Such insights, especially when unflattering, may have occurred to him before, but in so fleeting a fashion that they have not been fully registered. Putting things into words . . . clarifies both what one knows and what one does not know. (1979, p. 24)

The first time round I wasn't sure how much psychotherapy would help, because I felt I knew a good many of the answers; although I realized that this knowledge hadn't made it easier to change, so maybe the answers were not correct or complete, and I hoped therapy could help me discover this. As a patient in Broadmoor said: 'Is psychotherapy the rediscovery of something you never discovered before? I knew it, but I didn't know I knew it' (Cox, 1978, p. 229).

Before I had any experience of psychotherapy I think I saw it mainly in terms of cognitive insight and positive gains. I didn't have much idea of the sort of relationship involved, or of the extent to which painful experience might be relived rather than just recalled. Since what one learns in psychotherapy does not only concern understanding, but much of it concerns experience, the relationship with the therapist is crucial. This is emphasized by many writers and psychotherapists, for instance Casement (1985, p. 168), Horney (1946), Lomas (1981) and Hobson (1985).

The quality of the relationship is particularly important since most people enter therapy when there is a crisis in their life and they feel at the end of their tether. They have usually been through the usual resources – GP, family, friends – and feel that it is no longer possible or permissible to seek further help or support from them, since they need the skill, time and confidentiality that only a professional can give. They may turn to psychotherapy only when they have tried everything else and nothing has helped, or because the help has been temporary or piecemeal and they are aware of some deep-rooted problem which remains untouched. Many are afraid that it will prove yet one more false avenue which leads nowhere and one, moreover, where the sense of failure might be particularly poignant, since it involves a personal relationship and the ability to communicate feelings, which are often fundamental problems in themselves.

In terms of the emotional energy, time and money invested it is a costly venture to embark on if one is not sure of success.

The process is moreover difficult to define, with such wide-ranging or nebulous aims (unless we are considering behaviour therapy) that success is difficult to determine. A good deal of research has been devoted to quantifying the success of various forms of therapy, 'measuring' the quality of change and benefits accrued, but these tests, statistics and questionnaires are mainly attempting to classify the imponderable and they tend to prove the tester's bias. Anthony Storr, a practising psychotherapist, declares: 'The evidence that psychoanalysis cures anybody of anything is so shaky as to be practically non-existent' (in Rycroft, 1966, p. 54). In context this does not mean that there are no benefits to be obtained from psychotherapy, merely that the idea of specific ills which can be 'cured' is misleading, and the aim of psychotherapy is now seen differently by many. Janet Malcolm (1980, pp. 129–30, 136–40) and Smail (1987, pp. 79–85), for instance, discuss the breadth of this interpretation, as do the essays in Horney (1946).

The nature of the initial maladjustment is given a radically new stance in the papers published by the Women's Therapy Centre in London under the title of *Living with the Sphinx* (Ernst and Maguire, 1987). The prevalent view had been already expressed by Strupp, Fox and Lessler: 'The view of therapeutic change taken by the people in our survey coincides with that of all analytically oriented therapists: it is seen not in terms of "symptom removal" but as occurring on a broad front and affecting a broad spectrum of life experience' (1969, p. 120). The problems do not go away, but one learns new ways of adjusting to them. They cease to become obstacles to happiness, at least to the same extent, and are seen from a new angle, so that energy that was burnt up in neurotic conflicts can be released for life-enhancing activities.

This would seem to be corroborated by my own experience. Initially, each plunge into psychotherapy helped me to feel much more positive about myself. After the first period of once-a-week therapy lasting three and a half years (in which I often thought I was getting nowhere), I emerged from what seemed a long period of undiluted misery into six relatively stable years during which I weathered several major crises, without feeling the need to scurry back to my therapist. It is difficult to say how much this increased equilibrium was due to the healing effects of time, to changed circumstances, or to the benefits of psychotherapy. However, I was sufficiently persuaded of the latter possibility to re-enter therapy after these six years, when a new crisis reactivated unresolved problems. I felt that many of the questions raised the first time round had reformulated themselves in time, and new ones had arisen.

It is not always possible at one stage in one's development to tackle all the problems simultaneously. As my first therapist said, when I expressed surprise at not being transformed overnight into a shining example of sanity: 'You can't expect to undo in three years the mess it took thirty years to make.' Certain specific problems were solved. I had reached a greater understanding of my own motives and those of others, which enabled me to be more tolerant and to come to terms with difficulties more readily. But the real gains were diffuse, consisting in a generalized sense of greater security and in more positive thinking. 'What the patient in psychotherapy acquires are new perceptions of himself and others; he learns new patterns of interpersonal behaviour and unlearns maladaptive ways' (Strupp, Fox and Lessler, 1969, p. 141).

I can best sum up my feelings about this by saying that I am no longer frightened of spiders. I was not in fact phobic about them beforehand, and certainly did not enter therapy with spiders in mind, or with any conscious desire to cure a fear which was no real source of anxiety to me (though occasionally a nuisance to others, who were asked to come and remove intrusive arachnids). I do remember, however, at an early stage in therapy, being quite unable to continue speaking or thinking because my attention was riveted by a Very Large Spider which had just scurried under a piece of furniture. Gradually, however, either during psychotherapy or shortly after it terminated, I realized that I was no longer worried when spiders, even enormous ones, hovered near my pillow or planned to share my bath. They seemed to me to have a perfect right to be where they were, doing the useful job of catching flies. It felt as if there were now *Lebensraum* for spiders and me. This was, I think, symptomatic of a more relaxed attitude to life and other people. Maybe no one but me noticed the difference, though I'm sure the spiders did. But it felt a good deal more comfortable.

In view of the divergence and subjectivity of opinions about the positive outcome of psychotherapy, there is no firm assurance that it will help. The corpus of opinion and research seems to suggest that it does, but of course those who have undergone it have as much vested interest as therapists in declaring that this is so. One does not want to have spent all that time and money for nothing. Certainly it can help; the evidence seems to suggest that for most people it actually does provide better conditions for long-term growth and stability, and is more likely to facilitate these conditions than the mere process of time or a change of circumstances would do unaided (although this is too difficult to judge, since each person's experience is unique and there can be no valid control experiments).

An encouraging comment is made by one of the clients at the Isis Centre, Oxford, quoted by Oldfield (p. 97), who had come for help at a time of acute distress and felt, looking back, that she had had 'an opportunity to learn something from a painful experience, rather than just suffer it'. Oldfield's survey found that counselling enabled the majority of clients to feel more confident, positive and open in their dealings with others, and more able to cope. (The relatively short-term counselling provided by the Isis Centre does not necessarily produce the same results, or have the same dangers, as more intensive psychotherapy over a longer period of time.) Similarly Carl Rogers, basing his statements on research evidence, declares that, in the non-directive client-centred therapy which he practises, clients develop much more positive attitudes towards themselves and others, are more accepting and autonomous, feel and seem more mature (1961, p. 65). Rogers (an avid tester and quantifier) affirms: 'Much more research needs to be done, but there can no longer be any doubt as to the effectiveness of such a relationship [i.e. the sort he advocates and practises] in producing change' (p. 36).

This all sounds very positive. However, not all people who have undergone psychotherapy would wholeheartedly endorse these views, and many who are hesitating about whether to embark on a course may still wonder if therapy can harm as well as heal. Horney (1946) and Ernst and Goodison (1981, p. 292) discuss this, and Storr pinpoints some of the doubts.

There are two main fears which deter people from seeking analytical help who might otherwise do so. The first is that they will become intensely dependent on the analyst, unable to escape from his clutches, and thus ensnared in a necessarily unsatisfactory relationship from which they cannot disentangle themselves. The second is that the analytical process will, by tracing the origin of their difficulties to their primary roots, destroy such adaptation as they have achieved, especially if this happens to be in the field of creative activity. (in Rycroft, 1966, pp. 81–2)

Storr does not think these fears are valid since they refer to false ways of adapting that have broken down and that will ideally be replaced in therapy by more genuine attitudes, a view shared by Horney and indeed most practising psycho-therapists. I do not, however, think these fears should be dismissed too lightly, since the temporary disorientation when previous defences have been undermined and there is not yet anything viable to take their place can be agonizing and even lead to destruction of the self or personality.

My own experience, at least in the second of three therapies, suggests that these dangers are real, while not inevitable. My views have been substantially modified over time. I used to think that psychotherapy was a fascinating experience which was beneficial to a greater or lesser extent to most people who tried it. My only doubts were whether the efficacity was really commensurable with the large expenditure in time and money it entailed. I did not see it as a painful or potentially damaging experience, as I now do.

In retrospect my first therapy, with a psychiatrist I shall call Dr Sybil Brown, seems relatively straightforward and untraumatic. It was characterized by positive, albeit nebulous, gains and few drawbacks. The second experience of therapy, with a psychotherapist I shall call Harriet, was, however, much more fraught with anxiety, characterized by regressed behaviour on my part, ups and downs in the relationship and 'an intense transference' as the therapist delicately put it (meaning that the strong emotions, both intensely positive and intensely negative, that I felt for her were really attitudes transferred from a significant figure from the past). I entered this therapy feeling overwhelmed by a series of bereavements and other, more minor disasters which had got confused with them. It seemed that this collapse at a time of crisis was a repetitive pattern, and one I wanted to break. Momentary relief was obtained and a very creative phase in my life followed, due to the positive influence of the therapy at this stage, and a good relationship with the therapist.

This phase lasted just over a year, during which I had twice-weekly sessions, with an occasional extra. Then I sank into the longest and most painful depression of my life, which lasted about two years, almost without alleviation. It is difficult to pinpoint the causes exactly, but they had much to do with the transference neurosis, and with the loss of all my previous defences; both phenomena were attributable to psychotherapy itself.

The force of the negative feelings in the transference became unbearable, as they had in my adolescence. They urged me to reject the therapist/my mother as useless and harmful, but if I acted on this rejection it would leave me without any security in the present or hope for the future. I needed her (both therapist and mother) too much to hate her. Although a fanatically independent person, who had always been very self-sufficient, I became abjectly dependent on my second therapist. Increasingly I felt that 'reality' concerned my sessions of psychotherapy, while 'real life' became merely an intrusion. I had no idea, even after the previous three years of once-a-week therapy with Sybil Brown, how frightening it could be to relive past traumata, as opposed to merely recalling them; to do so, moreover, without the protection of any of one's previous defences. There seemed to be an increasing conflict between the regressed self, uncovered by the analytic work, and the demands of the outside world that I should be responsible and efficient. I became prey to a continual feeling of panic; a sensation of overwhelming dread at some unspecified disaster.

During this period I became much less able to cope with things which had always been a source of strain but never before proved unmanageable, like stress at work or ill-health. I became unable to enjoy any of the activities I had previously taken pleasure in, unable to eat, unable to do anything creative (initially only outside professional activities, then the depression affected these too). I eventually became acutely suicidal and in need of hospitalization in a nursing home. During this period I lost a good many of my friends, who could not face the continued depression and felt that the bouncy character they had chosen as a friend had been replaced by a dreary, self-absorbed individual they disliked as much as I did myself. From being an outwardly coping and well-adapted individual, then, I had regressed, when none of my previous defences seemed feasible, to a degree of inadequacy that made me temporarily unable to function in my career and private life. This made me seriously doubt the value, or at least the wisdom, of psychotherapy.

It is difficult to say whether I would have become depressed anyway, or that the depression was due to age, physical ill-health or circumstances, more than to psychotherapy, or whether I would have fared better without psychotherapy.

There is no control experiment. Certainly, if no psychotherapy had been available, I would have wanted it. I can only state that, during therapy, I became worse than I had ever been before and there seemed for a long time no way out of the vicious circle. Rationally, I felt I should stop therapy since it seemed to be doing more harm than good. Emotionally, I couldn't bear to abandon this one hope of security or improvement. At times I still felt that this was a relationship I wanted to work at, and that it was important to do so, however difficult or painful this proved. At other times I felt I could take no more of it and that it was creating more problems than it solved. We tried reducing the sessions from twice to once a week, in the hope that this would defuse the intensity of the transference and diminish the anguish. Instead I felt bereft and desolate, as if I'd lost something precious. It might have been a source of anguish, rather than security, but it had felt significant; and there was only an absence in its place. I felt I needed to stay in psychotherapy since otherwise I would be completely adrift during a crisis; yet that was precisely when it failed to be therapeutic. I had invested too much energy in the process and become too attached to my therapist to quit. And the more I hung on, the more incapable I seemed to become of leading a normal life. I am still quite surprised that I am alive to tell the tale.

The vicious circle was eventually broken by seeking help from another psychotherapist I'll call Simon, and seeing them both concurrently for eighteen months. Perhaps just by bringing new light on to the problems Simon changed my attitude instantly. Perhaps he had special skills. I can't even be sure that the previous therapy had done me no good because I might have been much worse without it. I only know that I had got into a dangerous and stagnant situation in, and partly because of, psychotherapy, which could not have been solved with the same therapist, quite possibly through no fault of hers. In retrospect the positive phase which followed the trough, and the knowledge that Harriet had stood by me during a very painful period for both of us, made the relationship seem very worthwhile, although I continue to doubt whether the depression itself was really inevitable, or can be seen as anything but a wholly negative experience.

Having experienced many of the positive gains that I sought as well as a level of pain I did not expect, I am now not at all sure that vulnerable people should be exposed to psychotherapy. This implies of course that most of those who need it may not be sufficiently resilient to benefit from it, given the strain it actually causes. This is a view likely to be dismissed out of hand by the professionals, but which I feel, from bitter experience, should be taken seriously. As Casement admits, 'with some damaged patients we take on a terrible responsibility. We could make things worse for them if we fail to survive at the point when they most need to test our capacity for survival' (1985, p. 145).

Psychotherapy has saved many and improved others, although few would claim to be 'cured' in the absolute sense. But it can also be harmful, without there being any very clear way of knowing in advance whether this will happen, or in retrospect whether there was any positive side to the pain. Psychotherapy is not necessarily a re-educative experience in a safe environment, which will lead to lasting change in real life.[1] It can merely be the replay of past traumata (become agonizingly present instead of forgotten) which leads to nothing. This probably is not the case if the sufferer sticks at the endeavour and overcomes the anguish, seen as a temporary 'transference neurosis'. But how many do not reach this stage, either because they terminate the therapy or commit suicide?

The dangers inherent in such a perilous undertaking, as well as the creative excitement which each new phase of therapy brought me initially, provided the genesis of this book. I'm not sure that insecure and damaged people are necessarily improved by such an experience. As Janet Malcolm discovered (1980, p. 130), it works best with the healthy. A strong core of sanity is needed to survive it, or benefit significantly from it.

2   CHOICE OF THERAPIST

'**M**y therapist is better than your therapist' is a party game much played in France and North America, and even in England, among the *cognoscenti*. It's like cars; we all think our own model is the best. The amazing thing is that, in spite of the dangers inherent in the relationship, a large number of people end up satisfied with their choice. It is, however, a relationship that can make or break the individual, and one only entered into by highly vulnerable people, usually at a point of crisis. So it cannot be undertaken lightly. Nor do I think it should be allowed to outlive its usefulness. There is no point in clinging to a mistake through habit or fear, although it is sometimes difficult to know at what stage in the proceedings the contract should be terminated. It's a bit like marriage and other close relationships. No one believes that these are perfect, yet many people are reluctant to get out of a bad match. Others, perhaps, are not prepared to work at the problems, and switch partners too readily.

My own experience leads me to think that I've been lucky, mainly by chance, with my three main therapists. But brief encounters with others, and the testimony of friends, suggest that there are such things as disastrous therapists (at least for that individual) and others who, while not totally inadvisable, were none the less not the best. And it does matter; it can matter very much. To quote Clara Thompson:

In my early years as an analyst, I was taught the idea that any well trained analyst could do a good job on an analysable patient. It is possible that some success can always be achieved, but I now believe that one analyst can sometimes take a patient further than another because his temperament and life experience fit him to understand this type of patient especially well. I think patients may unconsciously react to this when they choose an analyst. (1964, p. 174)

This question is also discussed by Fromm-Reichmann (1950, pp. 62–3) and Kelman (in Horney, 1946, pp. 135–57).

My own experience of the varying efficacy of therapists and psychiatrists suggests that bad encounters can be disastrous and should be avoided. The first psychiatrist I did not get on with fortunately saw this straight away and referred me to someone else, so no harm was done, except that the referral took six months to be processed (probably through National Health Service [NHS] bureaucracy). Meanwhile I went through a traumatic loss in my life, without professional support, and felt totally abandoned and rejected by the psychiatric profession. As a result, I arrived on the doorstep of my first psychotherapist, Dr Sybil Brown, bristling with resistance. I wasn't given any choice about being referred to her, though I think the referring psychiatrist exercised some skill in selecting her and the choice proved a wise one. We got on well and the therapy was productive.

However, it took me a long time to feel at ease with her and I did have misgivings about certain aspects of her technique or approach. I didn't verbalize them to myself at the time, because I had nothing else to go by, knew little about psychotherapy and it was not in my interest to be too critical. These misgivings didn't consciously make me choose my next therapist, Harriet, but they were responsible for an enthusiastic response to her. I chose her largely because she had time to see me at once, which felt important, both in terms of present urgency and the effects of delay the previous time. I also chose her because she sounded nice on the phone. The ability to communicate warmth and caring on the telephone became very important in this therapy (and transcended our mutual phone phobia) as there were several periods of separation through her absences or my illnesses during which I found it helpful to keep in contact this way. I found her relaxed and friendly approach very congenial. I never stopped liking her, even in the very worst moments of an intensely negative transference and negative experience. But I'm not at all sure that liking her always helped, particularly after she had confirmed my perception that it was important to her to be liked. The good rapport did not encourage rigorous discussion of problems, especially if either of us felt this might bring an element of antagonism into the relationship. It made it difficult to express anger or criticism. It also made it very difficult to leave the therapy when I felt it had become destructive. Maybe this was a good thing.

By the time I came to my third therapist, Simon, I had a much clearer idea of the sort of person I wanted. I knew that I required flexibility and warmth, coupled with strength and detachment. I needed someone who could himself bear, and help me face up to, my currently strong suicidal impulses. I did not want someone who was frequently absent, or absent for long periods. So this time I clarified in the first interview these issues which seemed to me crucial, and asked questions about orientation before going to see him. I was also more determined to avoid, if possible, getting into yet another situation which I felt was counter-productive, but which became difficult to change. I did not want to create a favourable first impression on him, as I felt I had been tempted to do with Sybil and Harriet in order to prevent them rejecting me. I wanted Simon to know the worst at once, so he would not become disappointed later. I showed him, therefore, the unvarnished despair which I felt had alienated others. When he shook my hand at the end of the hour and said, 'It's been nice meeting you', I replied grimly that he wouldn't think that after a while, since no one did. Simon continued to seem pleased to see me, however depressed or antagonistic or angry I became.

This first interview was largely indicative of the subsequent course of the therapy, characterized mainly by surprise at the unexpected. I began talking about one of my students who had just died; the third to die that term. 'How did she die?' he asked, after listening receptively to my grief. 'She fell asleep at the wheel of her car', I answered. 'She was driving herself?' asked Simon, 'You are, aren't you?' This did, however, condition me to expect him to refocus problems instantly, and to get impatient when this did not happen. However, his obvious wish to be helpful and accommodating, apparent in the first interview, usually enabled me to keep things in perspective when my dislike of constraint made me see him as inflexible or authoritarian, and to realize that this was largely a transferential reaction. There was a sense of adventure in many of his propositions, yet within a climate of security.

Each of these therapists had a somewhat different approach, each of which was well suited to my needs at diverse moments in my development. However, this became apparent gradually, rather than being so during the early interviews. Dr Brown challenged everything I said and made me look afresh at the tenets of my life until then, particularly those of my childhood. This often made it an uncomfortable experience, but it encouraged change. By systematically making me re-examine everything I said, or that had been said to me, it became possible to sort out true from false motives more clearly. In this way she eventually helped me to build up more self-esteem and confidence. However, this only came after the disorientation of having the views I had accepted from my mother exposed as false. It was not made clear to me that I was not being accused of lying, merely being told to re-examine the basis for the views I had formed. For instance, my remark that I had not been allowed to go to boarding-school because my parents could not afford it met with the response: 'You must know that is not true.' I immediately felt guilty; caught out in a lie. It was not for some months, and after many similar exchanges, that I realized that the lie was my mother's, and I was being accused of lack of perspicacity, rather than of mendacity.

Harriet, my second therapist, took my statements more or less at face value. This made her a pleasant person, and created a friendly climate, but it didn't help me get anywhere fast in therapy. We agreed with each other too easily and so I was not impelled to re-examine my views. For instance, when I complained that I had been bored and miserable at all the parties I had attended recently, she cheerfully commented that parties **are** often boring. I felt immediately reassured about my normality. But we did not touch on the underlying anxiety that I had lost my capacity for enjoyment (which became a serious problem in the ensuing months). I felt that I was left to provide my own insights and to reach my own revisions of judgement more or less unaided, though warmly supported. This wasn't always quite enough. But I could not have known this from a first interview, or even after a trial period. Much of the time the warmth and ease of the relationship was in itself sufficiently therapeutic to facilitate my own discoveries and for the lack of a more stringent analysis not to be serious. At a time of acute crisis it became a reason to look for another therapist, but this was not apparent until we had remained stuck in an impasse for some months. The positive aspects of this therapy were, however, sufficient for me to continue with it productively even after establishing a good working relationship with the next therapist.

Simon paid attention to the overt or anecdotal content of my discourse, but rarely commented on it directly. Instead, he focused on the underlying meaning, the hidden content of each communication, and the possible thread linking it with other communications in that session. In this way, he often helped me reach the core of an experience and to see a pattern in apparently disconnected phenomena. This sometimes annoyed me because I felt he was imposing a pattern where there was none, reading a pre-existing text into my personal discourse; but this could be discussed openly, given the climate of mutual honesty and receptivity.

These three approaches each had their productive side. Some fairly durable growth was achieved with the first therapist, and I needed to test it on life before doing more analytic work. I stopped therapy, then as later, because I felt I had got enough out of it for the moment; but it was always at the back of my mind that I might re-enter it at some later stage, preferably on a more intensive basis. When I did resume, the greater depth provided by more frequent sessions was important. But maybe I did not react quickly enough when the second therapy became destructive rather than productive. It is easy to say this with hindsight, and I think it would have been difficult to assess the long-term value of each approach and each relationship during the first few sessions. Psychotherapy, like any other relationship, changes over time, and its course is often unpredictable. However, I am certain that my instant reactions to the three other psychiatrists I saw (positive in one case and negative in two) were indicative of how the exchange was likely to go on; also that the one instance when I did not terminate the contract soon enough, largely because I was in no state to do so, was extremely counter-productive. One cannot, then, predict the strengths of a relationship, or what its limits might be, but if it is likely to be wholly negative this will be apparent from the start.

The therapist's warmth, acceptance and naturalness were not a guarantee of therapeutic success or a necessary and sufficient condition for a good therapeutic outcome, but lack of these traits was a fairly reliable predictor of a poor therapeutic outcome. (Strupp, Fox and Lessler, 1969, p. 101)

Nuances in attitude to communications can only gradually become apparent and their relative helpfulness only more gradually assessed. Other factors which are more readily evident include theoretical orientation. Maybe this does not make much difference since people tend to adapt to most things, and even to benefit equally from most approaches. This is a consumer view, not necessarily shared by therapists, who tend not unnaturally to favour their own orientation.

I found my first therapist, a self-styled neo-Freudian, eclectic in approach, yet rather rigid regarding those views she had adopted. She disputed this, in later conversations. Maybe her technique evolved over time or changed according to patients. At the time I did not consider her approach doctrinaire; I only did so in retrospect. I had not yet challenged the strong parental dictums or entirely thrown off the obedient little girl. Nor was I sufficiently secure in my own views to challenge anyone else's, at least in the field of psychotherapy, of which I was largely ignorant. Perhaps significantly, this therapist steadfastly refused to discuss theory or to enter into any sort of argument with me, and never allowed me to discuss books, on the grounds that all this was 'intellectualization' and would allow me to operate in a field with which I was familiar and experienced few problems. I felt that this prevented me from bringing the whole of myself into therapy. Books are as large a part of my life as children are for their mothers, or a career is for any professional. I subsequently wondered whether, had I been a dancer or football player, instead of an academic, she would have refused to let me talk about the tools of my trade. My guess is that she would have felt less threatened by something so much further removed from her own profession, and also more interested in it. But her veto on intellectual discussion was probably helpful in putting me more in touch with my feelings, and follows accepted analytic practice.

Curiously, however, my second therapist, Harriet, entered enthusiastically into discussions of theory or books, yet the relationship involved far more re-enaction and expression of strong feelings and early experiences. I think this may have been partly due to the greater frequency of sessions, partly to my having already worked through a period of intellectual insight with my first therapist, and being emotionally ready for something deeper; partly to the greater warmth I perceived in Harriet.

It seems that the amount of improvement noted by a patient in psychotherapy is highly correlated with his attitudes to the therapist. Indeed, psychotherapy was seen by our respondents as an intensely personal experience. More important, the therapist's warmth, his respect and interest . . . emerged as important ingredients in the amount of change reported . . . the more uncertain the patient felt about the therapist's attitude toward him, the less change he tended to experience. (Strupp, Fox and Lessler, 1969, p. 77)

I was much more critical by the time I entered this second therapy and consciously wanted a more flexible technique, with more room in it for me to express myself as I wanted, and to experiment with different approaches. As Harriet herself laughingly commented, near the beginning of the therapy, I was playing her off as the permissive parent against Sybil Brown, cast as a more authoritarian one. This relaxed sort of exchange encouraged greater frankness in my dealings with Harriet but it also made me reluctant to show any negative feelings. Her tolerance also jarred at times. 'That's alright, isn't it?', she tended to say to everything. On one occasion this referred to my current conflict about whether to abandon psychotherapy, as I felt it was doing more harm than good. I felt that her cheery comment was a flippant response to my genuine dilemma and angrily retorted, 'No, it damn well isn't. I feel dreadful about it.' The difference between her attitude and Sybil's was pinpointed for me by their separate reactions to my periodic moan, when depressed, that I was too miserable to swim. Sybil did not recognize that for me 'not swimming' means doing twenty lengths instead of the daily mile, and said 'You must force yourself to swim.' (I should point out that this was many years after she had ceased to be my therapist and become a friend, with, therefore, no obligation to be tactful.) Harriet, underestimating the correlation between swimming and the urge for life, said 'That's alright, isn't it?'

As Kelman points out (in Horney, 1946, p. 151), 'Your analyst's philosophy of life is important because it will influence you in the course of your analysis . . . you will be influenced in analysis as in any intimate relation of long duration.' Sybil's willingness to put duty before everything else impressed me, but it was too close to my parents' ethos for me to wish to imitate it any further than I already had (which was quite far). Harriet's insouciance attracted me, but also annoyed me. The decision not to become like either of them was a factor which enabled me to separate when the time came.

I don't think I became sufficiently close to Simon to be influenced by him, in the much briefer therapy of only once-weekly sessions. However, his courage and audacity struck a chord in me, and occasionally unleashed a recklessness that other people thought I didn't need. He seemed willing to explore almost any idea or method fully, however outlandish. He didn't abandon his own views but was open to new suggestions and did not dismiss them before due consideration had been given to each one according to its merits, regardless of accepted opinion. This operated at least with reference to social conventions; I sometimes detected a readiness to fit me into psychological textbook categories, which irked me. Moreover, it took a fairly unorthodox therapist to agree to see me concurrently with the previous therapist, co-operating with her while operating entirely independently. It does both credit that they accepted this arrangement without demur and were genuinely glad when it seemed to be productive, not only in terms of my improved sanity but also in the way in which each therapy fed positively back into the other, and advances with one person tended to produce new insights with the other.

A basic consideration with many people is that of gender. This is considered in some detail by Kelman (in Horney, 1946, pp. 143–9). Once I had got over the initial disappointment that my first therapist was female (and American, as I'd been told, and not male and Viennese, as I had fantasized), I rationalized this in a favourable light and thought that it would be a relief to talk over certain things with a woman. Up to that point my close friends had tended to be male. There was a certain amount of collusion with this female therapist against male behaviour in relationships, against the treatment of daughters by mothers and social attitudes to the education of girls, as well as regarding female sex experience. I thought at the time that the attachment was quite strong enough as it was, and that I would feel threatened by that sort of one-sided attachment to a man.

So the next time round, though I seriously considered going to a man for a change, I again chose a woman. I found that, contrary to my belief, the intensity of the attachment to a woman was agonizing. I had no model for it in my adult experience. I didn't know what to do with that degree of emotion directed towards another woman and, although I had no serious doubts about my own sexuality, became intolerably guilty and anxious as a result. So much so that I did not dare even discuss it. Moreover there **had** been a previous model for attachment to a woman – my mother – and that had been a very destructive relationship. So the transference became damagingly negative without my realizing it, since the superficial difference between the two women and the demonstrable niceness of my therapist blinded me for some years to what was really going on.

The particular difficulty women experience in separating from our mothers, and the similar experience of intimacy and separation in the therapeutic relationship, is imaginatively and thoroughly explored by Eichenbaum, Orbach and Ernst in papers based on their work in the Women's Therapy Centre contained in *Living with the Sphinx* (Ernst and Maguire, 1987).

I did definitely opt for a male therapist the next time round and the experience proved stimulating in ways I hadn't envisaged. I had been prepared for an attachment that might be inconvenient, but felt that if this did happen it would be a relief to direct any feeling, however inappropriate, towards a man instead of a woman. Before any attachment had time to develop, however, the gender difference had more interesting results. The immediate effect was to pinpoint my attitudes to creativity, carrying, holding, emptiness and such generically different experiences; attitudes which I and my female therapist had perhaps too readily taken for granted. (Though I don't think her being female need have obscured this from her.) The therapist's insistence on this gender difference often irked me, because I felt he was stressing it to the exclusion of other factors, and using it to imply a relationship that did not exist. But it was invigorating because it did not reflect my spontaneous way of seeing things. The frankness with which Simon designated possible associations or unconscious forces (which I would not have detected by myself, or mentioned if I had) was analytically productive. I felt that if he was scrupulously honest, bringing his own possible reactions into the open as well as mine, I could be too. It provided an incentive for discussion, in a context that made it safe, because words could only lead to an exploration of feelings.

Theoretically, it should have been easier and safer to talk about emotions with another woman. In fact, it wasn't; partly because she **was** another woman and so it did not feel natural, partly because she herself was the target of my emotions, whereas Simon wasn't, and partly because I sensed her own inhibitions checking me, whereas Simon's lack of inhibitions released me. It also generated in me a new curiosity in living. With a therapist of the same gender, and a not dissimilar personality, I had been going round in increasingly stagnant vicious circles. It took someone of a different gender and also a more markedly different personality, who responded to my differences, to galvanize me out of this and help me find the impetus and the means to change.

There was also a positive spin-off regarding the previous therapy, and relationships in real life, in that I rediscovered how valuable and reassuring the **sharing** of experience is with someone of the same gender, through the rediscovery of the more adventurous exercise of becoming conscious of difference. It is probably no coincidence that I became actively involved in the women's movement only after I had been in therapy with a male therapist for a year. Simon's attitude was in no way oppressive or patriarchal, but I became aware that he did not experience some problems in the same way as I do, and that no man could. I also became aware of how irrelevant my father had been in my childhood. My relationship had mainly been with my mother, and it was the strong tie of love and hate with her that I had to work through with a female therapist. This largely accounts for my remaining in therapy with Harriet while seeing Simon, and not changing to him definitively, as had originally been the intention.

This brings to the fore the whole question of identification. With any therapist, the understanding of what the experience means to the other person is what counts, rather than his or her own persuasions or experience. At times I have even found with therapists, as with friends, that identification is a bar to real understanding. Someone who has herself experienced bereavement may extrapolate from her experience and not fully grasp what it means for the other person. I felt diffident in talking about the problems of childlessness with Harriet as she was the mother of a large family, but I think she was prepared to enter into what the experience felt like to me precisely because she did not have any personal identification with it. In the same way I found that a male therapist was able to shed new light on this same problem, because he viewed it from a different and more conceptual angle than I could, as a woman and hence potential mother.

I do not, then, think there is any point in trying to look for the blind, one-armed, Rastafarian, homosexual, terrapin-loving therapist who will identify with all one's problems, any more than there is in looking for the ideal mate in the data print-out of a computer test which fails to take the essential qualities into consideration. There is no guarantee that the specifications of the imaginary ideal therapist will cause the relationship to be more effective than with one chosen more or less at random. I think that if anyone had described the socks of either of the male psychiatrists I saw I would have rejected them outright, and lost more important qualities in doing so.

The question of choice of both therapist and mode of therapy is addressed by Ernst and Goodison (1981, pp. 276–88), mainly in the context of women's needs. They give more space to bio-energetics and encounter groups than to individual therapy, although they also regard this sympathetically. Janet Malcolm (1980, pp. 144–5) deals with the differences between analysts of various schools, and how this may affect those who consult them. Karen Horney's *Are You Considering Psycho-analysis?* (1946) also has several essays on the topic. It is thoroughly and sensitively dealt with by Lindsay Knight in *Talking to a Stranger: A Consumer's Guide to Therapy* (1986). She also provides a useful list of addresses to help people select and obtain psychotherapy or counselling, with a guide to 1986 prices. Her book does not discuss the process as thoroughly as Horney, but is more basic, practical and up to date. It is however selling psychotherapy quite hard, although it does point out the dangers too.

There is a difference between the needs of the consulter in short-term counselling for specific problems and a more analytical therapy, ranging over a wide variety of situations. In the counselling situation it might well be that someone who has faced the problem from the inside, as it were, is likely to inspire more confidence than the outsider. Racial integration is one such situation; specific religious doubts are often best discussed with someone of the same persuasion; those suffering from physical disabilities or illnesses often wish to share an experience with others similarly placed. For instance, the patients in the National Spinal Injuries Unit set up a counselling service in 1975 in which ex-patients, who had coped with living with the results of spinal injuries, shared our experiences with those who were newly having to come to terms with them. It was felt that only those who had actually faced the problems personally were entirely credible. We were less likely to minimize the difficulties, more likely to know just what could reasonably be achieved and what problems to expect than the medical experts who, from a vertical position of perfect muscular co-ordination, explained how easy it was to organize life from a wheelchair.[1]

The value of shared experience is significant when something like a disability is at stake. It no longer obtains when deeper psychological problems of adjustment are the main issues. The really important factors here are whether the therapist has the requisite personal qualities of empathy, genuineness, receptivity, tolerance, tact, warmth, intuition, which obviously have nothing to do with creed, gender, or other personal characteristics. This is stated by Lomas (1973, p. 55) and borne out by the findings of Strupp, Fox and Lessler (1969, pp. 17, 77, 101, 117) and by those of Frischer (1977, pp. 152–4). Frischer concludes from her survey of analysands' views of their analysis that positive relationships in which the analyst is perceived as warm and friendly tend to produce the most favourable long-term benefits and the most productive analysis, whereas a perception of the analyst as cold, rigid, insensitive or inimical leads to minimal progress.

There still remains the problem of when and if to change therapist or cease therapy if the experience seems negative. Sometimes it is worth persisting in spite of one's inclinations, as with every relationship. Sometimes it might be more sensible to cut one's losses and end the contract. As most people in therapy are very vulnerable and have invested considerable time and money in the enterprise, abandoning it is not easy.

It can be easier to transplant oneself across whole worlds than to find the courage it requires to terminate a therapy, with all the self doubt that this implies and the paranoid anxieties that are inevitably multiplied by such a unilateral step. (Herman, 1985, p. 106)

The decision to quit involves the further dilemma of whether to try again with someone else. Even if one is not yet convinced that the whole thing is pointless, and one is motivated enough to make another attempt, the agony of going over the preliminaries yet again with a new person and risking perhaps another stalemate can deter even those who are surer of their own values than most people in therapy are likely to be. A friend of mine, discussing her 'trial period' in therapy, pointed out how difficult it was when the therapist said, after some months of getting to know each other, 'It feels OK to me, how about you?', to reply that actually it felt dreadful. She didn't even know whether this meant that it might be better with someone else, or just as awful. She could not in any case bear the thought of starting again at zero. I felt much the same when, after a year or so of what seemed to be an impasse, getting more and more depressed, with insights that led nowhere, I contemplated the alternatives. No therapy at all seemed unthinkable; starting again with a new person too exhausting and without success guaranteed; continuing as we were, pointless.

[I had] a deep sense of frustration that my problems lay untouched . . . I was hoping . . . that all this could be analysed to its neurotic origins and my unrest could recede . . . The thought of breaking off treatment filled me with horror, more and more. Yet the more ardently I stayed the course . . . the more insistently did the imperative for change assert its urge. (Herman, 1985, p. 108)

I was lucky in having a therapist who was willing to experiment with a shared therapy. This could just have been confusing, but in fact I found that the new person was not only able to give me the necessary breakthrough, but also to clarify certain things in the other therapy, which could then get sorted out with the appropriate therapist. Simon released me from a sort of bondage and set me free for new growth, both with him and with the previous person, in a way that would not have been possible had I not had this opportunity. It might not have worked for everybody or with every therapist. But it did work very well for me. There was unfinished business with one therapist that could not have got so satisfactorily sorted out merely by changing. There was a need for a radically new approach, which could not have been fulfilled by remaining in the same claustrophobic unit.

This does not mean, however, that I switched therapist as soon as tensions arose. I commented to Harriet that if only I'd worked half as hard at real life relationships as I had at the one with her, I'd have got somewhere in life. This lesson in how to work through problems together was (potentially) very salutary. It might be difficult in real life to meet someone as patient, or as prepared to take criticism without retaliating. But at least the experience of that possibility, albeit in an artificial set-up, was enlightening and strengthening. It also made me more tenacious when things were difficult between us. There is no easy answer to the dilemma of whether negative feelings are a reliable sign that this is the wrong person or situation, or whether they are a transitory stage to be battled with, like many other problems one encounters in the course of therapy, and which lead to insight if one can survive them. I can only say that I'm very glad I did put up with the awfulness of those bad moments, but also that I did not just submit passively, without trying to change the situation radically. I was lucky to have found a way out of it without getting right out; and I was lucky with my helpers.

3 THE TIME AND
THE PLACE –
AND THE COST

*If we are to search for a paradigm for our work, we should
look to that of friendship rather than the application of
scientific theory . . . non-technical qualities are **central** to
healing.*
Lomas, *The Case for a Personal Psychotherapy*, pp. 6–7,
author's emphasis

The main focus in the present work is on the type of
relationship which is, or could be, built up between the
therapist and the person seeking help. It is on the human
qualities of the exchange and not on technique. However, since
the insistence on technique has tended to submerge these
human qualities and to inhibit their appearance in the
relationship, some space will be allocated to examining the
various conventions governing the practice of psychotherapy,
on a purely practical level, to see how these affect people's
experience of therapy.

For the whole question of how the transaction is perceived
by the lay participant, to what extent and in what aspects it is
felt to be therapeutic, and what obstacles impede this at times,
involves material as well as psychic factors. Oldfield stresses
repeatedly that 'The healing agents are more likely to lie in the
pervasive and not entirely conscious effects of the counselling
relationship and less clearly in the cognitive work that is
done' (1983, p. 104, author's emphasis; see also pp. 80, 125).
While she is speaking here mainly of the relationship, as
opposed to the cognitive process, things like the length and
frequency of interviews, as well as the setting, can have a
bearing on the ease, or lack of it, with which people approach
the encounter and the benefit they obtain from it. These

factors may cause some to abandon therapy prematurely, when it might have been of some use to them. These practical considerations become less important after a while, and they are not the main issues to which I wish to address myself, but they are particularly important at the beginning of psychotherapy, and may continue to prove irritants to some people throughout the encounters. The package is designed for the consumer, but there is so far little consumer feedback about its appeal or drawbacks.

THE FIFTY-MINUTE HOUR

One of the main conventions of psychotherapy, which has given rise to many jokes (largely because it has caused a good deal of resentment, and laughter has seemed the best way of defusing the situation), has been the existence, nay, dogma, of the fifty-minute hour.

As Winnicott says, playing, that is, learning to live creatively (i.e. therapy) takes place in time, and it needs time in order for it to occur. It uses time (as opposed to wasting it) and it cannot be hurried. This is a recognized fact, and one which presumably accounts for the considerable length of time taken by every in-depth therapy or analysis. These are not quick, problem-solving sessions, but a gradual re-education through experience, an unlearning of obsolete habits and relearning of new behaviours, which have to be tested and retested, both in the laboratory conditions of the therapeutic set-up, and in the real world.

All therapists recognize this (see particularly Winnicott, 1971, pp. 47 ff., Horney, 1942 and Reik, 1936, pp. 107–10). What they have less patience with is the no less common affirmation that it is very hard to function effectively in fifty-minute spurts, especially as they do not occur as and when the mood takes one, but by prearrangement. Worse, the time-limit does not correspond to emotional need or the demand of the discourse. Most people are politely resigned to this, but at least occasional resentment at being turfed out on the dot, after fifty minutes, must be universal. Winnicott goes so far as to assert that 'Hate is expressed by the existence of the end of the "hour". I think this is true even when there is no difficulty whatever, and when the patient is pleased to go' (1958, p. 197). This is so because it is a brutal reminder that the relationship is not exclusively based on the client's needs. It is not entirely real; or it is only real within strict time-limits and in a space divorced from everyday reality.

Sometimes, it is true, one has run out of material, or is hoping to avoid bringing something up, and so the guillotine can be quite a relief. Sometimes it feels just about the right length of time. But there are occasions when it can be extremely counter-productive. For instance, when one has just reached an insight towards the end of the hour, or at last got round to voicing something painful. This familiar phenomenon is usually treated as a 'resistance' – that is, the devious patient stores up material until drinking-up time, and hopes to wangle extra minutes, or make a point about heartless-therapists-throwing-out-needy-patients. This might often be the case. It is also possible that many people genuinely find it difficult to unwind from their preoccupations or activities of the previous hour and to pick up the thread of discourse from the preceding session. This takes time, and people function at different rhythms, a truism not much allowed for by psychotherapy. Some people are only just getting warmed up by the end of the hour, while others who may have started off with a cornucopia of conscious material only find out where it is leading after fifty minutes. As one of Cox's patients said: 'It takes me time to climb into myself' (1978, p. 232).

This problem can build up considerable frustration and a sense of futility regarding the whole enterprise. It can to some extent be circumnavigated by a flexible use of time (occasionally offering longer or more frequent sessions), as well as by 'homework' done on the part of the client. Schneiderman (1983) pointed out how part of the rationale behind the brief and unpredictable length of Lacan's sessions was that much of the process did not take place in, but between sessions. Rogers (1951) and Horney (1942) repeatedly indicate how fruitfully the time betwen sessions can be used to continue the work of the therapeutic hour. I have myself often likened the process to that of piano lessons; the amount learnt in the actual lessons was variable, but without them I would never have practised regularly, or had corrected the bad habits which I got into when playing alone.

Quite possibly some people would still be dissatisfied if sessions continued indefinitely, so the imposition of a time-limit is doubly necessary for practical reasons: the therapist could not function without it, and the client would not necessarily benefit from its extension. However, circumstances outside the session are often not conducive to following up trains of thought at a deep level, so postponed exploration gets forever pushed aside, as Proust found in his fugitive re-surgences from the past. No doubt this is just a regrettable fact of life; but this need not necessarily prevent it from being examined critically, in case it is avoidable.

There seems to me to be an element of double-bind in the conventions governing psychotherapy. On the one hand, the overt aims are the creation of a more autonomous, critically perceptive person, confident enough of his or her own values to throw off the shackles of blind conformity to others' expectations. On the other hand, most therapists expect unquestioning obedience to the laws that require prompt departure on the hour; equally punctual appearance at the beginning; the exercise of restraint in asking all the questions you are supposed to be dying to know but not expected to find out; polite acceptance of the therapist's interpretations, etc. If, in addition to all that, you produce shiny new insights with regularity, do not regress into psychotic states, pay your bills without quibbling, refrain from cancelling engagements, don't bother the therapist by phone calls, and generally abstain from making demands, you will be well on the way to becoming a model patient and therapist's delight – and to exemplifying the kind of compliant child who (according to the theories of R. D. Laing, David Cooper, Gregory Bateson and other exponents of anti-psychiatry) may later become schizophrenic, due to the conflicting demands of its parents.

It could be alleged that this is a caricature, and that not all therapists do require this degree of compliancy. However, many do. Moreover, the issue underlying the caricature presents the genuine problem of finding a balance between flexibility and the need for a structure. As Peter Lomas eloquently points out:

The conflict between control and freedom, discipline and permissiveness, regulation and autonomy is an age-old conflict and one despairs of finding any satisfactory solution; yet everywhere we turn we are faced with the problem afresh.

The simplification involved in a psychotherapeutic convention ensures that too much energy is not wasted on inessentials, and, in addition, it brings the sense of security which accompanies ritual . . . We need, however, to continually question the degree to which, in any particular encounter, formality is justified or not. (1981, p. 125)

Winnicott also appreciates the need to be flexible about conventions, and to use time creatively rather than restrictively. He gives a detailed account of one of his sessions with a patient who had had a long treatment on a five-times-a-week basis for six years before coming to him, but found she needed a session of indefinite length. They settled for a once-weekly session of three hours, later reduced to two hours. He gives a detailed transcription of one session as 'a plea to every therapist to allow for the patient's capacity to play, that is, to be creative in the analytic work' (1971, pp. 66–7). This mainly involves great patience on the part of the analyst, and the withholding of interpretations until the patient makes them herself, but the length of sessions is not irrelevant, as he observes at the end of the description:

Somewhere soon after this she was able to go away. The work of the session had been done. It will be observed that in a fifty-minute session no effective work could possibly have been done. We had had three hours to waste and to use. (1971, p. 74)

Winnicott also describes in *The Piggle* (1977) how, in his treatment of a small girl over a period of years, he used interviews of varying length and with different intervals between them.

The problem is a tricky one, because therapists are busy people and there are too few of them to go round, at least in Britain, and especially outside London, so they cannot usually offer three-hour sessions; nor could many people find the time to attend. Besides, the regular provision of lengthy sessions still does not cater for the occasional, spontaneous need to continue the process already under way. The provision of a supportive relationship on demand, and the creation of an unstructured form of psychological help, is described by Michael Barnett, *People Not Psychiatry* (1973) and the collective work *The Radical Therapist* (1974).

The time-limit causes a frustration which does constitute a negative aspect of psychotherapy, but usually it provokes mild hostility rather than trauma. The inflexibility of the fifty-minute rule is a more severe problem on occasions when a person is acutely distressed, either due to a depressive phase, or to some painful occurrence during the hour. To be told, however gently, 'OK, it's time now' and be forced to snap out of whatever sort of pain you are in, go out into the street and the claims of the outside world, might be part of the process of growing up, but it can be very hurtful. It reminds you that you have not been talking to a friend, or to someone who can allow herself to show her care about what you really feel like, but that you are participating in a business contract, which is strictly circumscribed and limits the sharing severely. Oldfield draws attention to this fact that 'Therapeutic work can take place only within the containment of such boundaries, but they also occasion, from time to time, fierce protests' (1983 p. 78) and she reproduces the evidence of one client who said:

One day I had been very shocked and upset; after the session I felt very shaky about leaving. I was hurt, then, by the cool, professional manner. I would have liked some warmth then – a cup of tea. I was very angry then – about the situation and with the counsellor. It was difficult to go off again and face it all. The professionalism seemed very unbending. (p. 80)

This is largely inevitable. There can be no extra time accorded to one person in distress, because there is someone else waiting, who might be in equal need. Even if there weren't, the rationale would be that it would encourage people in bad habits and they would act desperate in order to obtain extra attention; or that, if they had once been allowed a five-minute grace, they would expect it as of right on future occasions and, if it were not accorded, this would give rise to resentment.

There is some truth in this. But it does not solve the human problem of the unhappiness of the person being sent away uncomforted and being left to cope alone with unbearable emotions; nor yet of the strangeness of a profession which requires on the one hand such high levels of empathy, understanding and sensitivity yet, on the other hand, such a need to feign insensitivity. Carl Rogers emphasizes throughout his work this need for a personal approach, and the concomitant fears it may arouse in the counsellor. He writes:

We are afraid that if we let ourselves experience . . . positive feelings towards another we may be trapped by them. They may lead to demands on us. So as a reaction we tend to build up distance between ourselves and others – aloofness, a 'professional' attitude, an impersonal relationship . . . In these ways . . . we can keep ourselves from experiencing the caring which would exist if we recognized the relationship as one between two persons. It is a real achievement when we can learn, even in certain relationships or at certain times in those relationships, that it is safe to care, that it is safe to relate to the other as a person for whom we have positive feelings. (1961, p. 52)

What solutions might there be to this dilemma? Two of my therapists, Harriet and Simon, did exercise some flexibility about the fifty-minute guillotine, although it did not usually extend with Harriet beyond a few extra minutes. Once she actually gave me an extra half-hour because there had been a cancellation and one of the reasons for my distress was that I'd been kept waiting a long time at the beginning of the session. This might of course not have been possible, and a more rigid therapist would not have accorded it anyway. It felt to me therapeutic and I did not expect it to be repeated. It doesn't necessarily follow that, given an inch, most people will take a mile, even in such a neurotically dependent situation, or assume that because they receive gentler treatment at a moment of crisis they will get it again. Clients as well as therapists can assess needs, and will probably not be offended if the rules are only unbent in times of dire distress. There is likely to be gratitude at the implicit recognition of the depth of disarray.

On many occasions the hurtful dismissal of someone in distress can be avoided by spending a few minutes calming the person down, letting her go away with a feeling of warmth and having had her pain understood, of not being rejected. I found that it helped if the last few minutes of the session were devoted to this. If I was allowed to continue expressing distress until time was up the ejection seemed brutal, because I had rarely been watching the clock, and the transition between inner and outside world was too brusque. At times the monologue had not left space for the therapist to intervene, or it may have seemed tactless to break into a fit of crying or a poignant silence. But a few minutes were not likely to make this easier, and the announcement of the end of the session was less devastating if there had been a 'drinking-up time' before closure, in which a caring attitude was made explicit. I found it helpful when the therapist made it clear that he or she too regretted ending the session, whether this was due to my distress or the fact that we were in the middle of something important.

Almost certainly the thought of keeping the next person waiting should be discarded, since it would be premature to assume that the next client's need is less than that of the outgoing person, and it would put the day's schedule out of skew for the therapist. The scrupulous punctuality of most therapists (mine anyway; Frischer relates many complaints from French analysands) is one of the therapeutic aspects of the transaction, providing one of the rare occasions when one's claim to attention and equality is respected by a professional. The fact that NHS consultants, bank managers, solicitors and other professionals all tend to keep people waiting, in spite of the anxiety habitually implicit in such interviews, is not a justification for the practice to be extended to psychotherapists. Jung's uncle is reputed to have said: 'Do you know how the Devil tortures people in hell? – he keeps them waiting.'

As well as respect for the next client, there is also an incontestable need for therapists to have a short break between engagements. There is a need to deal with urgent phone calls, perhaps make notes of the session, and digest one heavy scene before the next. As Harriet put it: 'I need to get back into myself.'

However, there are analogous cases where flexibility is part of the system and does not seem to have harmful results for either party. The Samaritans, for instance, have to keep their callers waiting sometimes, though all are in distress. University tutors (as opposed to student psychiatric counsellors) also exercise considerable latitude about consultations, either on moral problems or for individual tuition. It is true that inconvenience is sometimes caused to those waiting, and that this plays havoc with the tutor's timetable. It is also true that undergraduates rarely exhibit the sort of emotional dependency on their tutors that people commonly display to their therapists. Nor is it always possible to postpone commitments in order to listen to a student in distress, or continue a fascinating discussion. But flexibility where possible does seem to be the norm. Students do not on the whole take unfair advantage of this, but benefit from the availability it implies. Treating people as responsible adults, even if they are behaving like children, is more likely to help them grow. There may be some suggestions in this for therapists. As Lomas points out:

The failure to recognize the degree to which the patient searches for truth, meaning and relationship even in regressed behaviour exaggerates the difference between him and the therapist: it is a denigration of the patient comparable to that which adults make of children and which widens the gulf between the generations; it encourages the view that the therapist – as a seeker of truth – is morally superior and it stands in the way of the acceptance by patient and therapist that they are ordinary and similar human beings. (1973, p. 92)

Lacan, indeed, and his followers practised sessions of variable length, to suit the current material, and decreed that a structured discourse, whose duration would be determined by the subject matter, should be substituted for the traditional fifty minutes. In practice, however, this seems to have led to ever shorter sessions, with less tolerance of longer ones. Schneiderman (1983, pp. 132–55) gives a detailed account of how Lacan's short sessions worked, and the rationale behind them. He expresses convincingly the positive effects these could have.

The gesture of breaking the session off was a way of telling people to move forwards, not to get stuck or fascinated by the aesthetics of the experience . . . the combined pressure of the shortness of the sessions and the unpredictability of their stops creates a condition that greatly enhances one's tendencies to free-associate. (1983, p. 133)

This structuring of sessions through limitation does not, however, solve the problem of distress caused by arbitrary endings; rather the contrary. Even in the case of a five-times-weekly analysis, when there is the assurance of being able to continue the next day, this does not alter the fact that continuity has been broken, or that dismissal at a moment of distress still occurs. Besides which, most psychotherapies do not involve daily sessions, and neither the therapist nor the client might be able to fit in extra hours unexpectedly. This might seem to be an argument for having frequent sessions, since it is easier to establish a continuity of discourse and to bear a state of crisis over short intervals. However, therapy, like most other vices, is addictive and the more frequent the sessions the greater the dependency. Hobson (1985, p. 256) mentions the danger of therapy becoming an addiction, while Herman (1985) gives an impassioned account of the awfulness of the weekend break in a five-times-weekly analysis.

People who only have weekly sessions may, paradoxically, be **more** able to survive the interval, because they are used to relying on their own resources, whereas daily sessions are likely to encourage the urge to bring all problems to that hour, and to see real life as happening in that room, instead of vice versa. Once-a-week therapy cannot address the more primitive issues that are invoked by daily sessions; the pain and anxiety contingent on such intensive therapy makes it much more consuming, as well as time-consuming, more likely to become the pivot of a person's life. With one therapist I experimented with changing our usual twice-a-week arrangement to either three times or once, as felt appropriate. We also experimented with longer sessions. On the whole I gained some relief from a reduction of the number of sessions per week, but felt that longer sessions were more satisfactory. This depended on a variety of circumstances. It helped to be allowed to try alternatives, both for practical reasons and on account of the understanding this suggested of the problem.

There are no easy solutions; but the clue must surely lie, in this as in everything else, in flexibility and humanity. The consolidation of a warm and trusting relationship, in which the therapist is seen as a caring human being and not a distant, solely professional figure, will enable the other person to overcome difficulties encountered both within the context of therapy and outside it with greater equanimity. The initial reaction of a very upset person on being reminded that 'time is up' stands a far better chance of speedy rectification if he or she feels fairly sure, at one level, that the therapist does really want to help, is not unfeeling and is sympathetically aware of her misery, even if there is nothing tangible she proposes to do about it.

FEES

Another basic practical consideration, namely fees, also emphasizes the artificiality of the relationship and its nature as a business contract rather than one based on disinterested care. This issue is regularly brought up in the literature intended for training analysts, but the client's feelings are largely dealt with in terms of the 'resistance' manifested by delays in paying bills or quibbling about the amount. Nothing is usually said about the practicalities of the question; for instance, the relative merits of presenting bills by hand or sending them through the post. People tend to be touchy on the subject of money, particularly in a situation where the debt is more of an emotional than material nature. Many may dislike being reminded that they are in fact paying for what most of us would prefer to think of as offered spontaneously. (See Suttie, 1935, p. 214.) Others may welcome the fee as a means of lessening the onus of gratitude, or increasing their defensive rejection of the possibility of another person caring about them. The main thing is surely that the therapist should not seem embarrassed about presenting the bill or receiving payment, if this is done directly, since a matter-of-fact attitude to the transaction will foster a similar attitude in the client.

However, before one gets round to paying bills for services rendered there is the initial question of whether one can afford the treatment in the first place, closely linked with the question of whether one feels it is a justified expense. This whole question is aired thoughtfully by Kelman (in Horney, 1946, pp. 94–7). Therapists are expensive animals, even on this side of the Atlantic, where the urge to sell oneself for the highest obtainable price is in conflict with the general professional ethos. If the criticism seems exaggerated, read Thomas Szasz *The Ethics of Psychoanalysis* (1965), Janet Malcolm (1980, pp. 25, 108–9) or J. Hayley *Strategies of Psychotherapy* (1963). So one needs to be fairly clear that one feels the expense is justified before committing oneself to a long-term investment of this order.

It is also essential to know what the fees are in advance. All the therapists I have seen have made this clear at the first interview, but one psychiatrist did not and then submitted a bill for **seven** times the amount I was used to being charged (by either therapist or any medical consultant seen that year). Warning of this could have prevented considerable embarrassment. As it never occurred to me that his fees could be so wildly out of step with those of his colleagues I did not think of asking at the beginning of the interview, nor was I well enough to be so practical. Few therapists take advantage of people in this way, but fees do vary, both from one therapist to another and because most operate on a sliding scale according to the client's income. It might be indelicate to mention the matter at the beginning of the initial interview, putting money before the emotional rapport, and perhaps prematurely prejudicing the issue. But it does put consulters in a difficult position if, at the end of the first hour, they find out that the fee is higher than they can afford or are prepared to pay. It would be difficult to refuse if the relationship had a chance of working; but financial problems are not therapeutic.

The concept, found in much psychoanalytic literature (again, mainly transatlantic), that the price of therapy should be punitive, that sacrifices are essential or the person will not value the help they receive, seems to me one of the more curious misconceptions of the profession. Obviously, speaking as a consumer, I have as much vested interest in keeping the cost down as the professionals have in keeping it up. (Except that I do not in fact wish to receive something for nothing.) Some compromise must be reached, and that is perfectly reasonable. What makes no sense to me is the association of healing and helping with punishment and sacrifice, or the making of a dogma, even a virtue, out of this. There is probably some truth in the dictum that people value things more if they have had to struggle a bit to afford them (although it doesn't explain why blackberries from the hedgerows have a special delight, never tendered by exotic fruits from prestigious stores, nor why most people enjoy sex more and have a better relationship with their partner if they do not have to pay for it).

But what is not so often mentioned in the learned textbooks is that having to pay too high a price for something can cause not only resentment but also tangible problems for someone whose life may already be over-full of them. Obviously, the question of whether or not the person can afford the fees has to be discussed, bearing in mind the fact that people are notoriously unreliable about their financial situation; yet also recognizing that distress about money is a common feature of depression and can aggravate suicidal impulses.

Even allowing for the multiplicity of devious as well as realistic attitudes to money, it cannot be denied that for a number of people the commitment to what could be several years' outlay of a considerable part of their income represents a sacrifice, not just of material resources, but also of time. The crucial question is inevitably: is it worth it? Obviously this is not an exclusively financial question but is closely bound up with one's whole attitude to therapy, which is why therapists treat reluctance to paying bills as resistance to the exercise.

On the only two occasions in four and a half years' therapy with Harriet (or indeed in eight years total) that I ever complained about a bill, I was quite obviously criticizing the service, but this was not picked up by the therapist. Once, at the end of the first session after she had been on holiday for a month, while I had been severely depressed, she handed me a bill for the month before her absence. I gave it back to her without a word and left the room. Services had not recently been rendered, that particular session had been a wash-out, and I thought it was tactless to hand me a bill at that moment. A few weeks later, for the first time in our encounters, I raised the question of her fees being higher than those I received. She countered this by saying that she had higher overheads. That was hardly the point. I was complaining about the value of the service. She knew this, but did not explore it with me.

While resistance is frequently mentioned in books on therapy for therapists, the equally important question of **guilt** tends to get ignored. One of the few writers to give this respectful consideration is Kelman (in Horney, 1946, pp. 94–7), who is not here writing for other therapists but for prospective clients. Many people feel guilty at spending all this money and time on themselves. There is the feeling that both should be spent on someone or something else. In my case the very thing which had sent me scurrying to therapy in the first place was my inability to cope with all the demands made on my time, so it seemed ironic to be diverting yet more attention from them. It is quite probable that neither time nor money would have been more profitably spent in actuality. It is also true that the most time-consuming inactivity of all is neurosis or depression, which leaves one with no energy to do anything. This does not alter the reality of the guilt about the self-centredness of psychotherapy, or the guilt of partaking of an activity that was, at least until recently, often accused of being a middle-class indulgence. Therapists are possibly too convinced of the merits of the exercise to be sufficiently sympathetic to the authenticity of this guilt. It too gets brushed aside as resistance.

SETTING

Et le troupeau de sphynx regagne la sphyngerie
(*And the herd of sphinxes returns to its lair*)
Apollinaire, 'Le Brasier'

While it is unlikely that the décor of the consulting room plays a large part in the choice of therapist, or outcome of the therapy, it is not a negligible factor. It obviously does matter to many people what the room looks like and how comfortable the chairs are. Janet Malcolm (1980, pp. 3–4, 47, 81, 87) is attentive to the rooms of the various analysts she interviews, deducing much about their character and self-image from the furnishings. On a practical level, adequate sound-proofing is also essential, as noises from outside can be distracting and remind one that voices from inside might also carry. Frischer, in her chapter entitled 'The den of the sphinx' (1977, pp. 139–45), discusses the question in some detail. She stresses the importance to many people of a neutral décor, not characterized by too many personal details, *objets d'art* or signs of luxury. She points out how some people are put off by overt opulence, and reminded of a class difference between themselves and the therapist, or have envy and resentment activated by this advertisement that the therapist earns more than they do. I suspect the attitude obtains more in France, where psychotherapy is increasingly a pastime of the intellectual Left, and much less in the USA, where conspicuous opulence seems to be admired.

The difficulty of achieving a neutral décor or of offending no one is considerable. My first therapist, Sybil, whose consulting room was, by my standards, unobtrusively furnished and decorated, told me that she has had wildly different reactions from patients, ranging from warm enthusiasm about the care with which the room was furnished, to angry outbursts about how tastelessly it was thrown together. Obviously these people were talking about their feelings towards the therapist. Yet personal taste as well as transference would seem to play their role. Harriet, my second therapist, seemed to me to provide a setting that was both very tasteful and pleasantly neutral. I thought it reflected her rather casually warm, artistic personality. Yet I heard differing comments from other people who visited the premises, whether as consulters or colleagues (who were presumably not in a transferential relationship).

There is also the question of where or whether to sit. NHS psychiatrists tend to provide utilitarian chairs and no couches. Orthodox analysts encourage the use of the couch, with the psychiatrist seated out of view. Simon tried this once and I hated it, feeling cut off from any human response; although at times of distress I would sometimes spontaneously crawl out of sight of Harriet. All three of my therapists provided both chair and couch, inviting me in the initial interview to use the chair. Sybil and Simon placed the chair at some distance from the couch and I only used it if I had an injured leg or back. Harriet arranged the chair in an adjacent position, so it was possible to switch easily from one to another according to mood. She also provided a flexible sort of chair, which did not oblige a rigidly upright position, but enabled one to loll or curl up and otherwise change position (mentally as well as physically).

Far more tricky is the question, which therapists seem to spend a fair amount of energy considering, of where to situate their consulting room and how to effect entrances and exits. Again, consulters are likely to have views on the matter, but I have not seen them recorded. If patients are seen in a hospital out-patients' clinic there is likely to be a communal waiting room, leading into various consulting rooms nearby. This practice can also be followed by people functioning privately in a group. However, although the therapist tends to be a gregarious animal in its living and social habits, it tends to hunt alone, and it is the division of living and operational quarters which customarily creates problems.

Many people set aside a room in their private house for consultations, sometimes with its own entrance, opening directly into it or through a waiting room, sometimes reached through the main front door. Therapists seem to dislike the latter solution because it detracts from the classical anonymity of the analyst; the patient may glimpse other members of the family, and the décor is too personal. Probably more people than therapists imagine would be reassured to find they have normal things like wellies or bicycles in the entrance, rather than anguished about meeting the husband, wife, lover or children. People live in houses, and it is going to be much easier to establish a personal relationship with a person than with a white coat in a purpose-made office. However, the therapist-person does constitute half the contract, and there is the rest of the family to consider too, so those who feel strongly about not mixing their private and professional lives must be allowed to keep them separate. This must be something of a wasted effort in a small town where everybody knows everybody else.

A solution favoured by some is to have a consulting room separated from the house, with its own entrance and waiting room, which obviates the need for anyone to open the door and preserves a certain amount of privacy for all parties. It also gives more autonomy to the client, who opens the door and announces his or her arrival, rather than having to hover on a doorstep or wait to be summoned. Some people also have a (different) separate exit, which may be greatly appreciated by some patients, who are shy about being seen by others, especially if they emerge looking upset. However, this tactful arrangement does at the same time risk fostering the attitude, rather prevalent in Britain, that therapy is a shameful activity. People not uncommonly find it difficult to admit, even to themselves, the possibility of any psychic disturbance, even mild depressions, and do not wish to be seen to give in to the weakness to the extent of consulting someone for treatment. There is the fear that you might be thought mad, that the carefully cultivated façade of coping will be shattered. However, this rigid segregation, with its acknowledgement of the likelihood of clients wanting – even needing – secrecy, seems to increase the nervousness rather than diminish it. It reeks a bit of attending a VD clinic, or visiting the secret police, rather than accomplishing a perfectly avowable act. Freud himself, in fact, likened the shame inspired by receiving psychological treatment to that of certain sexual activities. It is of course an attitude of society, not the therapist, if psychological problems are thought of as a shameful disease; but that is no reason for encouraging it. It might even be alleged that it is actually quite an important function of therapy to persuade people who are riddled with guilt and insecurity that their anguish is indeed permissible and nothing to be ashamed of. Significantly, several of the clients in Oldfield's survey mentioned, among the factors considered most helpful in the experience, that of being in a situation where they could drop the coping front. 'What a relief it was to be able to say to someone – no, it's not alright', said one woman (1983, p. 73).

Departing and entering through the same door does not usually create any problem if the therapist operates alone, since sessions have ten-minute gaps between them and the next person is relatively unlikely to be already waiting. Moreover, the chances of meeting them tethering their bicycle to the fence outside are just as great, in my experience, even if you have exited from a different door. If the building is used by a group, rather than just one therapist, the risk of clients overlapping is much greater, though it could be minimized by staggering hours, so that one person begins sessions on the hour, another at a quarter past, another at half past, and so on; this way there is no noisy stampede at ten-to and on the hour.

It is not possible to generalize about whether people do or do not mind meeting others in this situation. More detailed reasons than mine are thoughtfully elaborated by Winnicott (1958, pp. 288–9). My feeling is that if you bump into another person destined for the same place, well, they have joined the club, and the feeling of relief at sharing problems might override that of embarrassment. But I am almost certainly being insensitive to the reality of other people's reluctance to confront rivals as well as witnesses.

There are, however, people who do not mind being seen in a therapist's waiting room, any more than at the dentist's; they might even welcome the chance of meeting other people with similar problems, and perhaps having the opportunity of discussing them. Why else do so many groups for problem-sharing exist? Or why do most people in therapy talk obsessively about it, preferably with a fellow traveller? The provision of a coffee machine might be a thoughtful addition to the potted plants which festoon most waiting rooms. The Women's Therapy Centre in London does in fact provide this facility, mentioned by Ernst (Ernst and Maguire, 1987, p. 103). When I suggested this to Harriet she chortled 'oral gratification!' I looked round for something to throw at her and could only find a used coffee mug . . . Maybe this sort of fraternization, which can easily degenerate into a game discernible as 'My therapist's better than your therapist', is precisely what therapists would like to discourage; but they have little chance of doing so, at least in a small town, or among the closely-knit social groups from which the bulk of their clientele are likely to come. Making the whole thing open could be healthier for all concerned. I discuss the role of cups of coffee in therapy later (see pp. 106–8).

Having experienced all sorts of arrangements, my own feeling is that the more natural the surroundings, the more they are part of a normal house, the easier the relationship is. But I am aware that this is a personal reaction not shared by all. My first experience of psychotherapy was in a hospital out-patients' clinic which I disliked because of its impersonality and the feeling of being processed in a sausage machine. I also disliked the association with illness rather than a desire for emotional growth. My first private therapist had a consulting room adjoining the house, with its own entrance and a different exit. I saw the advantages of this but did not like the furtive feeling it gave me, as if I ought not to want people, even co-consulters, to know where I was going. My second therapist practised in a group who shared a house, and it felt friendly and natural to enter through a door giving on to the street like any other house, with a kitchen where various therapists congregated for coffee. My third therapist reserved a room in his house, with a private entrance. His wife and children were not infrequently visible in the garden and this too felt friendly and natural. I liked it, but I am aware that some people might find it embarrassing. Some people want to see the therapist as a real person, while others are anxious not to know any biographical details which might destroy (or excite) their fantasies.

Having set the scene for two real people to meet in an identifiable room, we now discover that these people are actors on a stage, playing roles which are not immediately identifiable to either of them and without a script. Who are these 'characters in search of an author', and what do they say to each other? The role playing is known as transference and is traditionally supposed to be the hub of the therapeutic encounter. But if you are speaking to someone who only exists in the false role in which you have cast him or her, are you really solving your own problem of whether 'to be or not to be', or merely reiterating Hamlet's question? – which may not have been Hamlet's but Shakespeare's.

Part II

EXPERIENCING PSYCHOTHERAPY

4 TRANSFERENCE OR UNREALITY

THEORY

*B*y *transference is meant a striking peculiarity of neurotics. They develop toward their physician emotional relations, both of an affectionate and hostile character, which are not based upon the actual situation but are derived from their relations toward their parents (the Oedipus complex). Transference is a proof of the fact that adults have not overcome their former childish dependence . . . it is only by learning to make use of it that the physician is enabled to induce the patient to overcome his internal resistances and do away with his repressions.* (Freud, 'Psychoanalysis: Freudian school', p. 674)

The sort of patronizing vocabulary in this statement by Freud (1944) and the reduction of the client to the status of child, as well as the narrowly Oedipal interpretation of the transference, are behind my misgivings about the concept. Very early on in therapy I felt that there must be a significant real encounter between two people, actually present, and that if they were to get anywhere it was more likely to be by meeting on terms of equality. Yet the traditional view of the analyst is of someone who remains as neutral and anonymous as possible, saying little, revealing nothing of himself, the better to reflect the attitudes of the other person. Since these have not been pro-voked by any actual intervention on the part of the analyst, they will reveal that person's habitual distortions and expectations.

The basic anomaly in the therapeutic situation is that two

people face each other, alone, over a long period of time. In classical analysis even this amount of confrontation does not obtain, since the analyst is not visible, but seated behind the recumbent patient. During this time, one of them pours out anything that comes through his or her mind, including things which seem very private and may never have been voiced before, while the other remains virtually silent and anonymous, vouchsafing no opinion and giving away no personal information. It is not, of course, always like that; some therapists are more active and communicative than others. But that is the traditional pattern, still observed by many, both as creed and practice. It is difficult for therapists, even liberal ones, to counteract this, and they may have their reasons for not doing so.

The theory is that, since one knows nothing about the therapist, who does not directly state his or her opinions, anything one feels about his or her character or reactions is a 'projection'. That is, one projects on to the blank screen/ therapist responses that one's previous experience leads one to expect but which, since the therapist has not reacted at all, are inappropriate and merely repeat one's habitual distortions.

My objections to this theory are twofold. Firstly, it devalues the consulter's perceptions of the therapist. These are not just neurotic distortions, based on fantasy, that repeat inappropriate past behaviour, but are also part of a real relationship, in the present, with a real person. One's deductions are not necessarily incorrect. Discussion revealed several times that my intuition, or observation, of my therapist's real reaction was accurate, although it had been unvoiced and at times not even fully part of her conscious attitude. Her frank recognition of this helped me to become more confident of the validity of my judgement, and less reserved about sharing my feelings, because they did not always meet with denial.

My second objection is that non-participation in this context is not and cannot be a neutral attitude. It can only too readily be construed as hostility. The traditional view is that only if the analyst presents a neutral, blank screen can the in-appropriate reactions of the transference be exposed. Therapists regard the profound unnaturalness of this stance as one of the positive benefits of psychotherapy, as outlined by Anthony Storr:

The comparative blankness of the analyst is the quickest and most effective way of disinterring what is wrong in the patient's present relationship, in what way his human needs were not met in the past, and what he needs and hopes from human beings in the future. (in Rycroft, 1966, p. 81)

It is true that, in the absence of a response, one tends to supply one, along the lines of those which one habitually attributes (rightly or wrongly) to other people, and the exploration of this uncovers the dynamics of one's usual relationships. This does not alter the fact that the core of the difficulties experienced by many people in psychotherapy is precisely this blank-screen technique, which causes them to perceive the therapist as cold, indifferent or even rejecting – a non-person. This is stated with lucidity and conviction by Lomas:

*At first sight it would appear reasonable to suppose . . . that the nearer the therapist approaches the identity of a blank screen, the more easily he will evoke the projection on to himself of undistorted images by the patient. But in personal relationships a 'blank screen' response carries with it a negative emotional charge which must of necessity affect the attitude of the patient. An apparent **lack** of emotional response by a therapist is more likely to evoke a standard set of reactions in most patients: hurt, anger, withdrawal, confusion, idealization and envy of a being who seems to be so free of the emotional disturbances which afflict him and the people he knows in his ordinary life. Such reactions are artifacts caused by the therapeutic setting, rather than pure manifestations of childhood experience.* (1973, p. 139, author's emphasis)

Complaints about this sphinx-like role, ranging from jocular protest to real fury or total disorientation, are almost universal among those in therapy. Typical comments are found in Oldfield's survey, such as:

The counsellor had to take a distanced stance – this stopped me. There was no feedback to help me express myself . . . I wish she could have told me what she thought of me, of my coming . . . I expected her to be more aggressive somehow – in the way of direct questioning. But she explained that this was not her way of doing it. I accepted this . . . the whole thing is rather mysterious to me: she was quite prepared to sit in complete silence, if that was what I wanted. (1983, pp. 62–3)

Since systematic rejection and frustration from significant others in our lives is exactly what has caused the distress which brought most people to therapy, can it be that there is any justification for this technique, the pivot of classical analysis? Would it not be more therapeutic that people who have found it difficult to communicate should learn from the therapist how to establish a natural communication with another person? Is it so certain that the dangers in the possibility of the therapist becoming more human, more approachable and communicative, would really outweigh the advantages? Psychotherapy is an intimate, in-depth experience. Can one have such a thing with a faceless stranger?

If one is to get anywhere in therapy it is less likely to be through playing with Rorschach blots in the company of a mute stranger, than through the establishment and discussion of a relationship. This will not be an entirely two-way contact, as in the outside world, but a form of alliance, in which someone who feels that many of the other relationships in their life have not been successful can search with safety for the reasons, in their visible reactions to an individual, for why this should be so. It should be accepted that these reactions are not always, or primarily, distortions of a transference nature. If they are treated as such the likely result is to make the other person clam up entirely and refuse to discuss the relationship at all – at least in my experience.

It is not just the popular imagination but also analysts

themselves (at least in psychoanalytic literature) who tend to see the transference more as a fixation on outmoded childhood models, thus denigrating the analysand's status as an adult, and interpreting the relationship solely in terms of the past (or distortions and inappropriate patterns) irrespective of what might be going on in the present between two people who are actually there. Quite probably many therapists will deny that this is what they believe; certainly some don't. But a great deal of the literature, and people's actual experience of therapy, suggests that this is a trifle disingenuous.

An example of this sort of dismissive attitude to a patient's response was furnished by one psychiatrist whom I simply could not stand, to the extent that I asked the staff of the nursing home to prevent him from visiting me after the first week. He immediately put it down to 'negative transference'. The hysterical intensity of my hatred indeed suggested that this must be partly the case, although I could not think of any childhood figure he reminded me of. I think it was more the case of successive unreasonable authority figures in my life, intensifying my resentment of authoritarian parents. But the fact that he evoked a similar response from many of the nurses (and, as I later learnt, previous patients) suggested that there was also a strong element of reality in this reaction. The man was quite simply a bully, unreasonable and brusque in the extreme. He treated nurses, patients, secretaries and even psychologists as if they were morons or criminals. This was confirmed by my observations, conversations with the nurses and Harriet's impressions of his attitude to her. The negative response he evoked was not necessarily due to transference, therefore, but was the natural and appropriate reaction to his threatening language and behaviour.

For it is in the resolute denial of the reality of the person's experience that the dangers of over-emphasis on transference seem to me to lie. As Lomas declares, 'transference must be given second place to a mutual exploration of each other's stance' (1981, p. 52). He refers to Thomas Szasz:

The concept of transference serves two separate analytic purposes; it is a crucial part of the patient's therapeutic experience, and a succesful defensive measure to protect the analyst from too intense affective and real-life involvement with the patient. For the idea of transference implies denial and repudiation of the patient's **experience qua experience;** *in its place is substituted the more manageable construct of a* **transference experience.**

Thus, if the patient loves or hates the analyst, and if the analyst can view these attitudes as transference, then, in effect, the analyst has convinced himself that the patient does not have those feelings and disposition towards **him.** *The patient does not really love or hate the analyst, but someone else. This is why so-called transference interpretations are so easily and so often misused; they provide a ready-made opportunity for putting the patient at arm's length.* (Szasz, 1963, p. 432, author's emphasis)

If, under the influence of Freud, transference were not considered the king-pin of therapy, there would be little point in making an issue out of it. But this is the case, and I think it is responsible for the excessive focus on the past and on fantasy, to the detriment of present reality. It is not that the latter is necessarily **more** important, but that it is **equally** important, and this does not seem to have been given due recognition so far. This over-emphasis on transference, viewed in a narrowly Oedipal context, is not helpful either to those already in therapy or to those contemplating it, who find this one of the more off-putting aspects of the exercise. No less a person than Jung himself stated this danger very forcibly.

The continual reduction of all projections to their origins – and the transference is made up of projections – . . . constantly destroys the patient's attempts to build up a normal human relationship . . . Quite apart from this major loss there is the danger of perpetually brooding on the past, of looking back wistfully to things that cannot now be remedied – though, obviously, reductive analysis **is** *also necessary and the doctor* **must** *probe as deeply as possible into the origins of a neurosis in order to lay the foundation for the subsequent* *synthesis. The transference therefore consists in a number of projections which act as a substitute for a real psychological relationship. They create an apparent relationship and this is very important . . . [but] the patient's claim to a human relationship still remains and should be conceded, for without a relationship of some kind he falls into a void.*

Somehow he must relate himself to an object existing in the immediate present if he is to meet the demands of adapting with any degree of adequacy . . .

The touchstone of every analysis that has not stopped short of partial success . . . is always this person to person relationship, a psychological situation where the patient confronts the doctor on equal terms and with the same ruthless criticism that he must inevitably learn from the doctor in the course of his treatment.

This kind of personal relation is a freely negotiated bond or contract as opposed to the slavish and humanly degrading bondage of the transference. For the patient it is like a bridge: along it, he can make the first steps towards a worthwhile existence. He discovers that his own unique personality has value, that he has been accepted for what he is, and that he has it in him to adapt himself to the demands of life. (1921, pp. 135–7)

My own feeling too is that there is a need to meet on equal terms. My view is that a realistic appraisal of the therapist helps the therapee bear the transference, which can at times be very painful, and reintegrate herself into real life as a less neurotic person. A more open participation by the therapist also enables the transference to be spotted more clearly by the consulter, not leaving the therapist as the only person aware of what is and is not 'real'. As Hobson says:

Unless at the appropriate time – and this timing is crucial – the therapist reveals what he is like, the patient has no opportunity to test out fantasy against fact. The patient is hindered in his efforts to discover his identity. Since all is illusion he can come to believe that all is distortion – his experience of himself and his perception of other people. Then all his emotional responses are 'neurotic'. There is no healthy bit left . . . The opaque mask may put the patient in an untenable, helpless position in various ways. (1985, pp. 202–3)

My attitude to transference, and the concept of the therapist as an opaque mask, has certainly been influenced by my childhood experience. (A similar resentment of the analyst's apparent indifference is to be found in Ronald Fraser's autobiography *In Search of a Past*. He too had parents who did not acknowledge his identity.) As Harriet, my second therapist, suggested, my parents had in themselves been transference-rather than reality-figures. My father was an almost psychotically detached individual, who did not seem to notice my existence, or anybody else's. My mother held up to me the roles of ideal mother and ideal daughter. I knew these were false, but I was expected to collude with this role playing. My dislike of unknown and unreacting interlocutors probably stems from this. My parents were absorbed in their own activities, never listened to me or played with me, never gave me a sense of existing as a separate person valued as such. When I go to see my mother now I have to hang my personality on the doorknob as I enter her house. She never asks me any questions about my life, and never listens if I speak. I am subjected to a lengthy monologue which abolishes my reality totally, and I suppose it was always like this. She treats me like a patient might treat an analyst – projecting on to me her own fantasies, oblivious of my identity as a real person. Hence, no doubt, my refusal to do this to a therapist. This could be construed as a transference reaction, since it relates to childhood. It is not, however, based on a false apprehension of reality, either then or now. It is on the contrary founded on a very real need to have my experience validated.

There is, then, on the one hand the transference – that is, the false attribution of certain attitudes to the therapist, based on those of significant others in the past. But on the other hand it does not seem reasonable to discount the existence of genuine interaction between two people in the present, which has nothing to do with projected roles. The point about transference, surely, is that it will happen anyway, whether or not the therapist facilitates it by offering the consulter a blank screen on which to project fantasies. Although in the analytic confrontation it can be an engulfing emotional experience in which we relive ancient traumas in an artificially created situation, from which it is difficult to escape because the affect is so powerful and its superimposition on reality so strong, it is also a phenomenon which occurs all the time in daily life. The therapeutic aim of creating a transference situation is to show how we **habitually** distort the reactions of others, due to preconditioned responses, and how this continually, in all sorts of circumstances, diminishes our ability to assess our own motives and other people's opinions correctly. Past experiences are, of course, responsible for this distortion, and need to be discovered and analysed. But the real focus should be on what we are doing in the present, in actual situations, and on how this can be modified in the future.

What are transferred to the analyst are primarily those urges of the self that have been denied experience, and the authentic self is concerned not merely with past frustrations but with present and future possibilities of relationship. (Lomas, in Rycroft, 1966, p. 133)

It would seem that this stands a much better chance of resolution in the context of a relatively normal interchange, in which the person feels free to explore their misconceptions with an equal, instead of exposing them to the scrutiny of a sphinx with a superior grasp of reality. It will be easier, too, to test the new, more accurate perceptions with someone who has always been just what they are, rather than Jocasta suddenly metamorphosed into the mother of the boy next door.

The therapist cannot, after all, remain entirely neutral or a totally unknown quantity, especially after prolonged contact. We all reveal quite a lot about ourselves, through our gestures, our clothes, our choice of décor and so on. The involuntary smile or frown, a twitch of the lips, the white knuckles of a tense fist in an otherwise impassive listener, the degree of relaxation with which someone sits in a chair, even the various modulations of 'Oh?', all indicate something of the person's attitude, and many people in therapy are hyper-sensitive to such shades of non-verbal communication. One gradually builds up an image of the various ways in which one is being encouraged in certain directions, even by a mainly non-directive therapist. Unless they remain totally silent and non-interpretative throughout all sessions, one quickly senses a more sympathetic response to certain subjects or moods, and, depending on whether one tends to be compliant or aggressive, cultivates or avoids those which it is felt might give offence or gratification to the therapist.

Patients do not see the analyst as a blank screen. They scrutinize the analyst, who aims to remain inscrutable, and they find many clues to the nature of this person they are dealing with. They sense the state of mind of the analyst and respond accordingly. (Casement, 1985, p. 58)

For instance, the appearance of the neo-Freudian antennae, accompanied by a glint in the eye at the slightest mention of sex, might either cause one to drop the subject, because this is obviously what they are expecting, so you lapse into cliché, or to dwell on it, because one is playing the good patient and earning parental approval. Most therapists get noticeably more enthusiastic when people talk about their relationship with them, either through narcissism or because they sniff the incense of transference. So again people will tend to offer or withhold the bait, according to temperament. This may be construed as resistance, but it is also a reaction to perceived reality, rather than fantasy. As Casement observes: 'What is not always acknowledged is that patients also read the unconscious of the therapist . . . every analyst or therapist communicates far more to the patient about himself than is usually realized' (1985, p. xi).

Halmos (1965, p. 91) mentions that the influence of comments of 'Mm-hmm' and of 'good' in the responses of interviewees and listeners was examined in an experimental study by Hildum and Brown (1956), who found these monosyllabic grunts powerfully reinforcing. Halmos declares that 'this cannot but undermine our confidence in the possibility of "not influencing"'. He also quotes Nielsen:

We cannot be neutral in our daily work as therapists; the research on counter-transference has shown that this attitude is virtually impossible to maintain. New methods of psychotherapy may be indicated putting more stress on guidance and re-education . . . we **have to realize that psychoanalytic therapy has always been directive, and that the directive force is the personality of the therapist and his value judgements.** (1960, author's emphasis)

Even a relatively silent therapist provokes some reaction, because their very silence arouses some sort of feeling in the other person. As Hayley declares:

Non-directive therapy is a misnomer. To state that any communication between two people can be non-directive is to state an impossibility. Whatever a therapist doesn't say to a patient as well as what he says will circumscribe the patient's behaviour. If a therapist refuses to accept the patient's request for direction he is obviously directing the patient not to ask him what to do . . . silence is inevitably a comment on the patient's behaviour. (1963, p. 71)

More usually, the therapist does take at least a minimal part in the proceedings and so conveys something of his or her involvement and interest (or lack of it) by their words or tone of voice, by the kind of occasions when they intervene, or refrain from doing so. One adjusts one's behaviour almost unwittingly to one's perception of the person one is confronted by, in this as in any other situation. The very fact that the therapist's reactions are more of a mystery than those of other acquaintances may lead some people to be unnaturally wary, others to be less considerate of their interlocutor's feelings than they usually are, on the grounds that one is not **supposed** to be paying attention to them. This too is a reaction to the actual situation, which has nothing to do with transference and indeed may inhibit transference.

Nor is it by any means certain that therapists behave in exactly the same way to different people, that they offer exactly the same blank screen to everyone. Different temperaments will cause them to react in slightly different ways. This may be called counter-transference; it is also an intuitive appraisal of what that particular person needs – gentleness, dependability, a matter-of-fact approach, more or less reserve. One cannot, then, discount the presence of an authentic perception of each other as people and the interaction conditioned by this, operating simultaneously with the transference.

EXPERIENCE

My own experience has reinforced these views. I was present, in a more or less similar form, in all of my three therapies. Yet the relationship was in each case different, as was the course of each therapy. This was not due to transference, but to the different character and style of each therapist. This conditioned my response to them and their approach to psychotherapy. There were, of course, transferential attitudes in each therapy, as I will go on to discuss. But I think that in each case an actual exchange in the present was a more salient feature of the encounter, and was also more therapeutic than any transference.

Nothing in my conscious experience with my first therapist (Sybil) had made me aware of a transference situation, nor do I remember discussing it. We both remained somewhat sphinx-like about our feelings toward each other. I gained important insights, and benefited from her non-directive, reliable, non-condemning response. But I felt the lack of her participation as a real person keenly.

My second therapist (Harriet) seemed to bring herself much more fully into the dialogue; she stated that she had been influenced in this by her own therapist, Peter Lomas. My early intuition of this, backed up by discussion of it with her, confirmed my view that psychotherapy could be more like an encounter between equals, based on a real interaction in the present. I felt it need not be an artificial relationship, in which the therapist is denied reality, both by their own abstinence and the other person's projections.

This view was entirely supported by my third therapy, with Simon, one of whose therapists had also been Lomas. I did not undergo any powerful transference in the eighteen months I was with him. He was at times cast in certain roles, we discussed our changing relationship, but the exchanges felt normal. This realism was a large factor in the therapeutic aspect of the relationship. It felt like an encounter between equals, of equal reality and intelligence, in spite of the artificiality of the framework – namely, that I came to consult him about my problems, and we did not meet outside the consulting room.

I am, then, sceptical that an intense transference has to exist; or that, if it does, it is therapeutic. Yet, in spite of my scepticism about the transference, after about a year and a half of psychopractice (as a friend deemed it should be called, when not therapeutic) a very powerful transference, both positive and negative, took over with Harriet. I went through a period of total disorientation, a prime example of transference neurosis, before I could begin to understand what was going on. I then began to consult Simon, since I felt unable to function in this regressed state, and Harriet appeared unable to guide me out of it. Simon restored my ability to function as an adult, and this was a vital factor in effecting therapeutic change.

I subsequently revised my views about transference. I now think that it is inevitable, once therapy has reached a certain depth, but that it need not be so painful or devastating. I wish to examine what factors are involved in precipitating and controlling the transference, and to examine why I feel that the cooler relationship I had with Sybil and Simon was far more therapeutic than the intense transference I underwent with Harriet. Although I was often depressed during my therapies with them, the depression never seemed to be triggered off by the relationship with the therapist, as it did with Harriet; nor did I experience the same sort of pain by reliving traumatic early experiences. At the same time, Harriet's greater naturalness and openness, like Simon's, were more productive than Sybil's reserve in helping me discover which reactions belonged to the present and which were merely responses conditioned by the past.

My different reaction to three therapists and three (exclusively medical) psychiatrists may have something to do with my own change over the years. It is also possible that an encouraging experience of therapy the first time round gave me positive expectations towards the second attempt, so one might allege that there was a transference in that respect on to Harriet from Sybil. There was also some measure of transference in that I was trying to establish a different contact with each therapist, that would to some extent counterbalance the previous therapy. Yet an equally important component must have been my sense of each person as a different personality who consequently elicited different responses from me. There was relatively little evidence to go on, regarding this conjecture, but I see no reason why it should be dismissed as a transference fantasy. The more plausible source was observation of actual communications, both of a verbal and non-verbal nature.

When I first began psychotherapy I hadn't read much about it, though I was vaguely familiar with the concept of transference. I was baffled by what seemed to be a blank screen presented by the therapist, who did not (it seemed to me) participate in the dialogue herself as a real person, with opinions or verifiable characteristics. After three and a half years I had very little idea of what Sybil was like and no idea at all of what she felt about me. Subsequent friendship revealed that she was greatly surprised that none of her feelings towards me had got across (I think it would have been much more helpful if they had) and that the personality which I had attributed to her was not altogether congruent with the person I then got to know. I do not however think that this was a transference projection. I think that Sybil did indeed manifest as a therapist certain characteristics which she did not show with friends, such as limitless patience and tolerance.

There was, however, a transference (which we never discussed in these terms) and which was complicated by the counter-transference, again not discussed until years later. A good deal of the therapy focused on my dislike of my mother, whom I perceived as domineering and possessive, prone to the martyr act and subject to manifold self-delusions. The therapist apparently identified with this, having experienced her own mother in very similar terms. I did not of course know this, although I was dimly aware of the collusion against my mother, hence in favour of my father. What I did not quite understand was that this unvoiced collusion complicated my attitude to this female therapist, old enough to be my mother, and indeed the mother of two people about my age. She was in every respect unlike my mother and therefore became to some extent an idealized mother image – the opposite of my real parent – and identified with my father, whose eyes were very similar to hers. I think I saw this at the time, but I can't be sure. It was never discussed, as far as I remember.

My father died during this therapy and she and her husband later became increasingly identified with the lost figure of a loved but distant parent I had never really known. The death of her husband (a colleague and friend in his own right) was one of the major factors precipitating the depression which led me to resume therapy with Harriet six years later. I was losing my father all over again; although this time it was both an idealized figure, who had none the less become far more real than my genetic father, and someone married to an idealized mother image. Gradual understanding of this in the second therapy helped me come to terms with the process of mourning. Since the element of transference in my first therapy remained largely unknown to me, it is difficult to see how crucial or how helpful it can have been. I think there was a re-educative value in experiencing good parenting for the first time.

As I mentioned earlier, the transference was in my case complicated by the probability that my parents had been more fantasized than real. My mother has always held up to me her ideal image of a mother and asked me to collude with seeing her in this role. There has never been anything authentic in our relationship. The dialogue has always been an attempt to reproduce the ideal daughter–ideal mother roles and we have never spoken to each other as real people. My father was a complete sphinx, whose thoughts and character were largely unknown to me. I could only conjecture as to his feelings. I had spent my entire life looking for an idealized father figure, who was not him, and for whom I had no model in reality. Whereas my mother was just about real enough and even sporadically good enough for me to have a very clear idea of the ideal mother I wanted.

To some extent this image of the idealized mother got transferred on to my next therapist, Harriet, but again because it didn't tally with my image of my real mother I denied the therapist's suggestion that I was seeing her as my mother. More immediately obvious was the casting of Harriet into the role of permissive parent as opposed to the authoritarian one represented by my real parents and first therapist. Subsequently, Harriet claimed that I saw her as the bad mother and a Samaritan who was helping me as the good mother. A claim with some validity, but, like the previous one, it over-simplified the truth. Because she was indeed the mother of a large family, although not old enough to be my mother, it was inevitable that I should see her to some extent as a mother figure. This role was reinforced by a number of mothering gestures early in the therapy. Yet it was obvious to me from the start that there was another transference at work, since she was roughly the same age as my elder brother and, like him, acted the role of infrequent playmate, as well as being a bridge between the adult world and the peer group. It took us both some time to realize that, female and communicative as she was, she also enacted the role of silent, unknowable father, secretly loved yet openly hated, because I had to side with my mother who was the strong one, 'the Boss' (as he called her), the one who set standards and made rules.

My mother had been the only really significant adult in my childhood. There were no aunts or uncles in evidence, only one grandparent (my mother, magnified) and a mainly silent and aloof father. My relationship with my mother had therefore been very intense. She was the only grown-up who expressed or enforced criteria, the only source of approval or censure, since nothing I did seemed to have much effect on my father. She was the only provider of material necessities, as she was always ready to remind me. Pleasing my mother was therefore a question of survival, particularly as she kept threatening to leave us and warning me that my father would not look after me, which was a realistic statement. Yet I was unconsciously aware from an early stage that I did not much like her or respect her views – something I consciously denied with vehemence. My childhood was therefore characterized by a strong but ambivalent attachment to a powerful mother figure and an unfulfilled nostalgia for a father which I couldn't express. It was also characterized by the absence of any grown-up who would listen to me.

My therapist therefore became the mother-who-was-everything, as well as the idealized mother, in addition to the father who might have been almost anything but never truly became someone. Added to that, she was also my elder brother, an adored but distant childhood god, who became in my adolescence a feared bully and hated rival for my mother's attention. That was somewhat overloading the transference; small wonder it became intense and unbearable to both of us!

All this seems crystal clear with hindsight. But it took us some years to understand. For one thing, Harriet might have believed in transference all along, but I didn't. I thought the whole concept was nonsense, and was determined from the start to obtain a fairly realistic picture of my therapist, so as to counter any inappropriate transference; an attitude I consciously reversed in my next therapy with Simon. This obscured the transference for some time. Yet I think it finally saved the relationship and prevented me from terminating therapy prematurely. It turned what had for years seemed a wholly destructive and damaging experience into a fruitful one – though I still wonder whether it was really necessary, or at least if it could not have been analysed and resolved sooner.

This salvage operation was only possible because I had a very definite sense that my positive feelings towards Harriet were realistically justified. Not only was there a certain amount of evidence in the therapy to suggest that she really was kind and considerate in her dealings with me, but we had a number of friends in common who supported the view that she was an extremely pleasant person. I was in no doubt about this. Simultaneously it was increasingly difficult for me to see the therapy as anything but negative. How is it possible, I kept saying to myself, that such an exceedingly nice person can be the source of such a damaging experience; was I deluding myself that she was nice? Or merely imagining that the therapy was destructive? Other people corroborated the first impression and real evidence, as well as powerful unconscious (transference) feelings, made it impossible to deny the second. In spite of that I tussled for several years with this conflict and refused fully to acknowledge how negative the transference was, because I felt it unjustified in relation to such a likeable person. If I hadn't had this apprehension of the reality, corroborated by others so I knew it was not just a fiction, I don't think I would have had the incentive to persist in therapy after the first few major hitches, much less through the unrelenting trauma of several years. It was only because I knew that this unreal experience (unreal because it had an element of transferred negative affect, yet terrifyingly real in terms of what it was doing to me) bore little relationship to the reality of the exchange that I could see the projections clearly at work, exposed for what they were – inappropriate reactions to the present.

Yet they were not entirely inappropriate. My therapist, by being helpless to alleviate my depression and allowing me to go into a nursing home and become the responsibility of a psychiatrist, was repeating a childhood situation when neither parent had ever been able to cope with my moods or problems. It is probably relevant that for two years in my teens I was hospitalized as the result of a fractured spine. My parents had to hand me over to the medics and watch helplessly while I suffered, both physically and morally. None of the doctors or nurses I met in those two years let me recognize that there was any legitimate cause for depression in suddenly finding myself paralysed. Instead they treated me as a criminal because I became severely anorexic, and took refuge from my physical problems by throwing myself frantically into study for my O Levels, rather than trying to play netball in a wheel chair as hospital policy decreed that I should. They would not let us recognize ourselves as different, or as having legitimate problems. This was initially helpful but ultimately unhealthy, because it involved a denial of reality.

The feeling of being repeatedly let down, that my depression was indeed unmanageable, now as then, was real enough, and not a fantasy. This made it very destructive. Yet something was salvaged when Harriet looked with me quite frankly at the element of counter-transference in all this. She admitted to her own narcissistic need to be seen as a nice person, which to some extent repeated my mother's narcissistic need to see herself as a good mother, coupled with her insistence that I concur with this false image. I had, of course, also challenged the hospital staff's wish to be seen as medical wizards.

Having, then, vehemently denied for months that there was any way in which I was going to identify Harriet with my mother, since they were totally unalike in temperament and views, it came as quite a revelation to me, and one which triggered off a whole series of insights, to realize that I was treating her in precisely the same way as I treat my mother, in spite of **knowing** that this was unnecessary and inappropriate. I was protecting her, my therapist, from my depression and my anger, because this was what my mother had always demanded of me. If Harriet had been less honest about the counter-transference, and her real similarity with my mother in this respect, I might not have understood so clearly just what was at work.

Unlike my parents and the doctors, Harriet encouraged me to look at my depression, to express it; yet she was not prepared for me to plunge into it so completely. Once I had understood that it was not logical to protect my therapist as I had protected my mother, I was aware of the need to face up to my depression fully, to identify myself with it, in order to emerge strengthened. But Harriet found herself too involved in the despair, and equally unable to understand it, so was unable to help me out of it. It was like someone watching a person drowning, having the sense not to jump in, but not knowing where to find a lifeboat. When I was mute with despair, and could only cry, both during sessions and outside them, the analysis broke down. Harriet admitted that there was nothing she felt able to say, or do; that she felt helpless. I would leave the sessions totally uncomforted, no more able to understand what was going on, humiliated and bereft. I felt shut out by her apparent lack of reaction. 'I have to kill myself, because I don't exist', I explained to her, after one such non-encounter. My parents had never listened to my need for someone to share both happiness and pain. Harriet could not quite grasp why this annihilated me to the point that when I was depressed I had no sense of self to hang on to, and no way of comprehending that I might matter to other people.

After much insistence I wormed out of her the frank admission that she found my depression 'unbearable'. Not me, she hastened to add, but my depression. As far as I was concerned there was no longer any real distinction, though I could see the theoretical one, and I felt extremely rejected and despondent about any help being forthcoming. If she can't bear my depression, and I can't bear it, I thought, where do I go for help in order to bear it?

This conversation sprang from an angry jibe of mine: 'Go and reread Winnicott on hate in the counter-transference.' To my surprise, she did. Then said that it wasn't really relevant, except for his discussion of ways in which the mother can find the baby's demands hateful. Not the baby, she insisted, but its demands. There again, I saw the distinction, but commented that that is the adult's view. It doesn't help the baby much, since it only knows that the demands are not being met, or that they arouse antagonism. I subsequently felt very raw and resentful about this admission and wished my therapist had been less frank. I simply did not know where to turn when in distress after this, and it reinforced my feeling that this was precisely the effect I had on everyone, starting from parents and teachers when I was a child, up to the present. This realization of a past pattern through the transference and counter-transference is indeed how psychoanalytic psycho-therapy operates. The crucial thing is that the interaction should be analysed, so that the person changes. Instead, Harriet shelved it by telling me that I had reached her limitations and had to reconcile myself to this inescapable fact.

Uncomfortable as it was, this realization, brought about by open admission of a counter-transference, could have helped me to change. We did not explore it deeply enough, so I only saw that it was true without being able to change myself. I went through a very negative phase in psychopractice, during which I constantly muttered that I was going to abandon the entire exercise, that it had been the most damaging and non-therapeutic experience in my life, etc. Poor Harriet had merry hell during this time, and her desire to be seen as helpful and pleasant took a severe knocking. Yet she did not give up on me (while putting no pressure on me not to give up on her), and continued to be patient and tolerant, even friendly, while openly admitting that she found my remarks very hurtful. Since I had never been allowed to criticize my mother, whose reaction when hurt was to intensify the martyr act and deliberately arouse overwhelming guilt in me, this in itself was quite a cathartic experience. For perhaps the first time in my life I had attacked a loved object who did not disintegrate under the attack, but accepted it and remained fundamentally undamaged. I was puzzled that she could take my anger so much more easily than my cries for help and my despair.

There was a re-educative element in this recognition of her **real** difference both from me and from my mother. The most therapeutic aspect of the episode was her wish to be truthful, rather than protect herself. What most helped was the open acknowledgement that my intuition, that had nagged at me for months, had in fact been correct. Namely, that she experienced my need as hateful, and was to some extent rejecting me, despite her denials. My feelings were validated.[1] Although I might have preferred to have been told the contrary, truth was better than lies. It could help me change in a way that kindly lies could not. Perhaps more than words at this time (particularly since it was a word that had caused the distress), I was helped by a very warm Christmas card and present, which stated clearly to me that *I* was not hated, even if my behaviour was. This again revised the parental attitude, which identified me and my behaviour to such an extent that I was seen as **being** bad when I was just behaving badly.

Another aspect of Harriet's **real** difference from my mother was also therapeutic, though it took some time to see it as such. She admitted, when I challenged her about the matter, that she had never been in the sort of despair I was, and could not fully understand it. This left me feeling alone, although again the admission validated my intuition, which helped. What was therapeutic in the long term was that this reassured me that Harriet was not threatened by my despair, as my mother had been. Harriet's real limitation was that she could find no way of helping me out of my depression, but her real strength was that she was unable to follow me into it. In the first respect she was intensifying the pain, by repeating my mother's failure; in the second respect she was counteracting it, by being unlike my mother, and making sure that I knew this. I could not have known it through conjecture; I would have been more likely to transfer on to her my mother's depressive tendencies. It was therefore therapeutic to be shown a real person, who was different from the transferential figure.

The strong element of reality in this relationship temporarily went some way towards rescuing me from the transference neurosis, then. It made it more baffling and painful while it lasted, but did help me grasp what was **really** going on. However, it could also be argued that it ultimately aborted the healing aspects of the transference because it repeatedly re-enacted a hurtful experience from the past, in an environment which was **not** safer, and without a sufficiently detached 'containment' (as Bion and Casement call it) to support me when I collapsed with the pain. The transference enabled me to get in touch with childhood traumata, but this unleashed powerful forces of the unconscious, which overwhelmed Harriet too by their magnitude.

Harriet's failure to 'contain' me hurt unbearably because it was related to the transference; it was repeating yet again my parents' continual failure to provide any moral support. Yet I did not experience this **only** in the transference, as she tried to pretend. She herself even admitted occasionally that I had perceived a real failing in her. 'You have come up against my limitations', she said. She tried to convince me of the therapeutic value in realistically acknowledging this. The reality was however unhelpful because of the powerful transference. She was not just any adult who had been unable to help, she represented my parents' repeated failure in my childhood to give me the support I needed. Her failure was real, in the present, it was not just imaginary. Yet it caused disproportionate distress in me, as an adult, because I responded again as the child being hurt. The message I had received in childhood – that there was no help available, however incapable I felt myself to be of managing alone – was reinforced by her attitude. If she had not so repeatedly failed me when I most needed help I would not have become so unable to look after myself in the normal way, to the point of being unable to function for a while. Harriet claimed, with some justification, that I **made** her helpless. My neediness provoked in her a reaction of refusing to be needed that much. This was true; but the truth in it was damaging, because it reinforced my childhood conviction that my needs could never be met. The hopelessness that this inspired could only end in suicide.

The experience with Harriet was, then, damaging because of the transference, but also because it was real. What rescued me from the nightmare was the **reality** of there being other people who could listen to my despair without becoming overwhelmed by it themselves. There was a female Samaritan, who provided practical mothering and a male psychiatrist, who provided practical help and advice, and who took up the cudgels for me with my employers, acting to some extent as the omnipotent father figure I had fantasized as a child. These too were to some extent transferential figures. But they were not just acting roles in my scenario; they behaved this way with other people, and they actively illustrated my perceptions of them. These two helpers gave me the hope that there existed people strong enough to hear my despair, alleviate it and not be thrown by it, and this enabled me to crawl back to life.

I think Harriet's inability to help me out of my distress precisely at times when I was unable to cope with it myself was almost as damaging as my parents' initial failure. I had forgiven them for it and become able to look after myself, until the bereavements which preceded my re-entry into psychotherapy with Harriet. It seemed to me that, with her, each successive crisis exacerbated, rather than relieved, the childhood situation, when I had had to realize that no support could be expected from my parents. I felt increasingly hopeless about there being any help available. Maybe I learnt all over again that I can go it alone, and this gave me some self-respect. None the less, I am not sure that I would be alive to say this if there had been absolutely no help from outside figures.

Another crucial figure who gave me back a sense of identity was Simon, my third therapist. Harriet, as a therapist, and Sybil, as a friend, had become unable to integrate my depressed present self with their previous image, or to communicate their co-existence to me. Nor could Harriet understand why, when I am depressed, I can no longer imagine or remember any other state; just as, when I am happy, I cannot remember being depressed. While in no way a split personality, in the technical sense, I am totally the present persona, divorced from my other being. Psychotherapy has taught me to integrate the two, and to understand theoretically that they are both equally part of me. Simon's spontaneous perception of me, in the first interview, as energetic and positive beneath the manifest despair, helped me to incorporate this knowledge into a way of sitting out the black moods, when they come.

In this therapy there was probably again an idealization, the projection of a fantasy figure – that of the ideal brother which my real brother had ceased to be. Simon was exactly the same age as my brother, ten years older than me. Yet there was less idealization and more reality in the relationship than there had been with Harriet. Simon brought himself into the therapy sufficiently for me to be sure that he meant what he said, when expressing ideas or feelings, and this was an extremely therapeutic aspect of our encounter. I knew very little about him and was not much interested in finding out. This was both a conscious and a spontaneous, hence unconscious, reversal of my reaction to my therapy with Harriet. Simon, however, made sure that I knew clearly how he was reacting to me and this told me quite a lot about the sort of person I am and the effect I tend to have on other people.

The curious thing is that I experienced no intense transference, painful or otherwise, with Simon. I was usually pleased to see him, but almost never thought about him in between sessions. I did not mind his absences; I never dreamt about him; I only contacted him out of hours on strictly business matters. He had as much, or as little, importance as any other pleasant and intelligent colleague. I experienced no difficulty in terminating therapy with Simon, nor did I think of him afterwards. Whereas I remained in frequent contact with Harriet and Sybil (after a gap of three years). I never separated from them, any more than I had from my mother.

One factor may have been that I only saw him once a week. My experience with both him and Sybil is that the relationship does not become so engulfing with sessions reduced to this interval. I did, however, become attached to Sybil in a much more dependent and artificial – that is, transferential – way, possibly because she was a woman. This does not however entirely explain it, since I had been intensely attached to the men I had been in love with, and those relationships cannot have been free of transference. An important factor was doubtless that my therapy with Simon ran concurrently with the last year of my therapy with Harriet, and I did not have the emotional energy to be so involved with two people at once. I was also heavily defended against any undue attachment to Simon because of my dislike of the dependency I had on Harriet, though the conscious defence would not have been sufficient to have countered strong unconscious forces if they had been at work.

I think that there was a real response to a real person operating here too. I did not get very attached to Simon because I experienced him as warm but basically detached. I tend to engage emotionally in the same gear as the other person. The very frankness with which we (mainly he) talked about our real or potential relationship testified to its relative coolness.

Simon tried consistently to make me see him as a man; that is, as the Other, and as a potentially desirable other. This usually annoyed me, because I neither desired him nor wished to do so, and I felt there was more mileage in discovering similarities of temperament beneath the differences in reaction. He saw the gender difference as a fundamental one, colouring all our discourse; I saw it as less helpful than his spontaneous empathy or congeniality. Significantly, through its Latin derivation the latter word means both 'likeable' and 'of the same species'. The word also contains the French 'con', meaning cunt. He was always trying to remind me that he had a penis; I thought it was more useful that he offered me a receptive space, in which we could jointly create something.

It might seem that I am here lapsing into the sort of vocabulary and clichés used by analysts to refer to transferential attitudes, and which conditioned my early resistance to the whole concept. I think they have a limited symbolic value, as my use here suggests, but that this has been over-exploited. Before I became aware of the transference in my attitude to Harriet I was annoyed by her insistence that it must be there. I noticed a book on her desk and got it out of the library. It was H. Racker's *Transference and Counter-Transference* (1968). In many ways I found it thoughtful and illuminating, but it infuriated me by its vocabulary. Almost every utterance or attitude of the patient is reduced to supposed desires for 'penis words' or wishes to seduce or castrate the 'analyst-father', and is subjected to interpretations like 'The splitting between the good and bad breast', 'rejection of the "sweet breast", so the patient could maintain herself free of guilt regarding the mother-analyst' (p. 102).

This resistance to stereotypes and narrowly sexual interpretations is behind my whole attitude to the concept of transference, and the way in which it is applied. There must be more room for the reality of the present situation, and for respect towards the adult who is still present in the regressed child. Maybe it is by building on this, on an exchange related to real life situations, and not a highly artificial and angst-making dependency, that there is most chance for growth and true re-education.

One solution to the problem of transference versus reality, on these lines, is provided by Carl Rogers' client-centred therapy. The interaction is much less unreal than the transference. The stress is no longer on the creation and resolution of an artificial transference, but on the exploration of real feelings, in a real situation. The therapist is still not acting like a 'real' person, in the usual sense of the word, but the client can test the inappropriateness of his or her feelings about a listener whom he or she **knows** to be open, receptive and non-judgemental. There is a subtle difference between this and the transference, in that the present reality of the therapist, as a genuinely neutral figure, is always kept in mind, alongside the inevitable projections or fantasies based on previous, negative experiences. There is no real confusion of the therapist with childhood figures and so the client's dignity as an adult is maintained, and the distortions are more readily perceived and investigated. This, at least, is how it feels to me, as well as being what is alleged as theory.

The initial misconceptions are the same as in the transference. 'The client projects on to the therapist attitudes of negative judgement, and reacts with fear and shame to those projected accusations of guilt' (Rogers, 1951, p. 202). But, because the client has always experienced the therapist as non-judgemental and warmly accepting, this 'leads to recognition by the client that these feelings are within her, they are not in the therapist [and] this is accomplished because the therapist has so completely put aside the self of ordinary interaction that there is no shred of evidence upon which to base the projection' (1951, p. 203).

This realistic appraisal of the therapeutic situation, by an autonomous adult, as opposed to the elaboration of a fantasy by a helplessly regressed child, leads to the spontaneous disappearance of the transference, perceived as meaningless, and obviates the necessity for a long working-out of a painful and degrading situation which has been artificially created by therapy itself.

Rogers does not discount the existence, even inevitability, of transference **attitudes** (that is, the projection of inappropriate responses on to a person in the present, conditioned by past experiences) in the majority of cases, and to varying degrees. What he does claim, however, is that these attitudes do not develop into a **relationship** which is pivotal to the therapy as with the Freudian model (1951, pp. 201, 209–10).

This shift of focus from past and fantasy, to the present and reality, seems to me a healthy one, designed to promote growth and decrease false dependency attitudes. It is also more in accordance with what really goes on. Rogers' approach does not, however, have the warmth and realism of the personal psychotherapy advocated by Peter Lomas, since it involves the counsellor remaining as neutral as the legendary blank screen.

Dr Lomas trained both Harriet and Simon, and I gained a lot from this. They were both always aware of transferential possibilities, but did not lose sight of the fact that ours was also a dialogue between adults, who reacted to each other as real people in the present. Through reasons which I think had more to do with their personalities than their gender, the discourse remained mainly intellectual with Simon. I did not 'act out' my unconscious impulses with him, as I had with Harriet. He helped me to grow, rather than regress. However, I still think that it was not the reality element in my relationship with her which was damaging. On the contrary, it enabled me to hang on to my positive feelings for her, which were based more on a real appraisal of her personality, than on fantasy. This was so even when the negative transference had become compounded with the reality of the counter-transference. The experience could have been destructive, and nearly was. Yet I was finally able to integrate the reality of her limitations with the reality of her strengths, because she had had the honesty to show me both and not repeat my mother's play acting.

My conviction is that, under every neurotic behaving like a child there is a reasonable adult struggling to emerge. One does not just project infantile fantasies on to another human being who is quite unrelated to them, but also appraises that human being with a certain degree of realism, keeping the real person in perspective, whilst at the same time distorting his or her image in terms of an idealized or rejected fantasy figure. The attempt to reproduce the anonymity of laboratory conditions does not facilitate this process. As I will go on to discuss, the need is rather to establish a more realistic and more personal relationship than that provided by the classical model.

5 THE THERAPIST AS REAL PERSON

*I believe that the whole climate of opinion that has grown
from Freud tends to inhibit emotional reciprocity in the
warmest of therapists, so that it is only with the greatest
reluctance, if at all, that he can allow himself to reveal the
feelings which the patient arouses in him.*
Lomas, *True and False Experience*, p. 139

FRIENDSHIP VERSUS PROFESSIONALISM

An example of an exchange which could be read at the level
of transference/counter-transference but which was, I
think, taking place almost entirely in the context of the
attempts of the two people concerned to work out a *modus
vivendi* (or *operandi*) and which, moreover, brings into
question the nature of this relationship, was the statement
made by Harriet after a few months of our therapy: 'You are
trying to make me into a friend.'

My immediate reaction was to feel accused, and therefore
guilty; the implication being that this was a reprehensible action,
or at the very least inappropriate. This could be, and indeed at
one level is, a classic case of transference. A superficially
anodyne statement is taken to be a criticism, due to habitual
feelings of guilt, activated by the real or imaginary tendency of
others to criticize. Consequently I felt hurt and attacked; my
inclination was to retreat into silence, repeating childhood
behavioural patterns, or into flippancy, pretending I hadn't
heard: merely a less straightforward version of silence, repeating a response (learnt later) to accusations I prefer to mull over
in my own time, rather than risking a premature reaction.

One might also say that there could be an element of
counter-transference at work. Since this particular therapist
had never seen me with other people in similar circumstances

she had no way of knowing whether I am more, or less, open, ingratiating, amiable, forthcoming, relaxed or teasing with them. I felt I was behaving naturally and treating her exactly as I would treat anyone else in roughly similar circumstances, given that I liked them and felt at ease with them. If she either felt this was an act, or that the attitude was inappropriate, this suggests that she was bringing to bear on me her expectations of how people in therapy should or do behave, and of what behaviour like mine might mean, coming from someone else.

This may sound like yet more twisting of a neutral statement into an accusation. However, my initial reaction, which was purely emotional and had nothing much to do with the content of the remark, but more to do with a conditioned readiness to detect censure, does seem to be borne out by a stylistic analysis. The use of 'trying' and 'make me into' suggests coercion on my part, and perhaps a certain unwillingness on hers, reinforced by the use of 'you' (subject: active agent) and 'me' (object: passive victim), as well as the implication of conscious effort in 'trying'. The words were not carefully chosen, and this may not have been the conscious meaning; but whether or not the above intentions were present, I am sure that the remark was not entirely neutral; it must have contained some affective content for the speaker.

We have, then, a relatively straightforward statement, which is, moreover, a not inaccurate assessment of observed behaviour, taken by the recipient to signify a reprimand rather than a mere comment. There is, in a sense, a double transference operating here, since I first of all project diffuse feelings of being in the wrong, habitually evoked in me by other people, and secondly project on to one therapist an attitude exemplifying what I think all therapists think (you ought not to treat them as humans or friends, but get on with the serious business of relating to a blank screen).

Awareness of the first projection brings a certain relief; a recognition that this is indeed how I react, and that it does not necessarily bear much relation to reality, so that in future it could be useful to consider whether the universal reprobation of which I feel the target comes from others or from within. This could lead to a more positive way of thinking and self-estimation. (It hasn't yet, but I live in hope.)

Awareness of the second projection, however, causes some teeth-gnashing, even now in the tranquillity of recollected emotion. If the remark was based on fairly accurate observation, it none the less seems to me that my attitude constituted a reasonable response to the actual situation. I had no reason to assume that this person was *un*friendly – rather the contrary – and while I didn't at the time imagine that therapists behaved like friends, this was a self-proclaimed non-sphinx, emitting friendly messages, and I accordingly reacted exactly as I would towards any other person whose manner was similar. This does not constitute a transference attitude, since it is not inappropriate, nor a stale repetition of past patterns, but a direct response to a present situation, showing moreover distinct progress from the past, when I would have been more wary. Yet the mere fact of making the comment indicates an element of surprise on her part; a suggestion that this is not how other people react, or how I might have been expected to react.

The implication is obvious: you are not treating me as a therapist, but as a friend; there is therefore a difference. **Here we have the crux of the matter, of the whole psychotherapeutic endeavour: does one want a therapist, or a friend?** The answer is less simple than it seems. Of course we all want friends. Some people come to therapy because they find it difficult to make friends, and one of the aims of the exercise is to enable people to relate more satisfactorily to others. It could also be that our friends are not necessarily good therapists, or that it seems unfair to claim that amount of undivided attention from a friend, a lay-person, who is not getting paid for it and who is requested meanwhile to set aside his or her own needs to listen to yours.

Without friends, most of us wouldn't get far in therapy. At

times of crisis, with or without a therapist around, one's primary need is for the kind of support that only friends can give, since no therapist is ever going to make the sort of comforting noises that a loyal and partial friend will make. However, most neurotic crises, as opposed to reasonable reactions to adverse circumstances, repeat a pattern of over-reaction, or relate in some way to a previous trauma, so that the supportive warmth of friendship, indispensable for weathering the storm, is not, alas, sufficient to enable us to discover the source of the problem, and modify our responses to the next trial. Friends, like antibiotics and hot drinks, get you over the crisis and may help you forget it until the next one, but it takes more than affection to heal the wound.

A detached yet sympathetic professional does therefore have a useful function, which cannot be fulfilled entirely by friends, because to some extent it goes against the nature of friendship. Friends are bound to be partial, to be affected to some extent by one's distress. Only at moments of extreme crisis (and with very forbearing friends) can one expect them to set aside their own needs and attend exclusively to yours, because friendship is essentially a reciprocal activity.

This was brought home to me when Sybil, some years after our therapy had ended, had become a friend. Although she was still sympathetic, she made it clear that she did not want to hear about my depression, and that I was not to 'treat her like a therapist'. I think the moral is that if you want friends who will listen to your problems, don't choose professional psycho-therapists, because they spend all day doing it, and want a break out of office hours.

Maybe the issue will become clearer if I rephrase it slightly. To what extent is it desirable that a therapist, who is not by definition a friend (though they may be friendly), should approximate their behaviour to that of a friend?[1]

The attitude of my three therapists to cups of coffee seems to me to illustrate this graphically. The Samaritans nearly always offer you a hot drink. Therapists generally don't unless they are of radical persuasion, like the Women's Therapy Centre in London, or confidently unorthodox like Winnicott.[2] Theory decrees that they should not allow 'oral gratification'.

Sybil would never have dreamt of offering me coffee. Once when I was very dehydrated by crying and anti-depressants I asked for a glass of water. She hesitated a long while before saying she would get it for me. Fetching it herself was probably a gesture of kindness. At the time I construed it as the wish not to let me see, or to be seen by, whoever was in the waiting room. I felt guilty and somewhat rejected.

Ten years later she said that she had been agonizing over whether, on the eve of her departure for a long break, she could give a cup of coffee to a severely anorexic therapee. I suggested (speaking as an ex-anorexic) that this could only be helpful, as a gesture of 'permission to eat'. She decided, however, that it would encourage too great a dependency. This seemed to me ironic, given that this person, after many years of therapy, was already dependent to the point of needing some sort of daily contact with the therapist.

Harriet sometimes made us both coffee when I was showing great distress. The first few times this happened I was immensely grateful for the kind and nourishing gesture, and the element of naturalness that this brought into the encounter. Then I reflected that the coffee (and the biscuit which she chomped on and I refused) was for her as much as me. It enabled her to leave the room when she could not bear my tears and satisfied her own need for oral gratification. So I became a bit sceptical about the altruism of the gesture, and saw it less as part of a natural relationship, since coffee was only produced in response to desperation.

Simon amazed me one day by spontaneously offering coffee as I arrived. I reasoned again that this was not altruism. It was mid-morning and the previous session may have been heavy; or perhaps he was anticipating a rough time with me. In the following months the offer of coffee became a kind of ritual greeting. But it was up to me whether I accepted or refused, though I felt it inhibited his wish for coffee if I declined. This freedom was part of the naturalness which characterized the relationship.

It also released my inhibitions with Harriet. Once, on the pretext that I had had to miss lunch in order to fit in the altered session time, I asked her if I might have a cup of coffee, feeling very daring. This timid gesture, and the alacrity with which it was gratified, gave me a disproportionate sense of control over my destiny and confidence that I was an acceptable person who could ask for things without fear of reprimand. It did more to eradicate a lifetime of feeling too unworthy to ask for anything than any analytic interpretation could have done.

The question still remains of to what extent a professional helper cannot be a friend, but must remain aloof, refrain from expressing sympathy or being overtly supportive, keep their own personality or problems out of a search which is exclusively designed to help the other person. These are separate and crucial issues.

My immediate reaction is that someone who is that aloof and detached is not going to help me much, in a real crisis, because if they don't care about me, neither do I about myself, and that is precisely what the problem is. It must be axiomatic that no depressive has enough self-esteem to think they are worth bothering about or worth saving, so that a fairly powerful message of reinforcement is needed from the other person. I would stress, however, that this is **only** the case during a crisis; even then, it will meet with denial and disbelief, but something will sink in and be stored up for future reference, while the absence of any sort of warmth or encouragement could be very damaging. At other times, there is little point in trying to persuade anyone who thinks they are the dregs that this is not necessarily the case, and obviously the usual therapeutic approach of a systematic exploration of why this attitude should have developed, and what experiences it is based on, is most likely to lead to a positive re-evaluation. Much, too, depends on timing. If Harriet had, during the early stages of therapy, stated that she did not reject me, I would merely have felt she hadn't seen me at my worst. It was only after some years in which the relationship had really been tried that I could find comfort in this statement, said moreover very gently and warmly, at a time when I was too low to respond to analytical rigour. When Simon also said that he valued me, I at first found this inconceivable. Yet, strengthened by Harriet and Sybil's esteem, and by other remarks made by Simon, which enabled me to have some idea of just what he valued, I came nearer to being able to believe in it. Acquiring an inner sense of worth was to me a question of survival, rather than just self-image, so it was an important part of the therapy to learn to believe these words.

CONVEYING UNCONDITIONAL POSITIVE REGARD

My point is that neither the demanding work of exploration, nor the perilous cliff-hanging during a crisis, can be undertaken satisfactorily without a considerable measure of trust. Yet people who come to therapy are precisely those who find it hard to trust anyone, because of their past experience, and so the establishment of a trusting relationship is a delicate operation. More than the majority, these are people who have become accustomed to expect rejection or betrayal. There is no reason suddenly to feel confiding and confident with a distant and perhaps rather authoritarian figure, who gives away nothing of herself, is invariably calm and never offers comfort or advice, in a supportive way. It just doesn't make sense. Yet these are the rules of the game; more surprisingly still, the majority eventually come to accept them. Anthony Storr underlines this dilemma:

The internal process of reconnecting with instinct is . . . repeatedly blocked or inhibited by the patient's failure to allow himself to talk freely in the presence of the analyst. People only reveal their most intimate feelings to another person if they can trust that person; that is, if no doubts, suspicions or fears intervene between themselves and the person in whom they are attempting to confide. However, it is just because doubts, fears and suspicions have alienated the patient both from other people and himself that he finds himself in an emotional predicament. If he had been able, in the past, to trust his own feelings and to trust other people with them, he would not have become neurotically disturbed. When therefore he confronts the analyst, he inevitably tends to treat him as he has treated others in the past; as some one in whom he cannot freely confide for fear of scorn or rejection. (in Rycroft, 1966, pp. 79–80)

Dr Storr concludes that the resolution of this conflict lies in the transference, facilitated by the reliable yet totally unknown and unknowable figure of the analyst, who resolutely keeps himself in the background. I would maintain, on the contrary, that this attitude is much more likely to increase the unease and mistrust and that, as our everyday experience suggests, it is only when a warm and natural atmosphere has been created that people begin to trust each other.

I trusted all three therapists implicitly in the sense that I was sure they would never betray a confidence, or dictate behaviour, that they would appear reliably at the appointed hour and listen to me attentively. I did not, however, always feel with Sybil the relaxed trust which, for me, facilitates disclosure, and which I felt later with Harriet and Simon.

'How can I talk to you?' I expostulated one day, a few months after beginning therapy with Harriet. 'I don't even know if you like spinach.' She laughed. 'I do, actually.' Pause; bright smile. 'But that is not really the question you are asking, is it?' The indirect message might have been: 'Well, you can't accuse me of being an uncooperative sphinx; I answered about the spinach, didn't I? I just don't happen to want to divulge anything more right now.' Or it could have been an invitation to try further questions, since the spinach got an immediate and straight response. In either case the spontaneity of the laughter and the first part of the reply established a friendly atmosphere in which the second observation could safely be made, without it being taken as an accusation of stereotyped analytic behaviour; the way was open to me to proceed to the underlying issues, if I wanted to. This and other similar exchanges gave me the space I needed to test what sort of animal was here, how it might respond in certain conditions, how safe one was with it, and to realize that this was allowed; the grown-ups had not (yet) decreed otherwise.

What is needed is a friendly acceptance by the therapist, the creation of a space where you are entitled to be just as you are, however defective. This is to me the core of the therapeutic process. It is perhaps best summed up by Carl Rogers' formula of 'unconditional, positive regard' which he defines as follows:

When the therapist is experiencing a warm, positive and acceptant attitude toward what is in the client, this facilitates change. It involves the therapist's genuine willingness for the client to be whatever feeling is going on in him at that moment . . . It means that the therapist cares for the client in a total rather than conditional way. By this I mean that he does not simply accept the client when he is behaving in certain ways and disapprove of him when he behaves in other ways. It means an outgoing positive feeling without reservations, without evaluations. (1961, p. 62)

It is possible that this sounds more reassuring in theory than in practice because, as Lomas points out (1973, p. 80), Rogers tends to underestimate the vulnerability of his clients (rather as Szasz does, in *The Ethics of Psychoanalysis*), just as Freud tended to underestimate their capacity for autonomous behaviour. Lomas observes that the flaw in Carl Rogers' stance is that it is just as unemotional and detached as the orthodox analytical approach which he repudiates. One suspects, from Rogers' book on encounter groups (1969), that there is something of a rationalized defence about it, as there is about most professional doctrines or technical procedures adopted by psychiatrists, no less than the better documented resistances of patients.

Elsewhere Rogers does himself aver that his attitude must extend to a willingness to accept that his clients should feel and even act out any impulses, however anti-social; that they should have the freedom to be (and not just feel) unrepentantly neurotic, suicidal, destructive and even murderous. (An interesting gloss on this total acceptance, in the therapeutic context, of actions we might normally condemn as anti-social, while sharing the impulse to commit them, is provided by Dr Murray Cox's book [1978] based largely on his experience as a psychiatrist in Broadmoor.) This confirms my feeling that what is required is an affirmation of one's intrinsic value, undiminished by one's criminal propensities; a respect for the person one is, whether or not the therapist actually likes that person.

While it is perhaps true that an unvarying attitude of acceptance, a 'cool-warmth' is desirable, because it removes any reinforcement of a particular sort of behaviour and renders the acceptance truly unconditional, I think a certain amount of reinforcement and encouragement can be very therapeutic. I cautiously announced one day that I thought I might be beginning to see some point in living; indeed might go so far as to toy with the idea of actually liking life that particular day. I was surprised, and touched, to find the news met by a big smile. 'Great!', said Harriet, flinging her arms wide in an expansive gesture. It is quite possible that what I took to be a sharing of my happiness had in reality nothing to do with me. Maybe the therapist was feeling cheerful anyway and vastly relieved that one person at least was not going to spoil her morning by moaning. This doesn't detract from the immediate effect of the reaction, which came across as perfectly genuine, and which I experienced as warm and encouraging. A neutral 'Oh?' would certainly not have achieved this, nor even a word or phrase without the gesture; it was the spontaneity and physicality which convinced me that this was not mere polite acceptance of my statement. It is true that, as this was very early on in our therapy, I was not expecting any reaction at all, so the absence of one might have gone unnoticed, and no harm have been done; however, a less positive result would have been achieved. Moreover, a neutral reaction might have had the effect of making me think that, since my happiness gave her no pleasure, my unhappiness would meet with no sympathy. This was not denying my right to be miserable at other times, or suggesting that I was less welcome on such occasions, but affirming that my states of mind were not a matter of complete indifference to her, as I had hitherto supposed. The reinforcing message, for me, came from the spontaneity of the gesture; and I don't think it matters that much whether it was due to her being in a good mood, or participating in my contentment.

There is, however, a danger in this sort of spontaneous expression of pleasure at certain states of mind. I always found Harriet's genuine delight in my being undepressed very gratifying. Concomitantly, however, I was very conscious that my depression depressed her, and felt bad about it. This is not however a necessary corollary. A psychiatrist I consulted about medication was also genuinely thrilled when I emerged from a bad depression, but always warm and accepting when I was depressed, so I felt under no obligation to feign emotions, or guilt when low. As I had been referred to him when very depressed he had never known me as anything but that. The value I was accorded therefore had nothing to do with my character or achievements and so could not be lost. This was truly unconditional positive regard. I was recognized simply as having a right to live, even if I didn't always feel able to exercise it. My unconscious logic therefore reasoned that I ought to go on trying to live, simply as gratitude for this trust, though I did not feel pressure to do so if the effort became too great.

However, although this psychiatrist never expressed impatience with my depression, or any blame, he did make it clear that we had a common goal, which was to get rid of it, and that he believed this a possibility. I did not share his belief, but it mitigated my despair, and above all motivated me to try to overcome it, both through psychotherapy and through tackling practical problems. The psychiatrist bestowed on me, then, 'unconditional positive regard', but it was not non-directive, as Rogers claims his counselling to be. There was a very strong directive: 'Get better. I believe you can.' And this was inseparable from the warmth that was simultaneously communicated. There is a contradiction inherent in the desire to be totally non-directive in a counselling situation, as Halmos points out.

It is difficult to see how any professional service can be stripped of the motive or desire to be instrumental in bringing about a change by doing a service . . . a perfect non-directiveness would be a negation of this motive or desire.

A scrupulous and sometimes ostentatious non-interventionism of counselling is obviously doctrinaire. And a 'doctrinaire permissiveness' which tries to give identical encouragement to every individual . . . advertises moral relativism. (1965, p. 92)

Carl Rogers admits to this desire to effect change, measured in terms of certain criteria which he obviously does think preferable to their opposites. This is apparent both in his predilection for referring to the bulk of research evidence which suggests how effective his client-centred therapy is (and how much more effective than other brands), and by the casual statement that, if you give people the freedom to do and be whatever they choose they will in fact conform! This is not of course how he phrases it, but that is the general message; although there is no reason to suppose that he is not genuine in his preparedness to see them behave otherwise, there is no doubt either that he is glad if they manifest positive qualities rather than negative ones.

However, although I do not share his preference for the impersonality of the counsellor I find my views aptly interpreted by Rogers, particularly relating to the security engendered by this 'unconditional positive regard', which provides a re-educative experience, rather than a merely supportive affection.

*It is this absolute assurance that there will be no evaluation, no interpretation, no probing, no **personal** reaction by the counsellor that gradually permits the client to experience the relationship as one in which all defences can be dispensed with – a relationship in which the client feels, 'I can be the real me, no pretences'.*

*This security . . . is experienced as basically supporting, but it is in no way supportive. The client [experiences] the fact that here is some one who respects him **as he is**, and who is willing for him to take any direction which he chooses. The security is not a type of 'love-relationship' in any of the senses in which this term is ordinarily understood. The client does not feel that the therapist 'likes' him, in the usual sense of a biased and favourable judgement . . . there is simply no evidence upon which such a judgement could be based. But that this is a secure experience in which the self is deeply respected . . . of this the client gradually becomes sure. And this basic security is not something the client believes because he is told, not something about which he convinces himself logically, but it is something he **experiences**.* (1951, p. 209, author's emphasis)

This last point, designating the gradual inner certainty one acquires during therapy of unconditional acceptance by the therapist and therefore of one's own intrinsic worth, is an important one, since it emphasizes the value of **experience** over words. The client is not told that he or she is worthwhile or likeable. One slowly acquires the inner conviction of this – perhaps still challenged by the conscious understanding, just as any protestations of affection would be, but none the less felt to be true, at a pre-verbal level. This may sound vague and unreliable as evidence but it is after all at a pre-verbal level that one first becomes aware of the double-binds prevalent in adult behaviour (**saying** 'I love you' but acting otherwise;

telling you that honesty is a virtue but living lies themselves).

Since the process is gradual, no specific examples can illustrate it. At the most basic level, it becomes apparent through the reliability of the therapist: to be there, and to be equally receptive, whatever the content of the communication, or whatever the other person was like the previous time. For a very long time I doubted that my reception could be more than cool after a difficult session, when I had shown anger or despair. It was a source of great reassurance to me to find that the warmth of the reception or quality of listening remained unaltered. It was also a relief to find that relapses into depression after respites of cheerfulness were not greeted by hurt perplexity, as they tended to be by friends, but accepted as inevitable. Steady progress was not expected, only the willingness to explore the limitations of progress.

The communication of a **warm** 'unconditional positive regard' would, then, seem more likely to facilitate trust than an impassive neutrality, which is easily construed as indifference or even disapproval. Many therapists, particularly those of the humanistic school, like Lomas, Hobson and Casement, would support this view, held also by Heinz Kohut (1977, pp. 253–5). It is of course difficult to convey this 'positive regard' to people who have grown to expect negative reactions from their entourage. Most people in therapy have such low self-esteem that we encounter great difficulty even in believing that our best friends, lovers or spouses truly like us, whatever the evidence to the contrary. As suggested above, this cannot be done directly through words, which are suspect; it can only be achieved slowly, through experience. Yet even the neurotic's perceptions of other people are not so distorted, unless going through a severe depression or psychotic phase, that he or she cannot easily detect genuine acceptance. The distortions common in depression, when it is impossible to believe in positive feelings, make it necessary for attitudes and communications to be adjusted at such times to accommodate the person's heightened vulnerability. Yet it is amazing just how much does get through, as long as the communication is inspired by genuine feeling.

With amazement I read (Lomas, 1973) of a patient asking 'Do you like me?' and receiving the answer 'Yes, of course.' Of course. This seems to me a non-question, asked directly; a double-bind if ever there was one. It would be impossible for a therapist to answer 'No' because that would be devastating. An affirmative answer cannot then be believed, since there was no alternative. It must be assumed that, within the context of the relationship, and with the reinforcement of non-verbal communication, such as tone of voice, facial expression, etc., the response was experienced as meaningful. For this is a question we probably all ask indirectly and, through our experience of the therapist's 'positive regard', the answer is usually conveyed. The extent to which one sees this unvarying attentiveness as warm and caring is of course variable, and depends a good deal on one's present state of (in)security; there are times when old habits die hard and one feels rejected however unjustifiable this may be.

At the end of the last hour of my therapy with Sybil I was allowed to ask one direct question. (I do not remember whether this was her limitation or whether, more probably, I only dared ask one.) I asked whether she liked cats. I did in fact want to know, since I had drawn her innumerable cats and talked a lot about my own feline. As soon as I had asked it, I realized that it also meant 'Do you like me?', since she knew I identified with cats. She answered 'Yes.' I said 'Thank you.' That was the end of the therapy.

Generally speaking, the most therapeutic part of the encounter is this gradual awareness that here at last is someone with whom you do not have to put up a front, who does not expect you to earn approval, but simply accepts without condemnation that you can't cope, hate the guts of those who can (including sometimes the therapist) and are a seething mass of monstrous emotions which everybody else thinks are unwarranted.

The similar absence of praise, and the fact that this person at least is not impressed by your manifold talents, your charm, your usual gambits, relieves the urge to impress, to achieve, to prove yourself, and leaves you free to be just whatever you are, without guilt or feelings of inadequacy. It is the one place in the world where your **function** is to be inadequate, at least in the early stages of the therapy. None the less, it took me a while to realize this, and to overcome my usual fear of being thought neurotic for behaving as I do.

The therapist's unconditional acceptance does not of course automatically extend to other people, who still tend to base their attitudes on merit-tests and conformity to their expectations. As Sybil reminded me gently, with a wry smile, when I sniffed, '**You** put up with me when I'm like this, why can't he?' – 'I don't have to live with you.' It is rather different coping with someone's tears, anger or pain for short periods and when you are not the cause of them. Perhaps significantly, she ceased to put up with them quite so readily when we became close friends and she was confronted by my depression, rather than just hearing about it.

A prerequisite for the communication of this unvarying acceptance of the other person and concern for them is that the therapist must actually feel this. Feigned interest would be immediately detected by most people and have damaging results, destroying trust as irrevocably as coldness or indifference. The sceptic may doubt the likelihood of this generalized concern, and the neurotic doubt the possibility of its being extended to them in particular, however much they can appreciate that it is virtually impossible to get to know and understand someone really well without respecting her individuality and acknowledging the validity of her viewpoint. Yet it is easier to believe in it in the context of psychotherapy because communication is taking place at an authentic level, without the usual barriers and masks of social convention, politeness or posing for effect. Yet, paradoxically, this authenticity which is considered so desirable as an attitude for the person in therapy and an ingredient of their growth, and which is also vital on the part of therapists (as they themselves agree), runs counter to the doctrine of a professional mask of impassibility. Therapists are dissimulating the emotions which they feel. This would seem to be putting considerable strain on the therapist and not be conducive to the creation of a warm and friendly atmosphere in which the other person will feel free to reveal themselves.

DISCLOSURE BY THERAPIST

The communication of 'unconditional positive regard' need not inhibit the display of emotion on the part of the therapist. Indeed, one of the most therapeutic features of the encounter can be the discovery that someone can still like or respect you even when they feel angry towards you. Certainly two of my therapists stated quite clearly when they were hurt or angry at something I had said; one of them also showed it when he felt moved. This could have made me more cautious but in fact it gave me greater security to express my emotions openly, knowing that they would be reacted to with equal honesty, and so our interaction could be discussed. This was far more useful to me in learning what sort of effect I had on other people, and how to avoid hurting them, when possible.

Sybil, an irascible character in real life (although I did not know this at the time), never showed anger or even impatience with me while she was my therapist. I think this was an important factor in my psychological growth at that time. Yet it made it very difficult for me to cope with her anger and annoyance when she subsequently became a friend. I had thought her patience was limitless; it was not. This was a lesson in realism which I learnt from life, but which psychotherapy had ill prepared me for. It led me to question whether the unreality of the situation in psychotherapy, when the therapist tries to be invariably tolerant in a way real people never are, is necessarily therapeutic.

Harriet, a far more equable character, but one with strong

views she was prone to express, did sporadically show anger. On one occasion she thumped her fist on the arm of the chair and said, 'No it isn't, damn you!' in response to my statement that her refusal to let me play was a rejection. The tone was jocular and I was more amused than distressed. I think, too, that she would not have said it had I been in a less resilient or aggressive mood that day. Curiously, this exchange gave me more self-confidence. I felt that if she could openly express annoyance I could more readily believe in her expressions of warmth. She also made a point of showing when I had hurt her, though when we discussed it later, rather than at the time. This timing was probably crucial. Although this possibly made me over-protective (a carry-over from the need to protect my mother, who could not take criticism), it also seemed to me a helpful reaction, because it was **real**. She was not refusing to let me say hurtful things, merely reminding me that there was a person on the receiving end, who had feelings like me.

Once, after a series of crucial but stormy sessions, when for the first time I had confronted Harriet with my anger, she said that it would now be possible 'for us to go on, to get somewhere constructive; if both of us can bear it'. This reminded me forcibly that she too was vulnerable and that those sessions must have been painful for her as well as me, although in a very different way. It seemed as if this having gone through an ordeal together created both a bond and a basis of trust on which to build. She had not rejected me, or refused to let me express my rage; but she had received it as a human being, not a detached professional.

Most therapists, even the traditionalists, agree that it is preferable to show anger or exasperation at times rather than attempt to cover them up – a feint which will almost certainly be perceived by the other person. What is less widely accepted is the possibly therapeutic effect of showing other emotions, such as tiredness or depression, sympathy or envy; in short of entering into the encounter as a person, with all the variability and vulnerability that that implies, with the partiality of an individual, a three-dimensional being, with his or her own past and present. I was always rather touched when Harriet admitted to such human things as dreading a visit from her mother or missing her husband when he was away, even being tired, as long as it was accompanied by a little smile assuring me that she was not too tired to listen to me. I was not so keen on being told, 'Well, you can't expect me to be alert late in the afternoon.' I was also agreeably surprised when she pointed out how there were enviable things in my life, as well as all the disadvantages I was moaning about. Earlier in the therapy, this could simply have been an unwelcome put-down, serving only to make me feel misunderstood. In the context, and towards the end of the therapy, it gave me a new light on some aspects of my experience. Instead of envying her, I suddenly saw how she might envy me, and I felt that I possessed something at last. The timing was, however, crucial here as many depressives, me included, are terrified of being envied.

Curiously enough, I did not always welcome Simon's attempts to bring himself into my therapy. I readily accepted the presence of his wife and children in the garden, or the occasional comment which showed how he reacted to me. I valued the fact that I could ask any questions I liked, and get straight answers. But I got impatient if he provided unasked for information, or drifted into anecdote. I felt this was turning the stringent analysis I wanted from him into desultory chat. Possibly this was an instinctive reaction on my part to rectify what was at times an overdose of reality in my relationship with Harriet.

It would obviously not be constructive for the therapist to use the encounter as therapy for themselves and to change client-centred therapy into therapist-centred, however much some clients might feel they would welcome such an interchange. The therapist need say very little; just enough to convey the impression of being human. Cox points out:

a patient may be more likely to discuss personal and hitherto

undisclosed aspects of his life if the therapist does likewise.
However, I regard the risks of this approach as infinitely greater
than the assets . . . probably one of the fundamental abilities of the
therapist is to be able to facilitate disclosures by his patient, with
minimal detailed personal disclosure on his part . . . Minimal
disclosure, paradoxically, makes the therapist more 'available'.
(1978, p. 173)

Some people would, of course, feel threatened by any sign that
the therapist was invading their space. They might find it
easier to reveal themselves to a person who had no existence in
his or her own right. It is in many ways a welcome luxury to
know that this one hour is devoted to oneself, to the
exploration of one's own problems with the temporary setting
aside of other people's claims on you, in a way that is not
possible in the outside world – which may itself have been a
contributory factor to the presenting problems.

However, this desirable and potentially constructive luxury
also sets up guilt feelings, which can be quite considerable, at
devoting so much attention to oneself and ignoring the other
person's needs. (This is more likely to be the case with women
than men, as Ernst points out [Ernst and Maguire, 1987].) It
instigates a new conflict, in that in most situations in daily life
consideration for others is deemed to be desirable, and the fear
of being selfish and greedy is often a contributory factor in
neurosis and depression. None the less, in therapy consideration for the other is thought to be out of place and treated as
resistance ('You don't want to talk about yourself'). If the
person is selfish in his or her daily life, whether or not they are
aware of this, it would seem to be of dubious value to be
encouraged in this habit. If she is not (unless she is carrying the
martyr act to neurotic extremes, in which case she is imposing
her unselfishness on others and could usefully be encouraged
to think of herself more), she is likely to become acutely
distressed by her apparently self-centred behaviour, and the
veto on any show of concern for the therapist. Moreover, the

person most worried by this will also be the one least likely to mention it, for fear of offending, overstepping the limits, trespassing on the other person's privacy.

Unless it is made clear to what extent the therapist regards it as essential that he or she should not obtrude on the proceedings, and whether it is permissible to ask questions, there can be some unease as to whether to risk a rebuff, or stifle one's concern by remarking, or refraining from doing so, on the therapist looking tired, or sad or happy. The usual reaction of neurotics will be to attribute the tiredness to themselves, and imagine that they have caused it by being boring or demanding, but this is best brought out in the open. My fear became especially acute if Sybil countered questions by comments such as 'You mean you don't think I am paying attention to you?' or 'You think I am not in tune with your mood?', which made the enquiry sound even more selfish.

If I thought Harriet was looking tired and said so, she generally corroborated the accuracy of my observation. If she had brushed me off with a denial of the evidence, this would have invalidated my perception. She did not launch into an account of why she was tired, as a friend would do, nor did I wish this. I merely wanted her to confirm my perception of reality, and allow me to show concern, before I inflicted my own moans on her. She did gently steer me into an analysis of why I needed to remark on her looking tired. I then realized that my mother was always complaining of being tired, and that I had been trained from an early age to put her needs before mine. Like many daughters, I had been groomed for my female role in terms of being a carer, and denying my own wish to be cosseted. There was, then, an element of transference in this attitude, but it also involved the normal reaction of one adult to another, or perhaps of one woman to another. (I don't remember ever having noticed whether Simon looked tired.) Her matter-of-fact acceptance of the reality element helped me feel respected as an adult while I explored the regression into the anxious child role.

It is evading the issue to claim that what one of the interlocutors thinks does not matter, but only what the other person thinks they think. The refusal to give a straightforward reply is a repetition of the authoritarian attitude that children or subordinates have no right to discuss opinions. The perpetuation of a sphinx-like pose is redolent of the very inauthenticity and rigidity which therapy is supposed to be discouraging in those seeking help.

Not being given reasons for things not only treats the other person like a child but can be positively unhelpful to both. Once when I was furious with Harriet for going away on holiday very soon after a long summer break, I discovered purely by chance, from a mutual friend, the reason why the holiday seemed necessary. I was immediately sympathetic and contrite. I felt dreadful at having kicked up such a selfish fuss. I think that if this had been explained to me, perhaps after I had had the chance to express my resentment, it would have mitigated my sense of abandonment and given me the opportunity to react like an adult, thus restoring my self-esteem.

Anthony Storr puts the case in favour of the traditional approach:

[the therapist's] refusal to correct the patient's misconceptions by revealing personal details about himself allows the exploration and discussion of those misconceptions in a way which would not be possible if they were to be immediately corrected.

Psychotherapy thus becomes what has been called a 'corrective emotional experience', in which negative assumptions about other people are gradually modified by means of the repeated analysis of the patient's changing relationship with the therapist. (in Rycroft, 1966, pp. 69, 72)

Sybil did not vouchsafe much information about herself, and discouraged questions. I stopped asking them, and became very curious about her past, and her life outside the consulting room. At first I felt the same curiosity about Harriet, but as our relationship grew more relaxed I found I could ask direct questions and get direct answers. Calm in the knowledge that I could always ask for information, I gradually ceased to be curious. This was also true with Simon.

It is a truism that disclosure begets disclosure, and so it would seem desirable that therapists should depart from the traditional anonymity and reveal something about themselves, and about their views and feelings. Basically, the more one is free to ask ordinary questions like 'How are you today?', or request anodyne information about whereabouts during absences, for instance, the less anguish there is likely to be, and the more one is likely to feel free to reveal oneself, and to trust the other person. It is impossible to trust a cool, guarded stranger. The more one knows about someone, the less there is a compulsion to speculate, with the concomitant fear of the unknown. The rationalization is of course that this hinders the transference, because fantasy is not allowed free play. I feel that paradoxically one may become **more** aware of the transference because one can see for oneself how inappropriate it is, although it will, curiously enough, still occur.

However, this feeling of being more at ease if one is dealing with a human being rather than a faceless official, of being reassured by a sensation of sharing, of reciprocity, all too often encounters the objection that this is rationalization, culpable yielding to curiosity and an immature refusal to put up with a necessary lack of gratification designed to increase one's self-knowledge. In view of the harm already done by systematic frustration and rejection to most people coming for therapy, it seems inconceivable that it should be considered (as it is by some) a corrective experience to increase the resentment and isolation caused by this; yet this is so. Cox admits that: 'Too little reciprocity results in the therapist being perceived as a cold, aloof, detached "professional" who makes the patient feel that he is regarded as "a card with bronchitis on it". This point is self-evident' (1978, p. 191), but he also affirms that:

successful therapy occurs most often where the therapist's personal involvement is limited to that of concentrated concern for his patient . . . The therapist's . . . implicit attitudes . . . personal values . . . must not intrude and prevent the patient's freedom of disclosure. (p. 190)

This point is also self-evident. Of course they must not intrude or prevent, but presence and intrusion are not identical. Much as I suspected that my therapists had interesting life stories to tell, which concerned me to the extent that I am fascinated by all biographies, particularly those of friends, and much as I might have wanted to know what they actually thought sometimes, I had enough sense and thrift to realize that there was not usually time to hear about them too, and I would rather concentrate on my own problems. But occasionally my ability to express these problems depended on my awareness that they are far from neutral subjects and that, however well-trained and hyper-analysed the therapist is, however much they may have their feelings under control, it would be presumptuous and insensitive to suppose that they do not have feelings.

In her paper 'Development of awareness of transference in a markedly detached personality' (1964, p. 118), Clara Thompson declares that the real breakthrough with a detached psychotic patient came when a spontaneous display of strong emotion on her part acted as a catalyst for the release of his own hitherto totally repressed feelings. Since she returns several times, in different papers, to this episode, one may suppose it made a great impression on her, and probably more in terms of the therapeutic effect on the patient than purely as a rare example of emotion being shown by her. This conjecture is borne out by her own writings and the testimony of those who knew her.

However, even admitting that a knowledge of autobiographical details or theoretical standpoints is not necessarily relevant or helpful to the therapeutic encounter, since it might inhibit the consulter, or enable them to pigeon-hole the therapist into stereotypes, there are times when the fear of hurting the other person's feelings on delicate issues can be very inhibiting. In such cases it would help to know something of the therapist's experience, so that one can discuss one's reluctance to inflict this material on them and present it as tactfully as honest self-disclosure permits. Is it fair, for instance, to talk of suicidal impulses or the joys of falling in love with someone recently bereaved? Theoretically I know that it is, but in practice I do not think I could have done it. Of course the therapist is sufficiently in touch with his or her own feelings to set these aside for the moment and concentrate on yours, and to realize that if you are treading on any corns it is probably without realizing it. This does not alter the fact that there are two people involved in the encounter, even if the aim is only to benefit one of them. There is some doubt in my mind as to whether it is right to expect inhuman standards of forbearance, stoicism and invulnerability from therapists, whether indeed the insistence on these does not operate detrimentally on the relationship, by making the therapist seem less sensitive to the other's grief or panic. (Only seem, but appearances are important if there is not enough visible reality.) The cult of the inhumanly perfect therapist could lead to the production of imperfectly human patients.

I certainly think that my confidence in my therapists and willingness to reveal myself increased the more I knew about them and realized that these calm, unruffled characters, who looked as if they never cursed when the soup boiled over, had faced far worse disasters and emerged relatively sane, presumably with some effort. That could have increased my feeling of inadequacy, because they were then confirmed as 'copers', and sometimes it did; but more often, instead of feeling ashamed at not coping, I felt more reassured that my problems would be understood. A big block was in fact reached with Harriet when she admitted, in response to a despairing question of mine, that she had never been really depressed and could not understand fully my despair. Though ultimately this helped, as I felt my depression could not swamp her.

The myth of the strong silent therapist perpetuates the parent–child syndrome and consequently increases the dependency and reduces the potential for autonomy of the other person. Babies have a right to be as selfish, demanding and inconsiderate as they like, because they know no better and are not expected to have a sense of moral responsibility, or to be able to deal with the concept of the other person's separateness. A severely disturbed patient will need to regress to this state, and it might even be alleged that many people in therapy have momentary needs for this sort of ruthless dependency. Ultimately, however, most of us hope to return to the world of normality and to assume our adult functions in it, among which due regard for the needs of others is essential. I felt that, if this was expected of me when I was not feeling too regressed, and conversely that I was allowed to be selfish and demanding at such times, this restored to me some sense of responsibility for my own actions.

One of the things which most helped me in a session when I was almost mute with despair was Harriet telling me of how, when her husband died, a priest had said to her, 'I can't give you faith if you haven't got it.' This had happened some years ago, and she was not asking for sympathy, but showing empathy. She added, 'I can only be with you while you try to find your own way forward.' This was the only thing which remained in my mind after the session, and the only thing which consoled me during it.

At certain stages in the relationship, then, (and it is important to bear in mind that growth is not a continual process but can fluctuate) it might be appropriate to introduce an element of sharing and mutuality, as part of the person's acquisition of self-esteem and ability to test their growth by acting on it, rather than just talking about it.

It would seem reasonable to suppose that this restoration of the patient's sense of being an ordinary person (potentially acceptable and understandable) would most readily take place in an atmosphere of ordinariness; in a relationship in which the patient feels valued for his ordinary human qualities, those which he shares with the rest of mankind: fundamentally, his capacity to experience. And in order to value him for these qualities the other person must have them and show that he has them: he must be an ordinary human being; he must not conceal his frailties.

In so far as the psychotherapist sets himself apart from his patient, giving the impression – even if only implicitly, by reticence – that he is a different order of being, his capacity to heal is reduced. (Lomas, 1973, p. 17)

This would seem to me, and probably to most other people in therapy, to be almost axiomatic; yet it is a very unorthodox view indeed and one, I suspect, unlikely to be shared, or at least put into practice, by most psychotherapists. Many seem to feel that just being discreet is not enough; that they should be regarded as infallible and perennially strong. If one is to believe the literature, that is; two at least of my therapists have not acted on this, and I have found their humanness helpful. It is probably relevant that both were trained by Peter Lomas. I was, however, horrified on one occasion when Simon alluded to my doubts as to whether he could cope with his own depression enough to bear mine. This was neither my conscious nor unconscious fear. It seemed to me an inappropriate remark, not reflecting the truth of the situation, and refocusing our attention from me to him. There could have been a transferential need for me not to see him as depressed, therefore like my father. But on this occasion I think that this should have been dealt with purely as transference and not reality.

It is true that the role of unshakeable strength is a helpful corrective to the inadequate parental support received by many people in therapy, and provides a stable background against which they can explore their own weaknesses but, if adhered to too rigidly, it risks becoming one more myth wielded by the 'Groan-Ups' to perpetuate the hierarchical set-up in which the child-patient is obliged to be dependent, grateful and unable to judge things for themselves. Those who want to lean on others and see them as capable and strong will cling to this idealized image of therapists as people who can invariably cope, with their own problems and ours; others will resent this imagined superiority. But the most dynamic situation might be one where people could learn to accommodate a certain duality in the therapist, as in oneself and everyone else one meets. It might help if one could gradually modify the image of the supremely stable and resilient therapist, although to some extent this must exist if one is to trust them and have confidence in their ability to guide us through the quagmire of our own conflicts, to encompass the knowledge, or intuition, that this sanity was hard won and not in-built. This knowledge is in fact truly therapeutic, as it has the corollary that, if they have achieved it, in spite of adverse circumstances or an unquiet nature, and partly as the result of their own analysis, there is some hope for the rest of us. It can therefore be quite reassuring to see the therapist as someone who was not, or even is not, always quite so serene as the sphinx before one.

Lomas, too, expresses doubts about whether the therapist is 'justified in hiding behind a mask of omnipotence and clarity' and maintains that 'the patient will be able to survive the uncertainty of the psychotherapy to a greater degree than is usually recognized. One of the ambiguities he must face is that he has to trust a person who is fallible . . .' (1981, p. 118). He goes on to discuss a case when he admitted his shortcomings: '[the patient] was not disturbed by the revelations of my failings . . . indeed, she gained a feeling of security from the belief that my preparedness to admit my failings increased the possibility of overcoming difficulties between us' (p. 120).

I would confirm this from experience. Yet I do think that there are limits to the limitations one can be expected to find tolerable. My confidence and trust in Harriet was increased by her frank admission of times when she agreed that she had mishandled a situation or been tactless. Since I would have felt this was the case anyway, nothing would have been served by her denying it, and my own willingness to admit failings grew. However, I was less convinced of the benefits when she declared that I must learn to accept her limitations, and that I was up against them when, for instance, I expected her to be supportive and positively helpful at times when I was in great distress. As I illustrated in the last chapter, it seemed to me that she here repeated my parents' failings by her inability to remain sympathetic yet calm. I kept pointing out how much more helpful were ordinary friends, who did not try to say anything profound, but merely made sympathetic noises. It was no use telling me that I was up against her limitations. If she had been a friend I might have found these endearing. But I had not chosen her, as I pointed out, for her weaknesses; I sought her out for supposed strengths.

What is probably desirable is some sort of compromise between the invulnerable sphinx and the averagely selfish and moody individuals most of us are. The therapist **does** need to be more altruistic and self-effacing, less unpredictable and inadequate in face of distress than most people. Professional and private behaviour are not, after all, synonymous. But the maintenance of this high ideal of conduct, in the interests of the other person's development, should not be at the expense of relaxing the reins occasionally when this could be in the interests of both parties.

6 THE OBJECT
AS REAL THERAPY

An element of creative play which brought into my therapy with Harriet a much needed dimension of reality, was the use of objects. This involved the exchange of objects, either as gifts or loans, which created a bond and made real a message. It also involved a creative use of an object which came to symbolize the therapy. It both belonged to and transcended the role of transitional object, as described by Winnicott (1953, pp. 77–89; 1958, pp. 229–43; 1971, pp. 1–30, 104–111).

Harriet said that she had never known a therapy characterized by so much exchange of objects, and concluded that I involve myself in the world in a very tangible way and am not happy with abstractions. Whether or not the interpretation was correct, this exchange of objects became to me the sign of something very positive about the therapy. It made it mine, ours, rather than just any therapy. It was also part of the dimension of serious play, which I will go on to discuss later.

At first the transfer of objects began with my bringing drawings, poems, stories which I wanted her to see – had indeed done especially for her, as part of the creative phase at the beginning of this therapy. It was part of a statement about myself, and also a statement about the productive effect she was having on me. Then I took to borrowing books from her, which was part of the general exchange of ideas with which I wanted to replace a one-sided analysis. Maybe this kept me too safely within the bounds of an intellectual discussion that I could to some extent control, rather than opening up the dykes

of the unconscious. Nini Herman is adamant about the danger
of this practice.

I began to borrow books from my therapist's own shelves, while he
colluded in my quest. This was generous and kind. But from the
standpoint of technique it mirrored a catastrophe: for by acceding to
my wish instead of analysing it, my Freudian therapist confessed
himself so far out of his depth that we now required help from the
lifeboat of literature. (1985, p. 107)

I don't see it like this; on the contrary, I took it as a mark of
confidence that Harriet was prepared to discuss books with
me, and to use their subject matter as a way of introducing
material in therapy. The reading matter we discussed often
provided the pretext for me to bring up some personal point,
which could be presented as objective criticism of a book; so it
also served a productive function in the therapy. Moreover, it
grouped Harriet among friends, or colleagues, rather than
impersonal professional helpers, and made me more trusting in
the relationship.

Similarly, a very non-intellectual use of objects served to
define her as a friend and playmate. One rainy afternoon, when
I was feeling non-verbal and resentful (about a changed hour
for the session), we spent the time making animals out of
Plasticine. At one level, this felt like a double waste of time: I
was there, when I should have been at work; and I wasn't
investigating any problems. At another level, it felt like a
shared experience; as if we were at last **doing** something
together (even making something), and this was moreover an
activity lost since childhood.

Gradually the field of exchanged objects became extended.
Postcards were exchanged during absences, both hers and
mine, and this greatly increased my sense of reciprocity in the
relationship and lessened the anguish at the one-sidedness of it
all. I felt slightly less resentful about the absences if I was given
this sign that I was not entirely forgotten and abandoned. The
postcards acted as transitional objects which reassured me

during absences or bad patches in the therapy, as did the occasional present of a book or other object. There was an element of play in this too, as the cards were often an allusion to some shared joke or experience.

Gifts of books or flowers also had an element of creative play. Beyond the obvious message of saying, 'You helped me; thank you', it made the helping into a joint creative act, rather than merely passive receptivity on my part. She gave help, I gave a flower, so the mutual contribution endowed help and gratitude with an objective, tangible life. We were playing with reality, inventing it, rather than just reflecting it. This sort of 'play' could also turn a negative experience into a positive one. Once, when I was feeling very despondent and there had been something of a non-session in terms of communication or consolation, Harriet said at the end, 'What can I **give** you?' – and gave me a very beautiful flower that had been on her desk. This meant more to me than any amount of analysis of my despair would have done. It didn't of course help me to understand the crisis or extricate myself from the nightmare, but failing that more desirable function, it did give me a positive memory to help me weather the negative phase of the next few months in therapy. The gesture was therapeutic, even if the analytical content of sessions had temporarily broken down. Moreover, I enshrined the ephemeral beauty of the flower in a couple of photographs, which preserved for both of us the beauty of the moment, transforming the pain which had preceded the gift into the happiness and creativity which it engendered.

The most important and complex of the shared objects was the seal. He was initially a splendid example of Winnicott's definition of the transitional object (1953, pp. 77–89; 1958, pp. 229–43; 1971, pp. 1–30, 104–11). The transitional object, usually a bit of blanket or a cuddly toy, has for the infant the magical properties of being 'me' and 'not-me' at the same time. It acts as a defence against annihilation anxiety, especially when the child is lonely or during periods of regression to an earlier phase of development. 'The baby creates the object, but the object was waiting to be created' (Winnicott, 1971, p. 104).

The seal came out of the toy cupboard on a birthday when I was feeling rather glum and in need of consolation. He also seemed to come in response to my otter mania. (I had decided to become one in my next life and meanwhile to make the otter into a cult object, largely because of its predilection for play.) It didn't make any difference that this was a seal, he was The Otter, as far as I was concerned, until such time as I chose to accept him as a seal. This was in itself a sign of the transition from fantasy to reality.

He (and it always was 'he') was not strictly speaking a transitional object, because for the first few months he lived exclusively in Harriet's cupboard and was only produced during sessions. He then accompanied me to hospital and thereafter came to stay with me whenever Harriet was away, or I felt particularly bereft between sessions. So he was at these times a transitional object. But his real role was more complex. And Harriet respectfully refrained from analysing it, after a few attempts which I firmly squashed. The seal was a useful form of non-verbal communication. Whether I asked for him, or picked him up; whether he was cuddled or simply held; whether I refused to notice him – all were barometers of my feelings. They were not so much conscious communications, as a way for me to get in touch with my feelings and communicate them directly. Above all he stood for a particular relationship which I didn't have with anyone else (nor, as far as I knew, did she). Otters and seals now meant something special for both of us, just as the words sphinx and chameleon to refer to therapists did. The object was part of a private language and creative game. It was a hallmark that proclaimed 'Ann, her therapy'. It was also a convenient way of expressing love or playfulness in a way that was both open and coded.

The seal was a sign, when the therapist was absent, that the relationship had a tangible existence that could survive separations, and which would not be threatened by negative feelings. It was a sign of the real things I would lose by quitting when the going got rough. During the period when I was experiencing extremely powerful negative views about the entire therapy, and thinking quite seriously of abandoning the exercise, I borrowed the seal and spent my insomniac nights hugging him; my mind was contemplating termination, but my emotions were obviously clinging on to the relationship. The seal enabled me to grasp this more clearly. At this nadir of our relationship, I was given a small 'portaseal' which could be carried everywhere, unlike his larger cousin. This seal, and the card which accompanied it, said far more to me than any analysis or direct words could have done about the quality of the relationship and the nature of Harriet's feelings. I wouldn't have believed words; but I could believe the object. It also transformed a very painful period for both of us into something playful, shared and affectionate. This encapsulated the tenor of the whole therapy.

The seal, the postcards and other exchanged objects were all part of the general dimension of reality in this therapy, making the relationship real as well as transference. There was an element of transference in that my own mother had not given me cuddly toys when I was small; she even gave away two teddy bears 'to the poor children' long before I had grown out of them. The gift was to the child in me, but it was also part of an on-going relationship in the present. Perhaps this dimension of reality accentuated the pain in the transference, and made it more difficult for me to understand how much of the attachment was to the real person, and how much to a fantasy figure. But I think that its value as a sign of something unique, comforting and valuable in the experience far out-weighed any disadvantages.

Being **given** something was truly therapeutic. But for the continuity of positive feelings which these gifts signified I might never have had the motivation to overcome my negative feelings. I would have had no proof that I mattered, and my childhood had been built on lies too much for me to have faith in words. It was perhaps relevant that my father had never given me any presents at all, while my mother used to shower me with gifts that I never wanted; things which she liked, or her vision of the ideal daughter would have liked, but which were quite inappropriate for me. One of the things which made cards and presents from Harriet significant was that they were all carefully chosen to refer to some joint joke or memory.

Obviously not all consulters are going to want cuddly toys. Yet there is something to be gained by generalizing from this personal case of object attachment. Hobson narrates how he countered the panic of a patient faced with his impending absence, and his own helplessness, by giving her a stone. For twenty years she held this stone in moments of distress and found she was able to cope.

The shape, the texture, the touch – the 'feel' – of a stone, can have a 'personal' quality. It can be an emerging symbol of togetherness . . .

In an emotional bond, embodied in the stone which 'joined' Betty and me, there is an intermediate (not quite literal, not quite figurative) pre-metaphorical language. (1985, p. 83)

This seems to me to illustrate effectively the role of objects in my own therapy. The general message, I think, is that people are liable, in therapy as in all other experiences, to find their own mode of expression and that maximum freedom is important. If one is allowed to bring into therapy all sorts of thoughts and feelings, why not also all kinds of objects? I didn't feel any need to share a seal with my previous or subsequent therapists. The precise nature of the discourse would not have been translated by such an object. There were things I never verbalized about the relationship which were presumably conveyed by the seal, just as Harriet's acceptance of me was symbolized by her enthusiastic participation in the seal game. It may not always be necessary or even desirable for the therapist to respond actively, but it should also be recognized that there are some essentially poetic experiences which should not be subjected to the scrutiny of logical analysis. The seal would have been destroyed for me if he had been reducible to words. The seal signified a playful, creative, also a loving side of me that I wanted to bring into therapy, actively yet indirectly.

7　THE SPACE TO PLAY

Foolish people think that joking isn't being serious.
Paul Valéry

Therapy is usually treated as a very serious subject, to be approached with a great deal of reverence and tackled with the grim determination of the north face of Everest in winter. It does actually feel like that sometimes, in practice; but that is no reason for regarding it solely as hard work and penance, or to minimize the more enjoyable aspects of the experience. There are moments of joy as well as moments of anguish. More important, since therapy is exploration, there are areas of creative play which need to be exploited if the individual is to grow. This has been given little recognition in the learned text books, though it is central to Winnicott's thought, notably as illustrated in *Playing and Reality*. He declares:

The reason why playing is essential is that it is in playing that the patient is being creative. It is in playing and only in playing that the individual child or adult is able to be creative and to use the whole personality, and it is only in being creative that the individual discovers the self. (1971, p. 63)

Play is of course a serious activity; it absorbs the attention of the player. It uses, as Winnicott says, the whole personality. There is a distinct need, to my mind, to bring one's whole personality into therapy. This is particularly true for someone like me with dramatic mood swings, who finds it difficult to integrate the depressed self with the buoyant self, and to realize that they are both the same person. If therapy is to be a treatment of the entire person, and if no subjects are to be taboo, then humour and joy, playfulness and creativity have their role, in direct proportion to that which they occupy in the personality, as well as sorrow and despair, inadequacy and destructiveness. As Cox observes: 'It would be a caricature of therapy if the therapist could only hear about impotence, failure or the fear of failure, and dismiss any joy and celebration as his patient merely being "defensive"' (1978, p. 61).

In my second therapy, with Harriet, I felt the need from the start (once I had emerged from the depression which made me re-enter therapy) to bring something of the more positive and lively me to the sessions. I felt that my previous therapist had got a false picture of me by hearing only about the gloomy side. This was not just a question of vanity (that I wanted to appear as a fun person) but more to do with the need to give my therapist as well as myself a yardstick for the depressions. Only someone who knew what I could be like and feel like when happy could, it seemed, appreciate the sense of loss and desolation I had when depressed, because only then could they understand the gulf between the two ways of being. The sharing of jokes, taste for word-play and clowning about of those first few months were part of the wish to present myself as a whole person, lively and positive, as well as negative and depressed.

If the patient is to be received as a whole person, rather than an 'utterer of symptoms', then to be 'taken seriously' implies that his laughter and humour is as much part of his presentation as his formal 'complaint'. It therefore follows that the therapist's appropriate response is not always that of sombre solemnity; indeed, shared laughter may facilitate third level [i.e. deep] disclosures much more rapidly than an emotionally neutral response. (Cox, 1978, p. 10)

I was not then just playing about, as my therapist sometimes wondered, and a friend declared. The friend assured me that she was making considerable progress in therapy because, unlike me, she treated the activity seriously and the therapist with respect. I can't deny that she made progress. But my view was that I also take my work seriously, as well as the activities of love and friendship, but I would no more wish to devalue my therapist than my students, colleagues, friends or lovers by treating them solemnly. Taking someone seriously involves being able to play with them; that is, to explore the possibilities of the relationship or to share together a creative attitude to life. 'The ability to laugh at himself is, paradoxically, an indication that a man is able to take himself seriously', says Cox (1978, p. 61).

My playing around at the beginning of this therapy was largely inspired by the desire to bring a spirit of creative imagination to the exercise; not to take the rules of the game as immutable, but to redefine them, to rearrange the elements and see if a new construct could be obtained. Carentuto comments: 'Experience with children tells us that play is a way of learning, of becoming aware of themselves and of the world' (1979, p. 124).

A humorous relationship is likely to be a trusting and sharing one, which encourages the consulter to open up. The element of shared jokes and laughter in all my therapies certainly established a climate of ease, in which I felt freer to reveal painful feelings. Carl Rogers also points to the likelihood of a humorous relationship being a trusting and sharing one, mainly because of the sense it gives of the therapist as being human and the client as being equal. To this end, it is not just the client's laughter which is therapeutic, but also the therapist's. He describes how one of his clients, who had been a bit startled by his laughter in an early interview, then came to find it therapeutic, encouraging growth and eagerness to get on with her investigations (1951, p. 112).

The constructive role of shared laughter is apparent in his example. It fulfils the multiple function of creating a bond between two people who are, after all, jointly involved in the endeavour; it favours the establishment of trust; it fosters the image of the therapist as a person, with authentic reactions, and it counteracts a feeling of hopelessness by instigating a feeling of optimism. The bonding function of laughter and play is crucial. As Cox states, 'all laughter is not a manic defence and it can be the strongest bond between therapist and patient which facilitates subsequent disclosure' (1978, p. 65). Not only does it encourage the person to explore painful areas, but it can also salvage the relationship when the pain becomes too great. It can enable you jointly to weather some of the storms the relationship will surely encounter. My experience of therapy with Harriet initially as fun made me reluctant to abandon the effort when the going got rough. It enabled me to put up with the times of frustration and despondency.

It is quite likely a question of temperament, but I reckon it has been indispensable to me to have had therapists who all possessed a lively sense of humour and saw the importance of play. 'What a relief; you let me run round in the garden before I do my homework', I said to Harriet, soon after the commencement of our therapy. It seemed an important part of the working through of the transference that here at last was a playful parent, or an older sibling, who would join in games and not remind me disapprovingly of duty. The breakthrough came with Sybil when, after what seemed to me like some pretty heavy early sessions, almost as fraught as life outside, I realized that here was no sphinx, but a human being with a great sense of fun. After that, of course, there was the constant temptation to make her laugh. But her perspicacity and sense of duty, coupled with my capacity for depression, prevented most sessions from degenerating into farce. Shared play was also valuable as a work incentive. Instead of the Protestant work ethic having a dampening effect, and curbing my spontaneity, I actually felt the need, now and again, to show how serious the playing around had been, and to balance the levity with spells of demonstrable progress. Similarly, I have observed in teaching that students apply themselves far more thoroughly to a subject they can see as fun, and retain much more if it is taught by someone who enjoys it.

François Weyergans's novel *Le Pitre* ('The clown'), based on his therapy with Lacan, makes it sound like a series of farcical games; but the linguistic inventiveness of the two and the amazing behaviour of the therapist certainly stimulated a new way of looking at things. Unfortunately we do not learn how effective the therapy was. There is a danger, as with a Beckett play, that the taste for verbal pyrotechnics and comic effects can mask the underlying seriousness but, as one Beckett character says to another, 'What keeps you here? – The dialogue.' There is not only the hope that the word-play (or '*charlacanerie*') will keep the attention of the audience or therapist (and there is a double meaning in the play; actors and audience are obliged to remain present and to make, or receive, utterances), but there is also the feeling that the entertainment value of laughter fulfils a deeper purpose. It compels attention and involves the participants. Also, in Beckett's theatre as in psychotherapy, laughter or playing is a way of not just accepting a depressing reality, which would lead to hopelessness, but of looking at it from different angles, inventing alternatives, freeing humans through this imaginative capacity.

The investigative role of play, as a means of discovering knowledge through examining the multiple possibilites in reality, is emphasized by Heinz Kohut (1977, p. 207). He discusses how, in psychotherapy as in creative science, 'play-fulness' involves a realization that the truth is unknowable, but that the way to seek it and express it involves looking at it from many points of view and describing it in a variety of ways. Psychotherapy, like science or art, tends towards the organiz-ation of structure and meaning from inchoate experience. Through bringing inspiration, insight and discipline to bear on the raw material something new comes into being. Psycho-therapy is therefore creative rather than a question of following rules or a leader.

This is well illustrated by the work of Marion Milner, in particular, *On Not Being Able to Paint* (1950), in which she analyses the need for the same sort of receptivity and authenticity in truly creative painting that one tries to cultivate in psychoanalysis. She elaborates on this relationship of the two activities in her detailed account of the treatment of a psychotic patient, conducted largely through the drawings she produced for each session (*The Hands of the Living God*, 1969). In an earlier article (1952) she relates children's playing to concentration in adults, and sees that they use the therapist as a play-object 'not only [as] defensive regression, but an essential recurrent phase of a creative relation to the world'. This view informs Winnicott's work, particularly as described in *Playing and Reality*:

Psychotherapy takes place in the overlap of two areas of playing, that of the patient and that of the therapist. Psychotherapy has to do with two people playing together. The corollary of this is that where playing is not possible then the work done by the therapist is directed towards bringing the patient from a state of not being able to play into a state of being able to play. (1971, p. 44)

This was amply borne out by my own therapy. Originally, I had been able to play. Harriet brought her own playfulness to the sessions, and this was productive both for my life and my therapy. She then clamped down on this, seeing it, with some justification, as 'defensive'. My life and therapy became devoid of joy and meaning, and I had to be brought gradually back into 'a state of being able to play'.

Although it was only too easy to see that this had happened, it was not obvious to either of us for some time why it had come about. I had always defined myself as playful and creative. These were characteristics I valued, and turned to good use both professionally and in daily life. They were present at the beginning of my therapy with Harriet. It took some years of 'therapy' (or 'psychomalpractice', as a friend caustically termed it) to kill this ability in me. The relation of this loss of my playfulness to anything in psychotherapy itself was not immediately obvious. The likely explanation (indeed, a real reason) was that I had become too depressed to enjoy anything. It was not for a long time that I connected it with a remark made by Harriet two years earlier. Although it had seemed unimportant at the time it had indeed rankled and had a deep and oddly destructive effect.

Harriet's reaction to the clown act one day had been to say with exasperation 'Don't you ever stop playing?' 'No,' said I, 'why should I?'. 'I come here to work and I think it's time you stopped fooling about.' My immediate reaction was to dismiss this statement as a stuffy grown-up attitude, or an example of the Protestant work ethic which I had spent my adult life defying. I was feeling playful at the time and translated this into the composition of a story about a kitten who was told not to play by a Boss Cat, and got its own back by isolating the Boss Cat from neighbourhood games. It was not until two years later, by which time my workaholic tendencies had reached such an extreme that I could no longer enjoy anything, could not stop working, even to sleep, and had become so exhausted that I had to be put under sedation in a nursing home, that I realized how I had introjected this half-forgotten comment made by my therapist. The obedient child in me had, unknown to my rational self, taken these words to heart and stopped being able to play. This was doubly ironic in that Harriet valued the capacity for creative play highly, both in herself and in me, and I had estranged myself from her by this obsession with work to the detriment of life. But neither of us realized this until I was virtually destroyed by it. Even when I did reach this insight I found myself unable to relax and enjoy things immediately. It was not until Simon, enlisted to extricate me from this impasse, spontaneously saw me as a 'free spirit' that I felt released from the cage and able to reaffirm my autonomous creativity. I had reached a state indicated by Winnicott in the words, 'We find that individuals live creatively and feel that life is worth living or else that they cannot live creatively and are doubtful about the value of living' (1971, p. 83).

This states clearly the relation between the need to play, in the widest sense, and the desire to live, hence the therapeutic value of an encounter where one works by playing creatively. The most therapeutic aspect of psychotherapy in the first year (with the second therapist) had then been my ability, and the permission, to use the space for play. This made me more creative in life and also made the therapy more productive. When this permission to play was withdrawn I lost my ability to create and live. I only regained both when another therapist, Simon, indirectly gave me permission to play; a release which was celebrated by a spate of creative writing, the resumption of musical activity and the return of my sense of humour. I would affirm with Winnicott that:

The essential feature of my meaning in this communication is this, that playing is an experience, always a creative experience, and it is an experience in the space–time continuum, a basic form of living . . . it helps us understand our work if we know that the basis of what we do is the patient's playing, a creative experience taking up space and time, and intensely real for the patient. (1971, p. 59)

8 THE SPACE FOR WORDS

Free association: the term the psychoanalyst uses to register his approval of the patient who talks about what the analyst wants him to talk about. The opposite of resistance.
Resistance: the term the psychoanalyst uses to register his disapproval of the patient who talks about what he himself wants to talk about rather than about what the analyst wants him to talk about.
Szasz, *The Second Sin*, p. 82

Psychotherapy does not aim at filling the empty space in one's life, as I learnt with some regret. It offers instead a space to be filled. But filled with what? While my need, as I discussed in Chapter 5, was to encounter a real person, who did not just present a blank screen for my projections but joined me in the therapeutic space, this does not imply that I wanted his or her reality to invade that space. It was better kept minimal, just sufficient to encourage me to fill the space. A problem encountered by people in therapy and not usually dealt with in books for therapists is the content of sessions. It is usually assumed that any material can be discussed and that there should be no taboo subjects. In practice this is not entirely the case; therapists do exercise subtle control. Nor is the mere permission to talk about anything automatically helpful to the consulter, who may initially find his or her anxiety is increased by this lack of structure. This is not supposed to be a problem, but it is one.

Moreover, there are also the questions of what not to say, of whether it is necessarily counter-productive to keep silent about some matters. There are the words which must be found to provide the discourse; there is also the need for distance, in which to preserve oneself. Again, this is not supposed to be an issue, because the rule is to spew out everything and hold nothing back. My fear was that if I handed everything over to my therapist, by bringing all my secrets into the sessions, I would lose my identity and become possessed by the other, no longer be discrete. I think obligatory total divulgence is an invasion of privacy. This may, of course, be why I still have blocks after eight years of therapy. The conviction is however strong enough, and the practice, I suspect, frequent enough for me to feel that it is worth discussing.

There is, then, first of all the problem of what to say; particularly of where to start. Most people come with preconceptions: that they will be expected to narrate their life story, starting with childhood memories; that dreams are obligatory material; that they should say why they have come. None of these apparently simple areas is without problems. Many people do not know very clearly why they have come, or feel obscurely that they should not be so worried or hung up about the problem.

My own initial feeling was that my problems were largely imaginary and neurotic (obviously an introjection of the parental view), that I had no right to bother anyone with them, and it was culpable to admit to finding them intolerable. I couldn't have said this, for fear of having it corroborated, and therefore being rejected before I had begun. Some people may resent having to go back to the murky zone of childhood, when they have pressing present-day problems, which do not immediately seem to be related. Even dreams can create a problem. A friend of mine with a Jungian analyst was expected to begin each session with an account of the previous night's dreams, in spite of her assertion that she never remembered a thing about them. She assures me that this was a directive, not an option. I tried to strike a bargain with her, in which I would narrate to her my memorable, technicolour dreams in five fun-packed acts of myth-laden tragicomedy, so that she could fulfil the important aim of pleasing her analyst by producing this rich dream life and I could relieve the burden on my own therapist – who was distinctly un-Jungian and only mildly interested in dreams – while maintaining an attitude of tolerant interest in my elaborate attempts at interpretation. ('Mm,' said Harriet, 'maybe Jung is right about kitchens signifying the unconscious. But they mean preparing meals to me.') Unfortunately, we could see no way round the dilemma; my unconscious and my friend's were unlikely to be very similar (however collectively archetypal at core), and so the interpretation wouldn't be valid and would interfere with the progress of her analysis.

This directive to present dream material was perhaps unusual. More generally, therapists would seem not to give any guidance. Some do not even make it explicit that there are no rules and so any material can be discussed. This in itself can create anxieties, since most people coming to therapy for the first time are tense and defensive. They may well feel that something is expected of them and be upset by not knowing what it is, or how to comply with the unvoiced rules that they feel must none the less be there. Oldfield mentions the prevalence of such uncertainty about what constitutes relevant material, and also the fact that this distress often seems to be underestimated by the counsellors. One woman summed it up by saying: 'I could never quite see what we were trying to do. I'm supposed to sit and talk, and I don't quite know what to talk about.' Oldfield comments on the varying degrees of frustration, anger or disorientation with which people met this lack of guidance. One of the interviewees commented:

There were some very difficult times; we just sat in silence. It felt a bit like the night before, doing one's homework: what the hell am I going to talk about tomorrow? . . . I was either too frightened to say what I wanted to talk about – or I couldn't identify a way through the wall . . . The problem was my reluctance to talk about, or my non-awareness of, important issues. There didn't seem to be the help I needed to break it down.

There were certainly times when I was very apprehensive about the sessions, and the responsibility that seemed to be loaded on to me to conduct them.

There was a powerful task imposed to bring in material, like a little boy doing his homework – else we shall sit in one of those interminable silences. I wouldn't have been here if I hadn't found it difficult to talk about things I felt vulnerable about or had buried so deep I couldn't dig them up for myself. It was a paradox – that I was required to do the digging by myself.

Her method was to make it my responsibility – perhaps she could have shared this in some way, so that I could respond? (Oldfield, 1983, p. 63)

This fact, that not being able to talk about problems often constitutes one of the presenting problems in many cases, is perhaps dismissed a trifle glibly by psychotherapists. The rationale is that suggestions or hints from the therapist would falsify the person's presentation of her own problems, and perhaps block them. This is reasonable, but a compromise needs to be found between this danger and the opposite one, of silencing the consulter through a perplexing silence on the part of the listener. Clarifying the rules (or absence of them) might minimize the time wasted on futile guessing games, such as those mentioned by one of Rogers' clients: 'At first I tried to figure out what he wanted me to say or do. I was trying to outguess him or rather to diagnose my case as I thought he would. That didn't pan out' (1951, p. 72). Part of the ethos of Rogers' client-centred therapy is that it gives the person back her autonomy and encourages exploration (see Rogers, 1951, pp. 72, 105). This is true, in many cases, but some people need more encouragement at first than others. This is also true of university teaching, where it would be uneducational to spoonfeed people, or stunt their enquiry by directing it too forcefully; yet embarrassed silences, when the student is groping for an acceptable comment, are not very helpful either.

The problem, after all, mainly concerns the first few interviews, when everything is strange and anxiety at the maximum, to an extent that is more likely to be an obstacle rather than an opening to any communication. As Cox observes, 'as the questions are asked, so the answers begin to crystallize' (1978, p. 85). This is one of the dynamic and productive features of therapy, but it is often not apparent for a long time, during which a great deal of not necessarily useful frustration has been encountered; moreover, at great expense. ('Bicycling in yogurt' is how one of Frischer's interviewees called this futile endeavour.) Hobson declares:

There is reason to suppose that a clear awareness of the task of therapy is beneficial to the patient. A client becomes unnerved and often persecuted if he sits under the eye of a therapist without a notion of what is expected or of what is likely to happen. We should spell out as far as possible what psychotherapy is about. (1985, p. 203)

Generally, the compulsion to talk about what is on one's mind will override other considerations. I would usually begin with these things, perhaps exploring avenues of suggestion they opened up, but with which I had not previously connected them. This seemed to work. But there are days when one's mind seems a blank, or when the current preoccupations seem terribly trivial. One feels a recurrent obligation to return to the headlines, as it were, to worry at the precipitating factors of a recent crisis, or the major long-term hang-ups; to talk about 'my ontological insecurity', rather than the sudden feeling of panic as you tripped over a black cat in the dark.

Therapists perhaps do not see this as a problem, since most would say that anything can be used as a starting-point. But this is to underestimate the active super-ego of most people in therapy. It is a misconception only equal to that which maintains that therapists give no directives about what material should be included in or excluded from sessions. Often it seems to the beginner that this is so. But one gradually becomes aware of certain topics which are more welcome than others, and I do not think this is solely a transferential projection. Both Sybil and Harriet steered me off talking about mutual acquaintances, although the communication had to do with quite important feelings and not just gossip. Sybil refused point-blank to let me talk about books, on the grounds that this was 'rationalization' and, since my intellect was functioning quite adequately, I ought to concentrate on feelings. Yet when she complained that I did not talk much about sex, and I alleged that this was because I felt I was functioning satisfactorily in that domain so there was nothing to say, this was not immediately accepted.

The only time I dared openly to discuss my suicidal impulses with Sybil she rounded angrily on me, declaring that the statement was 'a threat', which was not at all how it seemed to me. I was made to feel wrong and ungrateful to be in such despair. I shut up. But I went on feeling suicidal, and not always sure why, since I had not had the chance to talk it out. Intimidated by the experience, it was years before I dared to discuss these impulses with Harriet, who also shied away from facing them, though without condemning me for feeling them or denying their validity. It only occurred to me some years later, and because someone else pointed it out, that maybe they had actually cared whether I were alive or dead. I can see, with my intellect, that this is a likely explanation for their resistance to the topic of suicide. But since I have never considered my own life worthwhile, nor have I ever been able to believe that I could matter to another human being, I still cannot understand this emotionally.

However, I can see that it might be painful for a therapist to be confronted by someone's suicidal feelings. But it is surely more painful for the other person to be feeling them. Not being able to discuss them is hardly therapeutic. With students, as well as friends, I have found that it is important to let the suicidal person express his or her despair, and neither to minimize it nor to panic about it. I found it has helped me, and I have helped others most, if the listener fully accepts the authenticity of the impulse, but tries to indicate another way of dealing with it, if possible. What needs to be conveyed is that life can still be lived, and that the person who wishes to die does none the less have some value to others. This cannot be believed, because a suicidal person has no value in her own eyes. But it will be stored up and can gradually help to build up more ego-strength to weather subsequent crises. As David Smail says, 'the greatest comfort derives from having one's view, however despairing it may be, confirmed by someone else who is not afraid to share it' (1987, p. 6). I was distinctly uncomforted once, when I reported to Sybil that a psychiatrist had said he could not get me admitted to a nursing home because they would not take suicidal patients, to be told by her, 'But you are not suicidal.' She was not at the time my therapist but I was even so amazed at this refusal to validate my feelings. In view of the difficulties I had getting therapists to listen to this problem, I would then claim that it is a trifle disingenuous of them to assert that absolutely all material can be discussed, without restriction.

Anxiety about the limits or limitlessness of the content of sessions is often matched by that about their unstructured nature. There often seems to be no thread, no beginning and end – just an aimless babble. It can be encouraging, as one of Oldfield's respondents stated, and as I found with Simon, if the therapist attempts to sum up the content of the session, to make some statement either about the possible connection between apparently disparate pronouncements or simply about their underlying meaning. Sometimes I felt he had actually got it wrong, and it was annoying not to be able to discuss this until the next session. More usually, I was intrigued by the thread he discerned in my seemingly random discourse, and felt reassured that it had not all been so inconsequential as I had thought. Often, his interpretation gave me a completely new slant on the attitudes I had revealed. Whatever my reaction, the feeling was usually relief that nothing I had said had been too trivial to be of potential use, and so I gradually became less selective about the material I brought to sessions. I had, in fact, suggested to Harriet the possibility of summing up sessions. She received the suggestion with enthusiasm, then groaned at the thought of trying to make sense of my grasshopperish pronouncements, or summing up in a few words the amount of information conveyed per second that my phases of overdrive produced. I saw her problem. However, I think this was indicative of the way in which she listened to the actual words, respectfully, but not with critical distance. Simon listened to the sub-text and so helped me to see what was going on at a more unconscious level.

These days of accelerated communication were in fact in my case almost more of a problem than lack of material. Sometimes I had had a spate of major insights in between sessions, on which I had been working hard, so I arrived bursting with eagerness to communicate all the findings, as well as the elaborate process whereby I had reached them. This had good exorcism value, and there was a creative feeling in having shared the discovery with my therapist. Yet gradually I came to realize that there is no need to foist all the details on the therapist, who may find it difficult to take in, during a mere fifty minutes, so much breathless information, which may have necessitated two or three days' hard thought on my part to formulate. It also left very little room for the therapist to comment, if I was intent on getting it all out. So, as therapy progressed, I tended to be a bit more selective about what I actually said, or to ask for extra sessions at times of overdrive. When this was not possible I sometimes resorted to writing it down and handing Harriet the pages. Perhaps not all therapists would agree to doing homework, but she was on the whole very accommodating. This sort of communication was also useful if I had major insights during her absences, as I often did. I would have resented having to keep them to myself while they were fresh and only being able to mention them when they had lost the thrill of novelty.

There were also times when I dried up and felt I had nothing to say. Sometimes this was resistance – usually it was because I was fed up with having to find the time for a session when I felt I had better things to do. Sometimes there simply seemed nothing to say because nothing much was happening inside me. Usually I found these sessions very unsatisfactory with whichever therapist. But occasionally it left them more room to intervene, and as none of them was a total sphinx the session could sometimes be oddly productive, because I was in a more receptive frame of mind and there was space for us to work things out together.

A problem experienced by many (see Oldfield, 1983, pp. 82–3) is the difficulty of attending at a specific time and day for the purpose of discussing highly emotionally charged subjects for which one might not feel at all in the mood, or which, conversely, one had desperately wanted to discuss between sessions, but had by now lost sight of. It is very difficult for most people to shift gear from their daily preoccupations and delve into their inner world at set hours on particular days; it is no more possible for the majority than it is to make love at prescribed times. The analogy is not an inadvertent toadying to the conventional view of the analyst as an object of sexual fantasies, but an emphasis on the depth of emotional involvement present for most people in the experience, and the importance of mood, as opposed to the merely mechanical side of the transaction. I was amazed at a colleague of mine who swore that she was able to dash off for a session of psychotherapy in between teaching, with no real break on either side. I felt I needed a space at either end to 'get back into myself', as Harriet had put it.

It was not so much that I wanted to prepare any topic, just that I wanted to turn off other claims on my attention and make myself blank before the session. Afterwards I needed a space to let things settle; at times of crisis or great insight I needed quite a long period of quiet afterwards. This made it increasingly difficult for me to hold down a responsible and demanding job while being very deep into the therapeutic experience, and I have doubts about the wisdom of people trying to do both. (Margaret Little [1985] discusses how she too found this a problem and it is alluded to by Herman [1985].)

This need for space around sessions was matched by my need for space within sessions. Perhaps because I have a mother with a powerful, possessive personality I have always felt a need to keep areas of myself private and this operated in therapy too. I did not wish to be lured into saying **everything**, and this was a potent factor behind my hesitations before embarking on therapy in the first place. Many people have a fear that the analyst will pursue each disclosure relentlessly until all the defences are down, and all the secrets exposed. While this is probably the aim of a full-scale analysis, and the literature on the subject (mainly written by analysts) tends to foster this view of an all-seeing therapist with almost supernatural powers of detection and perspicacity, I don't think I have ever met an analysand who admits to having been quite that thoroughly analysed. Not only are most neurotics heavily defended, but most therapists are only human too, and not as infallibly sharp as they might wish. Given time, and total cooperation from the consulter, the two will get to the bottom of most problems in the end. But people often have a vested interest in hanging on to a few private areas, and they are only persuaded with great reluctance to abandon what have always seemed to be very necessary defences, virtually guaranteeing survival.

This need for space and privacy is not, however, merely my neurosis. Not only have I found in discussions with therapists, my own and others, that it is a need shared and respected by many, but this is also attested by David Smail (1987, p. 124). Robert Hobson, in his *Forms of Feeling* (1985, p. 203), discusses the 'intrusion' involved in being 'too intuitive and empathic' which 'can make a client feel invaded by a magical, all-knowing therapist'. He affirms:

It is important to avoid a forced confession of fragile 'secrets' which . . . are experienced as a 'core of the self'. Secrets should be valued and respected by therapists, by parents, and by husbands and wives. We need an 'inner space' and a 'space-between'. (1985, p. 201)

Moreover, there quite simply isn't time in most present-day therapies even to work through all the material which is accessible, let alone buried under layers of resistance. Ideally, one does continue until it has all beeen unearthed. In practice, it may be so deeply submerged in the unconscious that it cannot be excavated during one course of treatment, but needs a lapse of years, and perhaps a crisis to trigger it off, before it can come to the surface.

An interesting example of this is the article by Guntrip (1975) about his two therapies with Fairbairn and Winnicott, subtitled 'How complete a result does psychoanalytic therapy achieve?'. He shows in this how two analyses, with highly skilled therapists, coupled with strong personal and professional motivation on his part, none the less failed to elucidate a childhood trauma and overcome amnesia about vital details, until time and a good deal of independent analytical work operated the desired effect.

Very few people have the leisure, or money, for the sort of intensive and prolonged analysis which would make it possible to unravel all secret traumata. Most of us are content to function a bit more effectively than before, to be a bit more in touch with our motives and feelings, and to have gained relief from the more pressing symptoms of distress.

There remains the question of to what extent the therapist should respect a notice, explicit or implicit, declaring 'Private; keep out'. My own feeling, which some therapists would term resistance, is that this should definitely be respected, just as the need for total confidentiality regarding one's disclosures should be respected. It might be possible, and is certainly desirable, to analyse together just why the notice is being displayed, and what motivates the need for a retention of secret zones. But it would be a violation of human rights, as I see it, for the therapist to insist on disclosure. Such an authoritarian approach would only breed mistrust, and people would take greater care on subsequent occasions to hide the fact that there is anything to hide. They would see the therapist as an invasive character, not to be trusted; a threat to the client's autonomy.

An interesting example of this, and of the need to break down the defences, is Peter Shaffer's play *Equus* (1973). It is a bit difficult to be entirely sure whether the need to do so is the psychiatrist's or the delinquent's; on reflection it is probably neither, but mainly for the audience to do so. The boy protagonist, in spite of his initial aggression and continued suspicions and accusations of 'nosy parker', directed at the psychiatrist, gradually lets his defences be broken down. This is effected mainly by his conniving at tricks, so that he feels he is not really responsible for what he has said and can deny it afterwards. Also, he develops an unwilling trust and liking for his inquisitor. However, the feeling that is conveyed here, through the psychiatrist's commentary, is that the boy is secretly longing to confess, only cannot bring himself to do so, because the original experience was so traumatic and shameful to him. There is then a conflict between terror of exposure and condemnation, and longing for the relief of sharing a burden. This may operate in other therapeutic contexts, and it is up to the therapist's tact, perception and knowledge of the person concerned to know just when and how much to probe. (It is to be hoped that off stage they don't play tricks like the ones in *Equus*.)

A crucial factor here is that the boy did really want to confess, but could not overcome his inhibitions enough to do so in a more normal way. The problem is perhaps more often one concerning minor secrets which one simply does not want invaded, perhaps as part of a need to maintain one's own autonomy. The acquisition of a new lover, for instance, might be something one feels ought to be communicated to the therapist, but that also needs to be kept private, since sharing it, at least initially, might destroy the magic.

It took years of psychotherapy for me to be fully aware of the extent to which I tend to hide my deepest feelings under a smoke-screen of words. Yet even when the façade of being lively and outgoing had completely broken down, so that I presented myself in daily life, as in therapy, as uncommunicative and withdrawn, I protected myself against psychic overexposure by avoiding distressing subjects in sessions. I suspect this was in part due to an intuition that Harriet had similar inhibitions to my own and was relieved to be spared embarrassing or painful experiences. She initially said this was a projection on my part and then admitted to its having some truth. We agreed that it was in part transferential, and due to my real need to protect my mother from distasteful facts she refused to acknowledge. This shared reticence may have been responsible in part for the long block this therapy reached. Simon, who was hired to get me out of the impasse, seemed to have no self-consciousness or inhibitions when tackling delicate problems and this immediately lifted my shyness. Not only was I able to broach subjects with him that I had previously found too alarming, but I then became able to discuss these things with Harriet, my concurrent therapist. As these things often involved my relationship with her, it was useful to have them both as therapists.

This ability to discuss things with one person which we would not mention to another operates in life as well as psychotherapy, and most of us have experienced it. In real life this is probably not transferential, but due to a realistic appraisal of the other person's sensibilities. I have found that in each of my therapies there were things I would not divulge to one therapist, which I could talk about with another, or to the same person when she was no longer my therapist. I think this had something to do with my sense of the other person's involvement. There might, I felt, be things someone would not wish to hear about because they affected them directly. As Simon pointed out: 'You can't talk about love with Harriet because you feel it.'

Paradoxically, this also related to the distancing effect the professional role has. There were many things which I could mention to friends, but not to Sybil, while she was my therapist. That is, a professional who would pounce on particular aspects of the admission, dissect them and toss them back at me with labels attached – labels, moreover, which tended to dispute my presentation of the object and rename it. She was often right; I just did not want to play into her hands. This was part of the transferential game of wishing to deprive the grown-ups of the satisfaction of saying 'I told you so.' When Sybil became metamorphosed from sphinx into friendly domesticat, the compulsion to be secretive out of sheer bloody-mindedness ceased to operate. However, I was again secretive with Harriet, chiefly about my feelings for her.

I found that I was able to talk to Simon about Harriet, mainly because she had become a problem, rather than a source of therapy. I needed to discuss this, but seemed unable to do so productively with her. I could not however discuss Simon with Harriet, except very obliquely. I think this was partly transferential; I had always tried to keep the men in my life well away from my mother. It was partly due to a different, though unformulated, distinction in my mind between their functions. Simon was my therapist; Harriet was the person I looked to for supportive comfort.

This admission of secretiveness will doubtless meet with disapproval. It sounds ludicrous and self-defeating, since the whole point of the exercise is to be completely frank and avoid no topics, spare no details. Certainly, someone who is not able to overcome resistance to this is unlikely to resolve their problems while it lasts. I find myself in something of a dilemma over this issue. My personal politics clamour for the individual to be respected, and that includes a respect for privacy. I do not think people should be forced to make admissions for which they are not ready, or which might make them feel worse. Yet I realize the drawbacks for therapy. It was, however, possible to discuss with Harriet just why she was not welcome inside certain demarcation limits, and why this embargo did not apply to all trespassers, but only to her. This was only possible because of the security accorded to me through her respect for my rights to privacy. It did not make me less adamant (at least at certain stages in the relationship) that the veto was not going to be lifted, but it turned the exclusion into a partly shared experience that could be lifted at a later stage because it had been recognized as valid. Yet I have to admit that by respecting my feelings, Harriet was also making it difficult for me to grow out of them. I lacked the incentive to become bolder. I think maybe there might have been ways of giving me more of a lead into various thorny problems. Here I was probably up against what she called her limitations (her reticence), which were also part of her positive qualities (her tolerance and respect for the individual). Simon seemed to take it for granted that many things said in therapy are not socially acceptable, but this makes it important to say them. It was his example, rather than his attitude, which inspired me to become more frank.

9 INTERPRETATION

Interpretations . . . are not merely ideas generated by a conceptual framework possessed by the therapist and fed by him into the patient's psychic apparatus, but also sentences uttered by a real, live person who is devoting time and attention to another real, live person.
Rycroft, *Psychoanalysis and Beyond*, p. 63

As well as the client having to find words in the 'talking cure', the therapist has to find them. What to say and what not to say present problems for both people. Presumably all who come to psychotherapy desire some sort of interpretation of actions or motives we have hitherto found baffling. We may wish to reach this mainly by ourselves, guided by the occasional prompt, or we may welcome explicit interpretation by the therapist. In either case, a well-placed or well-timed intervention can act as a revelation, just as an ill-timed one can be very damaging. It is well known that an interpretation which comes too soon will meet with resistance, and that that resistance could be lasting. As Casement declares:

*It is all too easy to cut across a patient's spontaneous finding of the therapist's presence by intervening too quickly. A similar error is to bring the patient's communications to a premature focus on to the therapist, which is often done in the name of transference. This . . . deflects from the patient's **experience of feeling** towards **thinking about feelings**, before the actual experience has been more fully entered into. (1985, p. 178, author's emphasis)*

This view is confirmed and expanded on by Hobson (1985, pp. 49–50, 201–2), who stresses the importance of not invalidating a person's feelings by a reductionist interpretation, as do Lomas and Smail throughout their work.

Right at the beginning of my first therapy I began to talk about the pressing problem of whether I could not get on with the person I was living with because of faults of my own, or because he really wasn't suited to me. This was a genuine issue in my life at the time, which might have called for some action – like ending the relationship. The therapist told me that I was really talking about my relationship with her. At the time I was not aware of how usual this response is from therapists, but even then it smelt of technical cliché. I felt the real life relationship had been disparaged, and that I was being rebuffed, made to talk about a relationship that didn't yet exist and which, as far as I could see, had nothing to do with the original problem. Both levels of communication were doubtless present, but it might have been more helpful if their equal validity had been recognized, so that the authenticity of the domestic situation was not denigrated. It was also, I think, too early in the relationship to tackle the transference, particularly with a person unfamiliar with the concept and therefore unreceptive to such an approach. When my third therapist started on a similar tack, I could see the justification for it, but was able to stand my ground more firmly about the fact that I was **also** talking about an outside relationship, which was causing me considerable distress in real life.

*A person always means what he says but he does not say all that he means. A psychotherapist should never even imply 'You don't mean that, you **really** mean this', but rather, 'Yes, you mean that but maybe you also mean this.'* (Hobson, 1985, pp. 49–50, author's emphasis)

Hobson also says:

Since the therapist believes that he is not there as a person, but merely as a 'blank screen', he may respond to all the patient's remarks about him as if they were merely manifestations of other relationships in the past, whether or not elaborated by fantasy. The patient comes to feel that all his productions are unreal distortions. Such a therapist nullifies the patient's attempts to distinguish those responses and attitudes that are illusory from those which are part of an actual situation in the present . . . he impedes the patient's movement towards a healthy reduction of his distorted perception of others, not allowing him to make the comparison between what is 'illusion' and what is 'actual'. (p. 202)

Ideally the therapist interprets as little as possible but waits, perhaps with a little unobtrusive guidance, for the other person to reach his or her own conclusions. The task must be as slow and frustrating as watching a small child learn to eat by itself. The temptation to prevent the mess and guide the spoon is constant, but obviously to be avoided if the infant is going to acquire sufficient dexterity. There is no need to be as bland as the non-directive school of Carl Rogers, in which the therapist's habit of repeating the client's statement ('I want to murder my mother.' 'You want to murder your mother?') seems, at least from the outside, to fall into the comic through its predictability. But a modicum of orientation can be very helpful and clients responding to Susan Oldfield's survey frequently stressed their appreciation of this, and their feeling of bewilderment or frustration when none was forthcoming. Sometimes this is an inevitable part of the awareness that there is going to be no spoon-feeding and that one will have to explore one's own motives. But moral autonomy, as well as physical, is more readily attained in a framework of supportive, though not supporting interest.

Most therapists are doubtless models of tact. They certainly intend to be, though the literature on the subject or revelations of friends can be distinctly eyebrow-raising. Yet it is also amazing how often theory or temperament can override this consideration. Even the most undogmatic of therapists are occasionally liable to pin labels on things, to attempt to straitjacket a complex and fluctuating state of mind into a neat category, to assume motives which would fit the textbook picture, but seem to be grossly inappropriate to one's own experience. The heavy-handed Freudian interpretation meted out to Stuart Sutherland (1976, p. 20), which violently disillusioned him with therapy at an early stage in the encounter, may sound extreme but, if the literature and the grapevine are anything to go by, is not so abnormal.

None of my therapists have used jargon, but I was not helped by Harriet's suggestion that 'the traditionalists' would equate the stories and drawings I brought her with the child's offering of faeces. No doubt excretion and artistic endeavour fulfil a similar function; no doubt I was trying to please the grown-ups by my offering. But I was not a child offering a turd; I was an adult who had tried to create something meaningful, to express a semi-conscious intuition through an artistic structure. If as an infant I had been able to offer the daisy chains and drawings, which I did indeed give adults at a later stage, I probably wouldn't have chosen the potty as a means of self-expression then.

Any objection to such pronouncements is likely to be countered by the accusation of 'resistance'. Racker, for instance, declares:

In other words basically the patient felt attracted to the Father-analyst's penis . . . the rejection of the analysis – the resistances against communicating certain associations or accepting interpretations – sprang from the fact that being seen, understood and interpreted was equated to transforming the danger of becoming the victim of a sadistic penis into catastrophic reality. (1968, p. 84)

and:

The interpretation breast was the more bad and feared the more the analysand had previously attacked the interpretations . . . the woman in the dream is the Mother-analyst . . . the patient did not want to recognize the goodness and capacity of this breast . . . she declared herself 'fed up with the uselessness of the analyst's interpretation'. (pp. 80, 103–4)

And who but an analyst would find this surprising? It is clear from the context that this is not just technical vocabulary being used by an analyst communicating to colleagues in a textbook.

The words were used to the analysand. Even if they had not been, I think there is a danger inherent in analysts communicating to each other in such jargon. It devalues the reality of the other person's experience as an adult (an issue which informs my argument in Chapter 5).

Doubts about an interpretation may of course be due to resistance, because it is seen as a threat; they may also be due to a dislike of jargon. Maybe if Racker had said simply to the first man, 'You admired your father because he was strong, but felt inadequate because you were weak and young', and the woman had been told, 'You want to preserve the image of your mother as bad, therefore you are suspicious of all women and resent or yearn for those who seem good', with the concomitant stress on the present situation of the individual, and the personal, as opposed to stereotypical past, the interpretations might have provoked less animosity.

Another example of this kind of technical vocabulary is 'The ideal-persecutor penis was represented in the analytic situation by the analyst's superiority in understanding – having destroyed the analyst's reason-penis the patient feared retaliation' (p. 87). At the risk of provoking howls of 'resistance' from the pundits, I maintain that none of this rings true. It just does not describe what I think is going on. I am not denying that there might be some validity in it, but it has been raised into dogmas of universal applicability, while it would seem to me to be purely relative. If I deny that this expresses what I have felt, the high priests are likely to reply that this cannot be so, the time-honoured pyramid of their cult depends on such oracular pronouncements, and I cannot have been properly analysed if I refuse to abandon my resistances to such consecrated truths. To which I can only reply that therapy worked sufficiently well for me to be sure of what I really feel, and of what reeks of inauthenticity. If the high priests don't like it, there may yet be some echoes of sympathy among the congregation or other heretics.

This sort of terminology may act as useful shorthand for analysts communicating to each other, but is very off-putting if addressed directly to someone in therapy, as it not infrequently is. Even supposing that people in therapy do not read books (which many of us do), this vocabulary perpetuates in the professionals who use it an attitude which gets passed on to the consulter. My insistence on this point is an attempt to counteract the common misconception on the part of the public that psychoanalysis involves falling in love with the analyst and being subjected to all sorts of far-fetched theories about the trials and delights of potty training, castration complexes and penis-envy. It doesn't have to. Kelman (in Horney, 1946, pp. 132–3) reviews the misconception (his word) about 'falling in love', while the feminists have entirely refocused the concept of penis-envy.[1] A lucid and sensitive critique of the dangers of reducing all motivation to sexuality is given, by an analyst, in Ian Suttie's excellent but neglected book *The Origins of Love and Hate* (1935). Jung also held this view. A more caustic attack, from the sociological and lay person's viewpoint, provides the main thrust of Ernest Gellner's *The Psychoanalytic Movement* (1985).

Both Simon and Harriet tried to persuade me that I was more prepared to accept his interpretations than hers because of the gender difference. 'You let him penetrate', said Harriet. No doubt I am physiologically and psychologically more receptive to male penetration, but I think the psychological reason has more to do with my personal history than the basic fact of gender. My father had never even tried to discuss anything with me. My mother invaded, or penetrated, my whole being. She covered the blank page of my identity with the rubber stamp of her own forceful views and personality. It was only under the influence of the peer group, of both genders, in my student days that I began to develop ideas which were truly my own. I think then that I am resistant to anyone who tries to impose his or her views on me, but receptive to people whom I respect, regardless of gender, who express different attitudes without forcing me to relinquish mine.

It seems to me important to let analysands work out their own hang-ups in their own words. This must surely have the effect of making us less reticent about bringing forward material which we feel is liable to get labelled with a cliché, or made less real as an experience, less genuinely ours, because it has been demoted to a stock response, a textbook syndrome. This is what we all are, no doubt; but people don't like to be told it, much less refused permission to perceive themselves differently.

At times, interpretations can quite simply be wrong, and it would be far more of a resistance to truth for the consulter not to realize this. For instance, my childhood passion for ballet, probably explicable in terms of peer-group influence, gaining maternal approval and exercising innate ability, was attributed by Sybil Brown to hermaphroditic yearnings, satisfied by the wearing of unisex leotards. I did not like to contradict my otherwise much-respected therapist by pointing out that I never once wore a leotard, but that we girls wore Greek tunics for class and rehearsals and tutus or three-quarter-length ballet dresses for performances; so, if anything, I was more likely to have been asserting my femininity. Later on in therapy I would probably have had enough self-confidence and felt sufficiently at ease in the relationship to mention this. At the time I was busy playing model patients and submissive children; in any case it hardly seemed worth quibbling about such a detail. But if she then proceeded to attribute to me hermaphroditic yearnings which I don't think I have, and to miss the extent to which I use silence as a weapon – a way of preserving my autonomy in the face of adult dogmatism and excluding the other person – the therapy may subsequently have got twisted.

Unwillingness to accept an interpretation is not, then, necessarily a refusal to acknowledge certain aspects of one's behaviour, but can be because of the way it is worded, or because it actually is wrong. Past experience has, after all, taught one that the grown-ups are not always right, and that one should not automatically accept everything they say as true. Therapy is, in fact, supposed to be encouraging one to be more critical and suspicious of motives, so it is a bit of a double-bind to expect unconditional docility to the therapist. As Peter Lomas observes:

[The therapist] is likely to work on the assumption that, because of his technical mastery, his own views of the interaction are right, the patient's wrong. This accounts for the very great emphasis placed on the patient's 'resistance' to interpretations. The concept of 'resistance' is based on the belief that the psychoanalyst's interpretations are correct and that if the patient is unwilling to accept them it is because they are painful to him; in other words, the determining factor in the state of resistance is avoidance of truth on the part of the patient.

It seems likely, however . . . that the patient is concerned with pursuing truth at least as much as avoiding it . . . therefore he may need to question the therapist with a degree of vigour that the latter may interpret as resistance unless he understands the encounter as one between equals who are searching for the truth. Even when the patient's challenge to the therapist's viewpoint is unreasonable this may originate less in an avoidance of pain than in a compulsive doubt of any interpretation owing to confusion in his early life. (1973, p. 141)

A similar view is to be found in Casement (1985, p. 17) and a sensitive response to the diverse reactions which an interpretation may evoke is shown by Karen Horney (1946, pp. 198–9). Yet the traditional attitude is categorical, as the chapter on 'Interpretation and its application' in Fromm-Reichmann's *The Principles of Intensive Psychotherapy* shows:

If a patient gets upset or angry about an interpretation, this is usually indicative of its being correct . . . otherwise the patient would not react so strongly to the interpretation. (1950, p. 151)

She also declares that too quick an acceptance on the patient's part means that there is no point in pursuing the interpretation for the moment. It seems you can't win, as a patient. While I am sure that sometimes anger does indeed indicate that a painful chord has been struck, revealing a truth the other person would rather suppress, it can also be a justifiable reaction to an erroneous statement. One friend of mine was furious when told how jealous she must have been of her much younger brother. This may have been true at a deep level she perhaps wasn't ready for. As an observer, I can only say that she gave every sign of genuinely loving her brother and that to suggest the opposite was to devalue the care and affection she bestowed on him, whether or not it coexisted with hidden hate.

Generally speaking, therapists do not go leaping into the skein of one's psychobabble crying 'Eureka! An Oedipus complex!' But it is by no means unknown for them to foist somewhat stereotyped interpretations on people too soon. For instance, while it is very likely that most people who come to therapy have not had ideal relations with their parents, and that the tensions in this relationship are likely to be acute in adolescence, my experience with students suggests that many of them are markedly reluctant to accept that there could be flaws in a relationship which may have been idealized up to the moment of crisis, particularly if the parent is paying for therapy. They tend to put on their blinkers and ear-plugs, to discharge themselves hastily from hospital after overdoses, or to discontinue therapy rapidly if premature suggestions are made along these lines. Therapists are not always as tactful in practice as they believe themselves to be in theory. They all realize that knowing something is true from the outside is not at all the same as feeling it is true from the inside, but don't always allow for the fact that someone in a highly vulnerable state may not be prepared to countenance from a stranger a suggestion which they may be battling against unconsciously. In any case, it is likely to provoke resistance simply by being a cliché and premature, as Casement points out (1985, p. 18).

Harriet's frequent allusion to envy struck both myself and a co-consulter rather in this way. We got a bit sick of being told we were envious, whether or not we felt this to be true. Sometimes we were merely being admiring (of the therapist's clothes, for instance). For a long time I growled whenever the word envy was mentioned, wondered if there were some truth in it, yet felt that there wasn't, much. It eventually dawned on me that the truth was perhaps more that I was afraid of being envied myself, and constantly driven to denigrating my own achievements, almost at times to the point of refusing to own or do anything which might be envied. This realization acted as a release in a way the previous statements had not, as I'd felt them to be at the most half-truths, telling me more about the therapist or her theories than myself.

A client in Oldfield's survey voiced the objection felt by many with the words: 'Being on the receiving end of such un-arguable interpretive clichés can be irritating, in so far as they defy logical discussion, even when this is appropriate' (1983, p. 78), and a similar point is made by Cox (1978, pp. 86–7). This seems so obvious it shouldn't need mentioning – were it not for repeated examples of the widespread use of this sort of force-feeding. It is an understandable temptation for someone who has seen daylight to want to communicate this illumination to another, particularly when they feel sure it can help this other. But people need to be allowed to reach things in their own time, and not to be fed with solid food before they have teeth. The dramatist, Antonin Artaud, declared:

I have myself spent nine years in a lunatic asylum and have never suffered from the obsession of wanting to kill myself; but I know that each conversation with a psychiatrist made me want to hang myself because I knew I could not strangle him. (1913–48, p. 38)

Artaud was lucky enough to be conscious of his anger and thus saved from either murder or suicide. But people in therapy do not always have sufficient ego-strength to defend themselves against authoritative interpretations, nor is it always easy to be consciously aware of one's own reactions, much less understand them.

To be told, for instance, 'That's greedy', is likely to arouse indignation, if felt to be unjust, or to reactivate shame and guilt if it coincides with past accusations or constitutes an introjected command from parents. I was most indignant when Harriet said this to me. In the context (my wish to diversify my professional interests) the remark seemed to me simply ludicrous. I did not think I was showing greed but intellectual curiosity, although this diversification did lead to my taking on more commitments than I could reasonably deal with. Greed is a heavily laden word; a more neutral comment might have been more helpful, such as, 'It might take a great deal of energy to do both things at once.' This could have been experienced as an accusation, implying that I had not the requisite stamina, but it could have acted as an invitation to self-examination.

The remark, however, hit hard at a deeper level. No one (except my brother, in childhood) had ever called me greedy. I had taken great care not to expose myself to this accusation. My mother had instilled into me the notion that greed, whether for food or for affection, was a cardinal sin. My first memories were of wartime, when individual greed was indeed a threat to collective survival. My father was thrifty and abstemious in the extreme, and my self-definition relied on identification with my father, in opposition to my mother and brother, whom I saw as greedy about material possessions as well as affection.

Here I was, then, being accused by someone I admired, a sort of mother figure, of being greedy. It mattered not one whit to me that greed in her (American) vocabulary was not a crime at all. 'It's nice being greedy,' she said, when I protested. 'Babies are greedy. I'm greedy too.' I thought that I had forgotten the comment. It was not for some years, by which time I had lost one-quarter of my previous body-weight and become more or less incapable of nourishing myself normally, that I suddenly connected the remark with my refusal to allow myself food. Zany unconscious logic had translated the remark about my intellectual appetite in terms of physical appetite. Nor were the two unconnected, since both were associated with the hunger for life and enjoyment which had previously characterized me but were now absent from my attitudes. Losing my appetite for life had not endeared me to my therapist or my friends, any more than getting thin had. Yet unconsciously I had thought it necessary to refute her statement in this devious way. Understanding this did not, however, enable me to give myself permission to eat. It was not until my next therapist spontaneously **saw** me as someone with considerable vitality and *joie de vivre* that I regained my appetite for life and started eating again.

The pseudo-anorexia during this therapy had complex causes; Harriet's comment about greed, as well as the lack of nourishment I felt in the therapy, were major contributing factors but not the entire explanation. Anorexia is commonly connected with the need for control. A period of severe anorexia in my teens had certainly been motivated by the need to gain control over my body and my life (I had been in hospital, partially paralysed, for over a year at the time). Conversely, my adult neo-anorexia was partly linked with a hysterectomy. The surgeon had made me unable to have children, my unconscious decreed that I should control matters myself by becoming so thin that my periods would have stopped anyway. Illogical as this is, it makes sense to me retrospectively. (Particularly as it was an insight of my own and not prompted by my therapist.) The hysterectomy made me feel no longer a woman, and physically unattractive, just as the depression had made my personality unattractive.

The first time I met Simon I was determined that he should not be disappointed by my appearing initially to be nicer than I really was, so I took care to show him the dreary person my other therapists had rejected. He gave the despair respectful recognition; he did not devalue the force of genuine distress but said, 'I can hear, however, a very energetic person speaking. You are depressed but not depressing.' That immediately changed my mood (I spontaneously ate for the first time in months), and it began a slow but lasting change. Likewise, I had been comforted and helped by another therapist (a stand-in while Harriet was away) saying, 'I can see that you are very depressed, but I don't find you depressing.'

Both Harriet (as a therapist) and Sybil (as a friend) had become swamped by my depression. They seemed trapped as helplessly as I was and could not help me escape. Simon responded immediately to the person I thought was dead, a self I could not consciously have brought into therapy because I no longer remembered her; he brought her back to life.

Simon interpreted more than either of the other two, but sparingly, and not usually until the end of a session or a communication. He would then attempt to abstract himself from what I had actually said, on the anecdotal level, in order to reach the core of meaning beneath it. I didn't always agree with his interpretations, but I usually listened with interest, as he did to my objections. Sometimes the very disagreement was productive, stimulating fresh enquiry on my part. The gentleness and thoughtfulness with which the interpretation was proffered probably had a lot to do with my receptivity. Initially a difference in temperament and approach was fruitful, as was his relative unconcern about agreeing with people. This was in contrast to Harriet, who valued similarity and agreement, in a way which made the encounters friendly but not always very searching. Schneiderman comments:

How much the analyst interprets depends largely on how much uncertainty he can tolerate. Lacan taught that you should never be too quick to fill in the blanks and to make sense of what you are hearing. He had confidence that with time the analysand would say what sense things had for him . . . Lacan, like most analysts, listened to something other than what was said . . . he never tried to find areas of agreement and accord but scrupulously maintained a fruitful, well-tuned discord. (1983, p. 119)

There must also be room for the quick, defensive negation of an interpretation, so that the therapist's apparent tolerance of denial facilitates an inner, unvoiced acceptance on the part of people none the less vehemently rejecting the interpretation, which they might be ready to half-accept, to themselves, but not yet to admit openly. The more the therapist can convey that he or she is not making categorical pronouncements, and that the other person's doubts are respected, the more room there will be for the two views to merge (if the interpretation is correct), and the more trust will be built up, so that the person can gradually become less defensive. I certainly found I became less quick to deny things out of hand, both in sessions and in the outside world, through this experience of tolerance. Neither Harriet nor Simon insisted on their infallibility. I don't think Sybil did either, as a therapist, although she could be very dogmatic with friends; so I gradually felt freer to say 'Well, what you have said doesn't make sense to me at the moment; I don't really feel it is like that, but I'll think about it.' People are of course different, and some only respect categorical pronouncements from an oracle, but if this desire is conceded too much they may fail to develop the appropriate autonomy. I certainly felt much more willing to explore things I was unsure about with Harriet once I had ascertained that she was not going to insist on being right, but willingly joined the exploration simply as 'the more experienced patient of the two' (a remark she quoted to me from Kopp, [1979, p. 43]), and would admit to error on occasion. Casement expresses it with eloquence and conviction:

*It is easy to rationalize that patients should not be allowed to control their own therapy, as if this might 'render the therapist impotent' – to use a familiar phrase. But if the therapist insists on controlling the entire therapy, might that not equally render the **patient** impotent? Sometimes, of course, a therapist has to stand firm with a patient. There are also times when a patient has to stand firm with the therapist, in the name of his or her own truth.* (1985, p. 19, author's emphasis)

There is a great deal of difference in the amount of directness one will take from friends or family and the amount one will take from a professional counsellor, who is supposed to have an extra capacity for tact, and is in any case precisely neither friend nor family and therefore has less liberty to criticize. They may furthermore stand for the grown-ups, whose views are suspect, whereas one's friends are peers and may be permitted to make disparaging comments which would simply be offensive from this stranger representing authority. Conversely, there is the danger that the person who accepts hierarchical roles may attach too much importance to the therapist's possibly idle words and be unduly discouraged by them, as I was by Harriet's remark about greed. Such over-ready acceptance of an interpretation blocks the route to autonomy.

Significantly, as I became more autonomous, Harriet left me more space. Perhaps she always had, and I had not at first known how to avail myself of it. Perhaps, as she suggested several times, I had changed her. Right at the very end of our therapy I said, 'There are some things you are frightened to look at.' She answered, 'If it feels like that to you, it must be right, for you; though it doesn't seem like that to me.' That seemed to me a very generous and encouraging response, which perhaps really needs to be heard in context, and with the tone of voice and facial expression that accompanied it. Simon also always left me room to be me, and did not criticize my views, although I often had a clear impression that he did not share them. He would show me that there was another way of seeing the matter, and leave it at that. It may have been that I was more receptive to counsel from others in the days when I saw Sybil, but I think she was in fact more directive.

This might seem at first to contradict my indictment of the concept of therapist as blank screen. I am now saying that I do not want to be invaded by someone else's views. But this does not mean that I do not want to know them. On the contrary, I think it is only by knowing with some degree of certainty which of the views being expressed are those of the therapist, and which are his or her reformulations of an attitude recognized as yours, that you can become surer of your own identity and of the validity of your stance. The other person must keep his or her distance in order to give you space in which to become yourself; but this does not entail an absence of space in which the therapist can also be him or herself. Nor does it mean throwing you into the terrifying vortex of unlimited space, which Nerval described so graphically in his sonnets, *Le Christ aux oliviers*, written eleven years before he committed suicide in 1855:

'La Spirale engloutissant Les Mondes et Les Jours'
(The vortex sucking in all planets and all time; author's capitals).

10 THE CULT
OF SILENCE

The danger of ill-timed interventions or ill-chosen words is considerable; it has however been well documented and therapists in general are well aware of it. Just as potentially dangerous is the cult of silence. This is less often discussed, mainly because it is an essential part of the technique of most therapists. Silence was for me the most traumatic feature of my therapy with Harriet.

One of the most universal complaints about therapists is the famous silence, giving rise to many analytical jokes, like the one about the woman who went to her psychiatrist for a year, remained silent throughout all her sessions, as did he, and at the end of the year shook his hand and said, 'Thank you, doctor, you have helped me a lot.' This was told to me by his daughter, who swears it is true; I have heard it from other sources too. Supposedly, like the cult of anonymity, this silence is conducive to the maximum revelation on the part of the patient, due to minimum coercion from the therapist. However, the plethora of jokes about it suggests that the situation is often felt as a threat, with a consequent need to defuse it by laughter which dispels the fear of the unknown and draws aside the veil of mystery to reveal rigid conformity to a stereotype.

Certainly, receptivity and non-coercion are among the greatest assets for a therapist, and one of the main differences between the professional and the gifted amateur is that the latter tend to leap in with advice and reminiscences, stopping the flow of thought, blocking one line of exploration by steering you along another. There is a big difference, however, between being non-directive and being totally or even mainly silent.

Firstly, silence in itself **is** coercive. It too is a way of acting (as opposed to being passive) and it is certainly going to be interpreted in a specific way by the recipient, according to his or her experience of silence in other contexts. 'Whenever I say something in therapy, or continue to say nothing, I am having an effect upon the patient', says Casement (1985, p. 59). Frischer (1977, pp. 149–51) also discusses how analysands react to silence with fear. Racker points out that 'the pressure of silence is usually **experienced as a threat**, [it is] a **coercive method**, something similar to a military siege' (1968, pp. 35–6, author's emphasis). Most of us can support, or even welcome, a companionable silence; but the therapist is not a companion, simply savouring the silence with you. You are conscious of the burden being on you to find something to say, when either your mind is a blank, or you are unable to express something which is too confused to be verbalized. There is the agonizing feeling of wasting valuable time, of not getting anywhere. One is often aware of how very expensive long silences are in this context. The longer the silence the more difficult it becomes to say anything, because it seems that the words will be invested with proportionally greater significance.

In some people, and certainly in me, as I show in the chapter on absence, a feeling of acute panic can mount up, inspired either by the silence itself, or by the feeling of pressure to break it, or the inability to do so, or the interpretation of the other person's silence as indicating hostility or coldness; quite possibly there is a combination of all these factors present. Cox emphasizes the facilitating aim of silence, its constructive aspect, which is a deliberate strategy on the part of the therapist, but one which may cause or accentuate distress, particularly to the neophyte.

[The] therapeutic space . . . becomes temporarily increasingly

frightening and bewildering, as established defence patterns change.
Such bewilderment and confusion may border on malignant chaos.
(1978, p. 54)

Oldfield highlights the dilemma for the counsellor faced, on
the one hand, by a strong wish for guidance from the client
and, on the other, by a resentment at too much advice or
direction, and who consequently

tries to balance sensitivity to the client's dependent needs and
longings, with respect for his capacity to reach his own decisions
about his life. Where these considerations are not successfully
clarified, there is a risk of the client experiencing fruitless
bewilderment and anger, and a chilling sense of still being very
much alone with his difficulties. (1983, p. 76)

It is this feeling of being alone which is one of the most likely
consequences of the therapist's silence. One of the main
reasons why I entered psychotherapy with Harriet was because
I felt that, in the present as in the past, there was no one to talk
to, no one who would really hear me; but also that there was
nowhere to turn when the pain of being alive became too acute
for me to find words with which to express it. A receptive
listener was not quite enough for this state of wordless but total
despair. At such times I felt that I needed someone to stop me
going round in vicious circles, to find the words which I
couldn't find alone, or to engage my interest in some aspect of
the problem beyond my experience of it. I needed the space to
express the despair, but I did this copiously in between
sessions, alone. I wanted, during sessions, to be less alone in
the misery, less overwhelmed by it. A silent therapist could
only reinforce the feeling of solitude.

For it must be remembered that the silence of others, the
non-communication that this signifies, has often been one of
the major contributory factors in the person's seeking help in
the first place. It is the failure to get through to other people
and to elicit a response from them that is at the source of much

emotional disturbance. Others have failed to 'hear' you, or to communicate their feelings; or there have been the greater silences of absence or death from a significant other. The therapist's silence is therefore often a reminder of this, a repetition of a painful situation, and is experienced as threatening, as hostile, or as a sign of indifference, even if this may be far from the truth.

An example of this is to be found in Guntrip's article, 'My experience of analysis with Fairbairn and Winnicott' (1975, pp. 145–51). He observes his own dislike of silent gaps during sessions, and his tendency to talk hard to fill them, relating it to his habit of ceaseless activity in daily life. 'Fairbairn interpreted that I was trying to take the analysis out of his hands and do his job; steal father's penis, Oedipal rivalry. Winnicott threw a dramatic new light on this talking hard' – by relating it to a childhood trauma, when Guntrip felt that his mother's depressive withdrawal and inactivity had been instrumental in the death of Percy, his baby brother. Winnicott pointed out:

'You're afraid to stop acting, talking or keeping awake. You feel you might die in a gap like Percy, because if you stop acting mother can't do anything. She couldn't save Percy or you. You're bound to feel I can't keep you alive, so you link up . . . sessions for me by your records. No gaps. You can't feel that you're a going concern to me because mother couldn't save you. You know about "being active" but not about "just growing"' . . . I began to be able to allow for some silences, and once, feeling a bit anxious, I was relieved to hear Winnicott move. I said nothing, but with uncanny intuition, he said: 'You began to feel afraid I'd abandoned you. You feel silence is abandonment.' (Guntrip, 1975, p. 152)

It is to be hoped that few people have suffered quite the traumatic experience of withdrawal that marked Guntrip, but the feeling of being abandoned by the therapist's silence is not uncommon. I certainly felt it acutely. And reacted similarly, in therapy as in life, by talking hard. In my case, as in others', it might be advisable to try and discover something of the person's previous experience of silence and their attitude to it, before inflicting this form of passive coercion on them.

My own attitude to silence was certainly coloured by having, on the one hand, an exceptionally silent father whose lack of response always hurt and baffled me and, on the other hand, by having a mother who used silence as a weapon. The ultimate punishment from her was to be sent to Coventry, sometimes for weeks on end. The veto on words was extended to other members of the family, so that the culprit was totally ignored by everyone until they showed ostentatious repentance.

Harriet was aware of how traumatic I had found this in my teens. Yet there were several occasions when she subjected me to silence. These were always times when I was very distressed and had regressed to the non-verbal stage, as she put it. At such times she felt that words could not reach me, or be of any use. My experience with friends was that any words helped; any murmur that assured me the other person was sympathetic, even if unable to communicate this verbally; any words that did not punish me by silence. Harriet maintained that she could find nothing helpful to say at such times, nothing that would not seem trivial or a cliché. I felt that almost anything would be better than the silence. Perhaps even if I had got angry at the inanity of her comments that would have saved me from the depression and anger of being left alone.

On account of my own experience of silence in childhood each experience of silence in therapy was to me painful and traumatic, although in real life I can take abnormal levels of silence and solitude. The only times I ever left the session early were because I couldn't bear the silence. Each time this happened I felt I could never go back and I became overwhelmed with suicidal despair, obviously an introjection of anger.

On one occasion I particularly remember the feeling of total numbness and unreality as I left early from a session which had seemed to become more and more mute on both sides. The silence in the room had grown unbreakable, shutting out response. I couldn't take the silence in which she left me, so I left. It was snowing fast and the streets seemed to be shrouded in silence too. I tidied my papers, wrote cheques to settle outstanding bills, then sat mesmerized by the snow falling silently on a distant, noiseless world, until it grew too dark even to see the snow. Then I took enough pills for me to sleep for two days and three nights, almost continuously. For two days more I remained numb; living my own death. Then I went through the motions of existence again. I'm not sure whether I ever gave Harriet or anyone else an account of those days. What was there to say?

This was not a healing crisis. It remained in my memory as a trauma which could prove fatal if it recurred.

Total silence very rarely conveys warmth or friendliness. Often all that is needed for the gaps in discourse to be experienced as potentially fruitful and not destructive is for them to be punctuated by the occasional murmur, or word of reassurance, or even the more systematic rephrasing or repetition of utterances advocated by Rogers. All that is needed is a reminder that the other person has not retreated into a private world, not abandoned you, not become hopeless and helpless when faced with your despair.

Simple phrases, which might seem clichés out of context, can be exactly what is needed when the panic at isolation threatens to become engulfing. Sybil had a trick of saying 'What are you **not** saying?', with a friendly little smile, when the silence showed signs of becoming self-perpetuating. I always fell willingly into the trap as it gave me an excuse for breaking the silence if I was finding it irksome, and it often pinpointed the cause for a silence, which was a certain reluctance to supply an association, or to make my private thoughts public. It was a formula, and she presumably used it with everybody, but it did not cause resentment, like a technical cliché, because it was her personal solution to a joint problem, and one which I felt worked; though it easily might not have done. The success of such devices probably depends a lot on the character of the person using them and the nature of the relationship.

Simon would sometimes say how the silence felt to him and then ask me how it felt to me (or reverse the statement and question). Both their ways of dealing with silence removed the onus from me and made me feel safer. I felt the therapist was 'with' me; not necessarily sharing my emotions, not upset by my pain or panic, but effecting a 'holding' relationship. I was reassured that there was another human being out there, a warm and caring human being, not a cool automaton or someone as out of their depth as I myself.

In this, as with other aspects of the relationship, people's needs and their attitudes to silence will be modified during the course of therapy, and change according to their state of mind and equilibrium. The silence of a stranger, which one cannot decode easily, is more likely to be felt as non-receptive or disorienting than that of a trusted friend. Someone coming new to therapy, and knowing nothing of the theory behind it, may be far more baffled and hurt by the experience than the more informed patient, and therapists sometimes take too much for granted in this respect.

In the early months of our therapy Harriet told me that I had to learn how to bear silence, since it was obviously so difficult for me. An ability to bear silence is certainly a measure of autonomy, of the ease with which one can be with oneself and one's own thoughts. This too is likely to increase during therapy, or to be present in the person's more serene moments, lost during times of stress and insecurity. Yet even so, someone who, like me, is perfectly capable of sustaining long periods alone with her thoughts, either in solitude or with a close companion, may still feel anguished at silence in the context of psychotherapy; partly through a feeling of distance from the therapist, and partly through a sense of obligation to say something, since this is after all 'the talking cure', and one does not really come to sessions just to keep quiet, or so it seems. This was certainly my own experience. I reckon I can take an unnatural amount of silence in real life, but was traumatized by it in therapy, in part due to the transferential nature of the experience, outlined above.

Yet with Simon I learnt that silences could be friendly and communicative. I even came to enjoy them. There was at times an element of excitement, or creativity, about these silences. The erotic potential of such experiences, which he was the first to point out, often served to stimulate me to new explorations and insights. I think the difference was that he looked at me during the silences, whereas Harriet had looked everywhere but at me. Simon used eye contact as communication and as a way of acknowledging my presence; Harriet seemed to discard me from her field of vision during the silences, and to avoid whatever they might communicate. Simon let silences speak in their own words; Harriet's inhibitions and good manners did not let her listen to this powerful non-verbal language. (Hobson [1985, p. 203] indicates with regret the 'taboo on looking' which our society inflicts on us.) More important, Simon did not let the silence prolong itself unduly but after a time ventured an interpretation or invited me to say what it felt like. He would also discuss what it felt like to him, so that the silences became potential communication, instead of blocking communication as with Harriet, who let them continue. Harriet said that she tried not to let the silences get too long, but it did not always feel like this.

Once more, then, flexibility is needed. It shouldn't necessarily be assumed that because a person is traumatized by silence at moments of crisis they cannot bear it when they are feeling perky. Most relationships contain bursts of confidence and a positive exchange of views, followed by periods of digestion, of simply being together. This is not so different in therapy. Some people positively welcome silence at such times and more generally; they are longing for a space in which their thoughts and repressed feelings can return, for a break from the continual clatter of voices, noises and demands being made on their attention which, in daily life, prevent them from exploring their inner lives. This must of course be respected.

Almost all psychotherapists talk too much or rather too loosely. They find it hard to subordinate themselves to a listening role. They interrupt the patient, prompt the patient, give him unnecessary reassurance, paraphrase his statements without essential clarification and otherwise socialize in a useless manner. (Dollard and Miller, 1950, p. 412)

It is well known that judicious silences can operate positively in psychotherapy, as Carl Rogers shows from a client's testimony:

During the first two interviews he interrupted pauses. I know that this was because I had mentioned before counselling started that pauses made me self-conscious. However, I remember wishing at the time that he had let me think without interruption. The one interview that stands out most clearly in my mind was one in which there were many long pauses during which time I was working very hard. I was beginning to get some insight into my situation and, although nothing was said, I had the feeling by the counsellor's attitude, that he was working right along with me. He was not restless, he did not take out a cigarette, he simply sat, I believe looking hard right at me, while I stared at the floor and worked in my mind. It was an attitude of complete co-operation and gave me the feeling that he was with me in what I was thinking. I see now the great value of pauses, if the counsellor's attitude is one of co-operation, not one of simply waiting for time to pass. (1951, p. 37)

Obviously, there are differences in the quality of the silence, and hence the need for reassurance, according to whether it is simply a pause, even a prolonged one, in the discourse or whether it represents an evident inability to communicate, either because the material is experienced as too painful or difficult to put into words, or because the person is afraid of crying or already overwhelmed by tears.

Tears, like silences, need careful and flexible handling. Some people cry more easily than others, but most of us are embarrassed by crying in front of a relative stranger. Most of us will need to do so in therapy, when particularly painful areas are reached, often for the first time. We have often been bottling up emotions for years and need to drop the pretence that we are strong and coping, to break the social taboo against adults weeping. Some of us, who may have an equal need to cry, are frightened of the criticism that this 'weak behaviour' has provoked in the past, or scornful of it ourselves, and would feel humiliated or liable to be rejected if we cried. We may therefore interpret the therapist's silent presence as a condemnation of our tears.

Again, it is not necessary to say much, or anything profound, when someone is that upset. It is perhaps the one time when reassuring clichés are more likely to be welcomed than despised. Nor is it necessary to transgress the professional ethos and make any elaborate show of affection or supportive gestures. Soothing words are usually enough, or a special tone of voice. Sybil used to make encouraging mutters like 'It's OK to feel that here', or 'It's safe to cry'. Although usually a very matter-of-fact character, who could even be quite acerbic at times, she used to produce a particularly gentle voice-for-frightened-animals at such moments, which was the verbal equivalent of being wrapped in a big rug and protected from all threats. Even if the content of what she said was irrelevant, it had the function of reducing psychic separation, while preserving actual distance, hence autonomy.

There is the possibility of some people using their distress manipulatively; a possibility which is analysed with considerable sensitivity and sense by Karen Horney throughout her work but made to seem almost the norm by Arieti and Bemporad (1978), who seem to forget that very few people actually enjoy being depressed. The vast majority of us, however, are likely to be feeling genuine pain when we show it, and to feel exposed or humiliated by showing it, so that to be faced at such times by a silent, apparently indifferent or even inimical figure can be extremely distressful. This is particularly so when cries for help, of whatever sort, have met with deaf ears before, as they repeatedly have with most people in therapy. Often therapy is seen as the last recourse, and failure to communicate or obtain any alleviation of pain or isolation in this context can be seen as the ultimate lack of hope. A silent therapist will then, at the very least, increase this feeling of being hopeless and alone, and might even precipitate a psychotic disturbance or a suicide attempt.

THE SILENCE

                    stretched
                    silencing
                            yet again
                            all attempts to break it.
You knew what silence meant to me
      yet silently
                    heard the pain.
I screamed my protests
                in silence
                        deafened you with need.
And between us all the words
I could not say
you could not find
                pushed us apart
                            again.
The ghosts of other silences
wedged in their shriek.
My mother's cry
giving birth in an air raid
My first scream of loss
      at dropping myself into this world.
I can't
            you said
                        but why
                            can't speak
                            can't find the words
no words
          I need
                your arms.

11 HOLDING

*There are times when people cannot cope [and] the help being searched for is always for **a person** to be available to help with these difficult feelings . . . In more human terms what is needed is a form of holding, such as a mother gives to her distressed child. There are various ways in which one adult can offer to another this holding (or containment). And it can be crucial for a patient to be thus held in order to recover, or discover maybe for the first time, a capacity for managing life and life's difficulties.*
Casement, *On Learning from the Patient*, pp. 132–3, author's emphasis

Winnicott and others have for some time stressed the importance of a loving and 'mothering' relationship with severely distressed patients, particularly children, and the probability of this being helpful in all psychotherapeutic contexts. There can be little doubt that the repetition of situations of emotional deprivation by an apparently unresponsive analyst is unlikely to help establish a climate of trust in which an insecure individual is able to develop a greater sense of worth and self-confidence. The theory of psychotherapy has often led therapists to be oblivious of the need for warmth and reassurance, and the different manifestations of this attitude needed by different patients or the same person at various stages of regression. Dr Lomas talks of the 'crippling limitations imposed on the patient by his rigorously scientific helper' and observes that 'the psychotherapist who tries to be natural with his patient needs to free himself, as far as possible . . . from the sense of distance which his professional training may have given him' (1981, p. 23).

Obviously, discretion needs to be used in the expression of caring and warmth. It must be remembered that many people who come to therapy have not experienced much mothering or love of any kind, and this deprivation has probably been instrumental in their maladaptation to life. Its absence is therefore liable to make them suspicious of sudden manifestations of this unknown commodity, particularly from a stranger. People who experience themselves as profoundly unlovable are not easily going to be convinced that someone else loves them. They will either refuse to see the suggestion at all, or they will see it as a lie or a seductive ploy. As Clara Thompson says:

The neurotic needs the love he never had, but he is no longer in a condition to receive it, should it be offered . . . on the other hand a patient who needs love may have become so distrustful that he cannot accept the simplest human friendliness without suspicion or panic. (1964, p. 80)

The danger, however, does not seem to me to lie in therapists rushing round to put blankets round people's shoulders, but in their being too inhibited by their awareness of their professional role to do so. They have been trained not to offer gratification, and to protect the patient from the facile desire for this, since acquiescence would impede autonomy. Yet, as Dr Lomas observes, 'our response should be less a matter of protecting [the patient] from the relationship – although at times we may do this – than offering him, if we have it to offer, the reality of our ordinary warmth and understanding' (1981, p. 127). This does not necessarily involve any physical contact. One does not tame a frightened animal by cuddling or (s)mothering it, but by gradually building up its trust, removing the fear of a threat and establishing the expectation of good experiences. To do this, more explicit expression of warmth than is customary in psychotherapy may be necessary. With some people this may take the form of extending moral holding, in the Winnicottian sense, to physical holding. Since this is not usually thought proper in the context of psychotherapy it is on this question that I propose to concentrate.

It is normally accepted that a very important part of parenting involves touching and holding a child. Nurses will not infrequently hold the hand of someone in pain, or put an arm round a person in distress. Yet doctors rarely do this, and presumably psychotherapists act on this model. One gets the impression from textbooks that no orthodox therapist would ever hold, much less cuddle, a patient. It is considered professional to keep a distance and remain impersonal, to analyse the need, but never to gratify it. Yet how many of us deliberately refrain from comforting a child, a friend or a sick person by some sort of reassuring contact?

There are some people to whom touching does not come naturally. There are also people who do not like being touched, perhaps by anyone, perhaps only in certain contexts, and psychotherapy might well be one. Their wishes should be respected. Obviously there can be no hard and fast rules, and what is appropriate for one patient or in one therapy may not be so for others. The stage therapy has reached is important, as is the relationship with the therapist. However, regardless of these differences in temperament, and regardless of the fact that we recognize how much all children and most adults need physical contact, orthodox therapists do not touch, or are not expected to touch, their patients. Perhaps they are right to be wary, and to confine themselves to analysing the impulse, as Winnicott shows in his 'Fragment of an analysis':

A. *A moment ago you put your hand to your face. If I were a sensitive mother and you an infant I would have known your face wanted contact and I would have brought your face against my breast, but you had to be the mother and the infant and your hand had to act the part of mother.*

P. *[after being overcome by sleep] I would be horrified if you actually did anything. You seemed to imply that you would have to make a physical contact . . . The conflict, wanting physical contact and being horrified if I got it.*

A. *Do you remember, in the incident of the headache you said that if I had actually held your head you would have felt it as a* *mechanical application of a technique? What was important was that the need was understood and felt by me.*

P. *At the level of feeling, I need physical contact, but feel horrified at the idea of getting it here. But I feel I ought to want it somewhere.* (1972, pp. 656–8)

Presumably, much too depends on nationality and background as well as temperament. There is first the relatively unemotional question of greeting or farewell. In England people tend not to shake hands, much less kiss, when meeting. Yet in most other countries it would be discourteous not to do so. For a therapist to shake hands would therefore seem more significant in Britain than in another country. Yet it is not uncommon for bank managers, solicitors or other sorts of medical consultants to shake hands (when seeing private patients; rarely, I note, with those seen on the National Health). The gesture itself simply means 'We are meeting or parting on good terms, as equals', so it would not be inappropriate in psychotherapy. Any signs of reluctance or undue enthusiasm on either side could be interpreted; and isn't that what the game is all about? A warm handshake from someone you otherwise found a cold fish, or a limp one from an otherwise friendly person could be indicative of what is really going on beneath the words. All such non-verbal communications are important signs of unconscious processes and should therefore be cultivated rather than ignored.

It has often seemed to me odd, after sharing what appeared to be an intimate experience, merely to get up and leave the room without any concrete acknowledgement of this. Words and facial expressions can express feelings but they don't always seem adequate for that degree of closeness. It might make some difference whether the psychotherapist is of the same sex, and whether one or both are female, since women in our society seem on the whole to be freer with gestures of affection than men, and since many people find it easier to touch others according to whether or not they are of the same gender (the taboos working differently according to individuals). (See Pratt and Mason's *The Caring Touch*, 1981, pp. 45–87.)

The attitudes of two people are of course involved. Psychotherapists might, for instance, fear that if gestures of warmth were permitted, those of anger or hostility would also be allowed. With psychotic patients they certainly are, and my guess is that Western society being what it is, many people probably find it easier to express or receive anger than love. Obviously there are all sorts of personal inhibitions and social conditioning which complicate the issue. However, I think that it is an issue, and one which needs to be aired, even if the conclusion is that each psychotherapist must behave according to his or her own temperament and that of the patient, whose needs may vary from time to time.

My first therapist, a woman, a mother and old enough to be my mother, never once touched me. It took several years of friendship afterwards before she even shook hands. I conclude that she is not a particularly demonstrative person. (Though she did tell me later that she let certain patients, mainly children and psychotics, touch her.) I remember thinking wistfully sometimes that it would be comforting if she were to put her arms round me when I was miserable, but the years went by and she never did. I got used to that as part of the frustrating experience inherent in therapy, exactly as I had seen as a child how other people's parents hugged them or comforted them and mine never did. As far as the psycho-therapy went, I don't think it did me any harm, though there is no way of knowing how much the occasional gesture of warmth might have been more therapeutic.

It might have encouraged greater dependence, but, in the same way that good mothering encourages healthy emotional growth, it might have given me a sense of being less repulsive and more acceptable. It seemed to me at the time that there was emotional dependence without gratification. I didn't become more capable of mothering myself or of receiving or giving affection. If anything, I became less confident of ever receiving it, in any asexual context, and more inhibited about showing it. There are some grounds for saying that I acquired a bit more self-respect during the course of this therapy, and became marginally kinder to myself, but this didn't last. There is no direct control experiment.

However, some fifteen years later, with a male psychiatrist – a medical adviser rather than a therapist – I found that a certain amount of physical contact was immensely reassuring and in no way encouraged emotional dependence. Possibly this was due to the rare ability of this particular psychiatrist to provide a warm, personal caring, while maintaining an entirely professional – even impersonal – relationship that was mainly concerned with medication and practical problems relating to health or work. This must be extremely difficult to achieve and not within everyone's capacity. The fact that this person had been a GP for over twenty years before becoming a psychiatrist may have accustomed him to the bedside manner, and to interest in the person, rather than a strictly clinical approach. (I certainly never found any other hospital psychiatrist so human, or so practically helpful.)

Whatever the reasons, however, all I can say from the receiving end is that it felt very reassuring to have the occasional friendly pat on the arm, or a strong, warm hand on my shoulder. The **words** of reassurance were there anyway, but how could I believe in words when my mother had systematically lied to me? My childhood was built on contradictions between word and deed, or unspoken wish. I wasn't going to believe any psychiatrist who said, 'I want you to live, I think you are worth trying to save', and did nothing about it. This one acted, in whatever ways of practical helpfulness were available to him, and combined word with gesture in a way that convinced me the words were not phoney. The words could have seemed empty in themselves, to my cynical and despondent ears but, accompanied by a gesture of warmth and by tireless patient efforts, they began to mean something, to give me a certain responsibility. Moreover, he did not insist on any regular contact when a crisis had been weathered. This response to my needs as and when they occurred felt to me far more natural than the rather mechanical regularity of psychotherapy. The ability and permission temporarily to stop consulting the person when the need no longer arose seemed to me to obviate the likelihood of emotional dependency or addiction which I think psychotherapy fosters.

This person, I felt, is not frightened of touching me. I felt protected and less repulsive. Nor did it in practice alter the relatively impersonal and professional key of the relationship, though in theory it might have done. The gestures personalized what I felt was intrinsically an impersonal caring – meted out to all suffering humans and not specially merited by me. Since professional relationships do not usually involve touching, or the recognition that the dialogue is **both** to an adult and to a frightened child, I didn't expect any gestures from this psychiatrist, and would probably have felt comforted without them. Their existence, however, and the absence of dependence in spite of this, made me question the whole issue of physical contact in psychotherapy.

There was no fear of misinterpretation of the gesture; it came across as utterly straightforward and natural and therefore it felt good. But it did not feel necessary. I didn't long for the gesture which never came, as I did in both therapies; this was an occasional part of the exchange, welcome but not vital.

This discovery came **after** I had spent months wondering why Harriet, my second therapist, never touched me any more. The problem would presumably not have arisen if she never had. But the contrast would still have been there. It was fuelled, moreover, by the experience of a similar sort of warm caring from one of the local Samaritans whom I saw frequently. She did for me all the things therapists are not supposed to do, because it would mean gratifying needs; things like bringing me food, arranging transport when I was ill, ringing up every day during bad patches, and other such practical kindnesses; above all holding me sometimes while I cried.

Yet her kindness and open display of caring did not engender any morbid dependency. I missed her when she was away, but not to the extent that I missed my therapist, who had much less place in my real life. I think this was partly because I knew I could count on the Samaritan for help when I needed it; I felt secure in the relationship. She was no doubt also a transferential figure of the ideal mother, but she lived up to the image. There was no anguish of loss or frustration. Her help was also regulated by my needs. When I was feeling reasonably well she let me go on living, and this gave me back some self-respect. When I was low she was available. The greater realism of her intervention in my life, signified both by her practical help and her response to needs at the appropriate time, made me much more able to accept my dependence and also to assert my independence when I felt able to do so. It would not even be true to say that it led me to no analytical insights.

On one occasion, in the depth of a long depression, I had a major insight into my suicidal impulses which I don't think could have come about without the security of her arms around me and her willingness to go right into the experience with me, which Harriet had never shown. Harriet even admitted that she felt the need to withdraw when I became so engulfed in despair, and could find nothing to say or do, because everything seemed inadequate. In vain I pleaded, 'Say **something, anything**!' She remained silent and helpless. Yet it had not always been so, and I think that was why I minded her lack of response so much, although the extent of my distress would have clamoured for some response anyway.

Because of my previous experience of psychotherapy and my reading, it had not occurred to me that therapists ever do touch people. I resented this and wished it were otherwise. It seemed to me like one of those stringent but unhelpful rules from childhood, such as not being allowed to have a grown-up stay with you until you went to sleep. Then one day the unimaginable happened. There was a pair of warm, steady hands on my shoulders as I cried. I went on crying, but it felt more secure, less terrifying and lonely. In retrospect it seemed the most beautiful thing anyone had ever done for me, partly because it was so unexpected. It probably wasn't the first time a friend had put their arms around me, but I couldn't remember whether or when this had happened (at least not a friend of the same sex, lovers being discounted because the relationship was in any case more tactile). Moreover, this person, though friendly, was not exactly a friend.

I didn't think the gesture would ever be repeated; it could just have been the recognition of a crisis. But the memory of it gave me a feeling of worth that enabled me to bear a forthcoming separation and to make some good new relationships during that time. However, the gesture was repeated, at rare intervals, and the feeling of inner warmth and worth lasted over the next separation. Some months later I became very deeply depressed. This was exacerbated by another long separation, during which I sank into a depression which refused to lift for two years. During that time there was no physical contact of any sort with the therapist and increasingly less emotional rapport. (Or so it seemed to me; Harriet remembers it differently.) Absences became unbearable. I seemed to cry all the time, outside therapy as well as in it. And I longed in vain for some sort of contact while I cried. What had started as a wish that did not have to be gratified often, as long as there was the hope that it sometimes might be, became an obsession. The longer the gesture was withheld, the less I could do without it. As I never mentioned this, as long as the need continued, I didn't know whether it was the result of deliberate policy or mere lack of inclination. Either reason seemed to me unacceptable. One was too theoretical and the other confirmed my self-hate. (For the therapist's view, see later, p. 202.)

I had never previously thought about whether I had been shown affection as a child. It now struck me that I had never met it until I was an adult, and then it had been sex rather than disinterested affection, which didn't feel quite so comforting. Moreover, it was usually in response to my cheerful self, and not an acceptance of the depressed me. This could have been a significant insight, leading to growth. In fact, all it did was reveal a lack of something important in my childhood which had not been remedied by adult life. Knowledge of this need did not appease it, but on the contrary made it obsessive and destructive, since I no longer seemed to be able to function efficiently in other spheres because of my crippling sense of emotional deprivation.

I kept wondering whether I had in fact had some affection shown to me as a small child, which had been withdrawn once they found out what I was really like. My rights as a child to unconditional affection from my parents had been abrogated because I was not a particularly nice child (or so my unconscious logic went). Harriet had in the past felt some affection towards me but she too had ceased to feel this because I was not a pleasant character, or because she felt as discouraged as I did by the continuing depression.

Being held might not have had this effect on someone else or perhaps even on me at a different time. I cannot say with any certainty that I became **more** depressed because of this experience, or that I would have been less depressed with more holding in the physical sense; though I think it was accompanied by a lack of holding in the Winnicottian sense.

There is no clear pattern of causality and no hard and fast rule to be drawn from the experience. Someone more used to a sympathetic understanding of tears in childhood would not have needed to make up for the experience in adulthood. Someone with more sense and fewer inhibitions would have discussed it with the therapist. However, many people, and not just those in therapy, have diminished common sense and odd reticences where deep feelings are concerned. Because it was so important to me, I couldn't possibly mention it. The longer I kept silent, the more it became impossible to talk about it. I tried obliquely once or twice, but I was never sure whether the message had been picked up and for nearly two years I lacked the courage to tackle it head on.

This was only remedied when I went to another therapist and found I was able to talk about it quite naturally with him. Significantly, I did not feel the need to be touched by Simon, although – or perhaps because? – he was male. His role from the start seemed to be more that of analyst and less that of mother or comforter. My main need with him seemed to be to have the re-educative experiences I had not found in my previous therapy, just as my need in that therapy had been to find the warmth I had not experienced in the initial therapy or my childhood.

It is possible that the gesture in itself had a harmful effect on the therapy and should not have been made. I am inclined to think that it was merely the discontinuation of it and my inability to discuss this which made it so harmful. Certainly it encouraged a degree of emotional dependency that had had little reality to feed on before that, and which I had not felt with my first therapist. The fantasy of being held had been there, but as something which experience and theory had taught me was impossible, so I had never let myself feel the force of the longing. When fantasy became reality, not once but several times, the wish became a need and its non-gratification became unbearable frustration. It seemed to me to symbolize my unloved state in the past and present (as well as future). It represented yet another of the basic human experiences that help people get through the hell of living and which I felt had been denied to me. If the therapist had maintained the traditional aloofness this crucial feeling of loss might never have come to the surface, at least with its primitive intensity. Having been used to emotional deprivation, I would probably have regarded it as another example of the natural state of affairs. But the glimpse of a sort of human warmth I felt I had previously imagined, but either lost or never experienced, made me acutely aware of this loss. This awareness could have been a breakthrough in the therapy; instead, it made me increasingly hopeless about life.

It is not, of course, possible to say how I would have reacted if the need had continued to be gratified. My feeling is that it would never have become as intense and anguished but would instead have continued to be a source of security. This is after all how such a gesture from a friend is experienced. It could be alleged that friendship is a straightforward relationship without transference (if such a thing exists). Friendship, of course, also implies reciprocity. But I don't think the lack of mutuality in the therapeutic relationship need inhibit this, since the transference usually operates as child/patient to parent/therapist. Not all children have to be the comforters of their parents. Perhaps it is relevant that I did. Many of my early years when I desperately wanted to be mothered and reassured were spent having to prop up or console my mother, who had herself never been mothered. As an infant I was never allowed to cry by the nanny and apparently developed fits in the effort to fight back the tears. As an older child I was told to stop making that dreadful noise, or to stop making a fuss about nothing, to keep out of the way until I had learnt how to behave properly. Learning that tears were permissible had been one of the most healing things in my first therapy with Sybil. Learning that they could be comforted was something begun and then lost in my second therapy with Harriet. I stopped wanting to be held, because I stopped hoping it might happen. But I didn't grow out of it, as I might have done with the extra warmth the gesture would have communicated. I shrank out of it, physically and emotionally. As Winnicott says:

If [a regressed patient's] need is not met the result is not anger, only a reproduction of the environmental failure situation which stopped the process of self-growth. The individual's capacity to 'wish' has

been interfered with, and we witness the reappearance of the
original cause of a sense of futility. (1958, p. 288)

We never got round to discussing this directly. Instead, I
showed Harriet the draft of this chapter. I was still seeing her
for psychotherapy, but we remained shy of discussing it. She
commented in writing: 'Perhaps I did hold back, feeling that I
was dragging you into a dependence which might become too
much. With hindsight it looks as if the dependence was already
there and the support should not have been withdrawn. My
memory is not of such complete or barren withdrawal as you
remember – but in addition a feeling that you were trying to
rid yourself of dependence on me and that, too, had to be
respected.'

Patrick Casement (1985, pp. 160–7) devotes some time to
analysing the difference between 'wants' or libidinal demands,
which should not be met either by parents or therapists, and
'needs', which have to be met for healthy growth. He believes
that, from infancy, people are searching for

what is needed for survival, for growth and healthy development. It
is when this search is frustrated or interfered with that we encounter
'pathological' response; and yet, even in this response there is a
healthy pointer to needs which have not been adequately met. I am
here making a distinction between **needs that need to be met and**
wants. (1985, p. 170, author's emphasis)

He points out how at birth there is no distinction between
wants and needs, but this gradually develops and the child's
maturation depends on the security which comes from having
needs gratified but wants dealt with by a caring firmness. This
distinction should also be recognized in therapy, he believes,
and the patient's demands should not invariably be met by
non-gratification.

Patients re-enact these different stages of growth in the course of
therapy. The therapist should therefore try to distinguish between
libidinal demands, which need to be frustrated, and growth-needs

which need to be met. I believe that some therapeutic opportunities are missed when therapists fail to recognize when it is growth-needs which are being presented for necessary attention. For instance, some patients need to have evidence of having had a real impact upon the therapist . . . A patient is let down if a therapist dutifully frustrates these needs, thinking that this is automatically required as a matter of analytic technique. (1985, p. 171)

He questions whether the usual assumption that psychotherapy should be entirely in the hands of the therapist is necessarily right, and affirms that patients do know what they are looking for, though the manner of the search is not direct or easily identified at times. Sometimes there are obvious clues as to what is needed. 'At other times, growing despair of finding this may be indicated by a pressure for further substitute gratification, as if this may be all that could be hoped for. None the less in this pressure it is often possible to recognize what has been missing for the patient' (1985, p. 171).

Casement does not, however, believe that gratification is always helpful, even when a growth-need would seem to be at stake rather than a libidinal demand. He describes (1985, pp. 160–7) the case of a young woman who was anxious for him to hold her hand. In this person's childhood her mother had failed her by fainting when she held her hand during an operation, so she was obviously trying to test the strength and reliability of this substitute parent.

In context, I am not very convinced by his argument as to why it would not have been a corrective experience for him to hold this woman's hand. Repeating a failure can hardly be corrective, therefore showing that the need **can** be met is likely to be more therapeutic. Yet the general principle is probably sound. 'When a patient has unresolved feelings about failures in parenting it becomes intrusive (deflective and seductive) if the therapist **actively** offers himself or herself as the "better" parent' (1985, pp. 172–3, author's emphasis). I think myself that one action or moment does not constitute an entire replacement act and that these things should not be confused, although I respect Casement's viewpoint.

Symbolic gestures, particularly when they are as important to the individual as this one was, can go a long way to remedying gaps in parenting and so providing a truly corrective experience, and I do not think they should be neglected. Margaret Little (1985) describes how Winnicott regularly held her hand during sessions, and how this was part of her psychological growth. In support of this view, Peter Lomas describes sessions in which he let a very disturbed patient hold him, and how this helped her both to overcome her feeling of acute panic and to 'reveal her despair more coherently than before.'

What gave Joyce comfort was, I think, not only that I 'held' her in a way that made her feel safe but that I did so in a way that made her feel that we were essentially similar beings. The kind of interchanges I have described were often repeated and we had to understand which inhibitions were inherently mine, and which occurred because she was unconsciously manoeuvring me to repeat her mother's failures of handling when she was a baby – yet desperately needing me to avoid these failures. It was not, however, until circumstances outside the consulting room forced me to 'hold' her in a different sense . . . that she really began to get better and to grow as an independent person. And even then our relationship continued essentially on the same lines. What made her feel safe and become more real was my spontaneous warmth. On the occasions when I held back – when a gesture or affectionate word failed to pass my censor – she became frightened and saw **me** *as 'not real'.* (1973, pp. 145–6, author's emphasis)

In a later work (1981, p. 61) Lomas also points to the dangers inherent in the Freudian doctrine of the 'rule of abstinence', namely the re-creation in therapy of the traumatic conditions which were responsible for the neurosis and the persistent refusal by the therapist to alleviate or obviate the trauma by gratifying the patient's desire for comfort or contact. As his own experience shows, it is not necessarily disastrous or non-therapeutic, threatening to either the patient or the therapist, to reveal human warmth, even to show affection at times. One does, moreover, wonder what sort of human being it is who can watch pain and neither say nor do anything to show their concern. A superhuman, no doubt, governed by superior standards of self-control and goal-directedness; but, in my weaker moments, I would rather just have a normal person – who might help me grow into one.

Yet even psychotherapists who agree that the sort of clinical distance advocated by orthodox analysts constitutes a barrier to communication and trust still rationalize their defences against any open show of warmth. This position is defended by Anthony Storr:

It is a truism to assert that neurotic difficulties spring from emotional deprivation in childhood; and it has often been affirmed, even by analysts themselves, that it is love which really heals the patient. This being so, it is arguable that what is needed is not understanding on the part of the patient, but love on the part of the analyst. Would not a conventional Good Samaritan approach be as effective, or more effective, than a technique in which the analyst simply interprets? The answer to this is simple, though singularly unappreciated. Analysis cannot be a therapy of replacement, nor is it desirable that it should be so. No analyst can make up for a rejecting mother or an absent father, nor can he be a lover. Implicit in the analytical relation is the idea that the analyst is a reliable, consistent person who will remain more or less the same during the patient's contact with him. But he cannot and should not offer love direct. (in Rycroft, 1966, p. 78)

I have quoted this at length because it presents the orthodox objections to those who **feel**, from their experience either as patients or as therapists, that the theory of deprivation is not always very comfortable in practice, and may not even be very therapeutic. It is not, I think, that Dr Storr is in any way wrong in his assertion that 'the analyst . . . cannot and should not offer love direct'. It merely seems to me that he discounts various alternative possibilities by postulating too extreme a polarity between clinical detachment and love. Or maybe the problem is largely semantic? There would seem to be a confusion here between love as 'agape' and love as 'eros'. There is a good deal of difference between a loving attitude, contained within the time of the session and place of the consulting room, and love in the wider sense. One does not expect the therapist to act out the role of loving parent fully, but only to represent one; nor do most of us wish for a lover in this context.

This view is amply demonstrated throughout Suttie's book *The Origins of Love and Hate* (1935), particularly in Chapter 6 ('The taboo on tenderness') and pp. 212–16, which specifically deal with the role of 'love' in psychotherapy. He declares: 'There can be no serious dispute that the physician's love is at least an important part in the treatment – in the allaying of anxiety' (p. 250). He also clarifies the term: 'The nature of the love being understood as a **feeling-interest responsiveness – not a goal-inhibited sexuality**' (pp. 212–13, author's emphasis). This is an important distinction of which much psychoanalytic literature and practice seems to have lost sight. For love, as Suttie argues, is not just sexual; it can mainly or even exclusively concern tenderness and the desire for companionship. Most people, I imagine, would be horrified to have their therapist (or their parent) actually become their lover, whatever their fantasies (although I read with amazement in Dominique Frischer's *Les Analysés parlent* how common this apparently is in France). The 'love' required in the therapeutic context is a warm, sustained concern which inspires security and is not afraid, at times, to express itself by human gestures, if appropriate to the relationship.

While I was in therapy with Sybil I think I was too insecure to believe I was lovable. It was only after I had secured her friendship that I began to believe it. Harriet's initial warmth had made me feel loved, but her subsequent aloofness activated a feeling of being unworthy. I did not need gestures or words from Simon; he managed to communicate to me a kind of 'unconditional positive regard' that was nothing to do with love as a personal emotion, which I would have experienced as threatening from a male therapist, but seemed to be more an attitude to life, like a desire to be kind to stray dogs. Yet Simon managed to be warm and personal in his detachment. He would say things like, 'You look as if you need a motherly arm around you', in a gentle voice. This openly recognized the need, so it did not become anguished, but provided a moral 'holding' that enabled me to hold myself.

Halmos states that in the more disturbed cases a certain amount of supportive care is vital **before** the person is strong enough to absorb any insights, much less reach them alone, and concludes:

The position that seems to be emerging is that, at all stages, psychotherapy has to be an appropriate mixture of mothering (management) and analysis (giving insight). (1965, p. 50)

My feeling is that I can more easily supply my own insights than my emotional needs; so, paradoxically, I needed first to be mothered in order for the analytical work to take place, either with Harriet or with Simon. This was the real therapy, at least from Harriet. I did not want or expect actual mothering from Simon. This may be due to my personal mythology, in which the Mother is affectionate, and the Father advises. It may relate to the lack of cuddling from my mother (or father) and the lack of dialogue, especially with my father. I was trying to re-create these original, idealized figures, with each therapist. The gender difference also operated in that I would have felt threatened by any physical contact with a male therapist, beyond a mere pat on the arm, but felt safe if, and sometimes only if, I could have some warm gesture from a woman.

A typical example of how much this seemed to help with Harriet is provided by a session in the last year of our therapy. I had been experiencing severe problems at work, and had applied for another job, which I was not sure that I wanted. I very much wanted to talk over with Harriet the conflicts this aroused. I tried to express them; she made no comment. I tried again, phrasing them differently. The comment she then made suggested that she did not understand the issues at stake. For half an hour I tried to explain to her why I needed so much to feel valued in my career, and how this had to come from outside, because I have no sense of inner worth. We had been discussing this for four years, and I felt that if she still could not see this she did not basically understand me. I felt I was up against a brick wall and could no longer communicate.

After half an hour I lost my temper and, for the first and only time in any of my therapies, stormed out, banging the door loudly behind me. I had only gone a few yards when I realized that I would feel dreadful for the rest of the day if our dialogue ended on this note; so I returned. We fell into each other's arms in the corridor. She made us coffee; for the first and only time I insisted that she should sit beside me for a while. Then at last I found the words which enabled her to enter into the dialogue with more understanding. As I left I buried my head in her shoulder, and that moment of closeness seemed to obliterate the psychic gulf that had separated us beforehand. The session proved to be a breakthrough. Because she had been able to accept both my anger and my affection we were able to talk much more frankly in the next session, both about my problems with the outside world and the difficulty of communicating within sessions.

Maybe I wouldn't have needed the gesture if Harriet could have 'held' me adequately, in the Winnicottian sense, through words. She seemed not to be able to do this, but found it difficult to accept the idea that the more literal holding did work, with me, and was our particular mode of communication, when language broke down. This session occurred one month **after** the dream I recount in the next chapter on absences. The identical gesture in the dream was not present in my conscious mind, but it was as if my unconscious were leading me towards behaviour which I knew would be restorative, and would turn the verbal breakdown of our sessions into a deeper communication. I was able to go forward in life and in psychotherapy only by going back, to a supposed time of symbiotic union with my mother.

12 ABSENCE AND LOSS

Why am I mourning you?
when you are still here
as much as you have ever been
which is to say as little

The inclusion in this chapter of prose poems, indicates that I regard separation and loss as a deeply emotional experience, belonging to a pre-verbal state. Poetry, unlike prose, is the attempt to reach beyond words, to what cannot be spoken or written; in this it resembles the child's first cry when it is born, and I will show in this chapter how my experience of separation anxiety led me to recapture the moment of my birth, which is to say the beginning of my depression.

In my second therapy I became traumatized by the therapist's absences, which seemed to me both frequent and long. This separation trauma was intensified both by the powerful transference and the extent to which the therapist was like a figure in real life, without actually being one. Harriet's absences seemed to me to be a very clear statement that, however caring she seemed to be when she was there, she didn't really care that much and was prepared to expose me to what we both recognized was an unbearably painful separation each time. It was also a statement that recreation and perhaps even reality existed for her in a space where I was not permitted to invade. The dimension of reality in the relationship here seemed to aggravate the sense of separation, although it was in other ways something which I welcomed.

Before I discuss the question of absences, then, it might be advisable to examine the question of how much presence is desirable. There is also the question of meeting outside the consulting room, and even of visits to each other's houses, introducing into the relationship a reality element which is not traditionally supposed to be there.[1]

Sybil told me jokingly of an American psychiatrist reputed to have said to his patients, if he met them at a social gathering, 'Are you leaving, or shall I?' I retorted that if anyone had said that to me I would have changed my therapist (Sybil no longer was my therapist). In fact, she and I did meet a few times during the course of therapy, as we lived in a small town and knew a good many people in common. She studiously avoided speaking to me on such occasions, which left me all the freer to monopolize her husband (whom I had known a long time, as he was the father of a former flat-mate and a colleague in his own right). After the first such encounter, when I had been in therapy with her for some three years, she said, 'You didn't tell me you knew my husband.' I pointed out truthfully that she had not told me she knew him. They marketed under different names, and I had felt hurt and furious when I heard by chance that they were married, as if she had had no right to be married to an acquaintance of mine without telling me. I also wondered how many times I had inadvertently put my foot in it by alluding to him. I noticed that Sybil took good care to tell me who Harriet and Simon were related to as soon as she learnt I was seeing them.

Harriet didn't seem to have qualms about socializing, and this seemed to me to characterize the general openness and realism of the relationship, to make it more natural and pleasant. Yet there were still areas in which I was, or felt I was, shut out from her 'real' life, and this perhaps hurt doubly because there was not always such a hard and fast distinction. I felt I was simply not part of her recreation, except now and again by accident, and so I belonged to chores and things which had to be escaped from periodically. The sense of exclusion was considerably greater in the case of this therapist than with Sybil, who had excluded me in a more deliberate and total fashion. The fact that Sybil and I became friends afterwards, and visited each other frequently, might imply that

I was trying to make up for those years of being shut out. The attachment possibly became greater and more possessive with Harriet because of the extent to which she was a real life figure, and not just a transference object.

As a form of self-protection next time round, I deliberately refrained from knowing much about Simon. However, he himself had no objection to vouchsafing information, whether solicited or not, and as his consulting room was part of the house there was inevitably a background of reality. This balance between the familiar and the unknown felt about right. I always had the certainty that any questions would be answered truthfully. This gave me security and prevented the need to know many answers. He in turn seemed remarkably incurious about any factual or biographical details relating to me, so there was a certain reciprocity of attitude. Informative details were provided by both, as and when they seemed relevant, but the focus was at all times on the emotional or unconscious content of my communications. I think that, for me, the anguish was assuaged largely because I felt that he had no *a priori* rules about not sharing his life with me, but that his behaviour would always be dictated by what he felt was good for the therapy and what accorded with his inclinations. Anguish, for me, came from being cut off from my therapist's life, or aspects of it.

Maybe everyone's wish is to have psychotherapy on demand, with a possible twenty-four-hours-a-day coverage, as with readily available parents or caretakers in childhood. Samaritans and GPs do in fact provide this coverage, although it is of course only possible because a large number of helpers or practitioners are involved. There is no assurance of continuity, but at least there is always a number to ring and the possibility of a sympathetic voice at the other end. It never occurred to me to ring Sybil between sessions. I somehow assumed that this was not part of the service, though I discovered years later that other people did ring her frequently. I suppose at this stage I had not yet learnt to recognize dependence in any sphere, and was also busy playing model patients. It took a while before I dared to ring Harriet, who seemed relieved that I had developed the sense to try and make contact with someone when desperate, rather than annoyed at this encroachment on her time. It certainly helped me to cope with separations or to feel that there was not too much of a gap between experience and discussion when I was going through a particularly stressful time. But I suppose it did lead to my missing her more when she was absent.

There is also the question of whether visits to the home are helpful, or encourage too much dependence. Traditionalists would allege that this introduces too much of a reality element into the relationship and spoils the purity of the transference. Yet the Samaritans don't seem beset by such qualms and I saw their visits as immensely helpful, without encouraging dependence. I particularly valued the fact that they occurred as and when I needed them, with no obligation on either part for their continuance beyond the crisis. The fixed intervals and hours of psychotherapy have always seemed to me unsatisfactory because unrelated to real need. The professional relationship with a GP is likewise not affected by home visits, nor does the demand for these usually exceed the period of need. A psychiatrist in charge of my medication also used to visit me at home. This was largely a question of practical convenience, but it was also a help to know that his visits were adjusted according to my needs, and that he was part of a more real environment than a consulting room.

This was not a question that had ever arisen with Sybil who, I am fairly sure, would not have visited me at home, though she did once make a lightning visit to see me in hospital when minor surgery unexpectedly prevented me from attending a session. 'I expect you are hurt that I am not staying any longer', she said as she left. I was; but it seemed I was not supposed to ask why she was leaving, and she did not tell me. She can't have had a prior engagement since it was my usual hour.

Harriet continued our sessions while I was in hospital after major surgery, and we both agreed that this had been a singularly productive phase of the therapy. Meeting on neutral territory, neither hers nor mine, seemed to make me feel safer, and I discussed during that period all sorts of things I had never felt relaxed enough to mention before. It felt more like a meeting between friends, so I consequently felt able to broach more intimate subjects than I had previously. There was also more of an exchange of views. There were subsequently various occasions when Harriet came to see me at times when I found it physically difficult to get to her place. As she remarked, these sessions were especially productive, as if I felt safer to discuss things when in my own surroundings. Once, during a crisis, she even came to see me at a non-session time and I felt greatly comforted by the visit. But my increasingly frequent periods of hospitalization always occurred when she was away. They were indeed often related to her absences, as if anguish at separation triggered off physical symptoms. The lack of a visit at such times increased my sense of deprivation. When it was possible to keep in touch via the telephone this did help, both as a supportive gesture and in maintaining communication when there would otherwise have been too long a gap in therapy.

Simon also once came to see me when sudden hospitalization prevented me from attending a session. Like all my encounters with Simon this was pleasant and therapeutic, but had none of the emotional charge of anguished necessity which distorted my relationship with Harriet.

Early in the second year of therapy, before I had begun to show distress about absences, Harriet remarked that she didn't understand why, if my experience of psychotherapy was as positive and gratifying as I maintained, I didn't feel more deprived or frustrated at the end of sessions or in between them. My explanation was that the 'good-enough Mother' image was sufficiently strong to be carried over from one session to another and even during long absences. As Simon sagely remarked much later: 'a sense of deprivation is not cured by more deprivation, but by the feeling of security and gratification derived from a need having been met.' Starvation never cured hunger, but feeding does. Perhaps symbolically I lost interest in food during a long summer separation (I lost one-quarter of my weight in a few months), and it took two years and a new therapist to help me regain my appetite.

I was puzzled by the extent to which I continued to mind separations since I did not remember feeling any anxiety when Sybil went away, often for equally long periods, though these were restricted to the summer and so were more predictable. I had not felt the need to organize my own comings and goings around hers, nor did I bother to ask where she was when she went away, much less try to get in touch. There was, however, a time when I was ill during a summer break and she herself rang me every day, which was a caring gesture that obviated the feeling of being abandoned. This relative indifference to absences also characterized my therapy with Simon. Maybe my distress about Harriet's absences was due to the different nature of this second therapy, involving a closer relationship, more frequent sessions and more of a re-enaction of past traumata, rather than merely an intellectual discussion of them. There was a more intense transference, but also a more real relationship. I had not realized until this second therapy how much I had resented my mother's frequent absences as a child, or the more crucial abandonment of her not even being interested in my life when she **was** there.

There had also been a change in my life circumstances, rendering me more vulnerable to separations. This included a number of bereavements, which probably affected the therapy too, making any loss seem definitive and non-therapeutic, since it reinforced an unpalatable reality. I think it was not so much the therapist I was mourning each time she went away as a lifetime of departures (absences or deaths), none of which I had been allowed to mourn at the proper time. Either the departing person had refused to let me express my grief, or the dead person (including my own father) was mourned by others (family or spouse) who claimed more right to grief than I. Harriet was the first person whom I had ever openly admitted to missing when she went away. By letting myself feel this deprivation I was acknowledging a long past of suppressed sorrow at separations. Without the trust in the relationship which facilitated this admission, the intensity of the feeling might never have surfaced.

It is difficult, therefore, to know how much of the separation trauma I experienced in this second therapy was due to a repetition of past anguish, how much to actual occurrences in the present, and how much to do with the tenor of this particular therapy. The past and present circumstances were obviously personal but the issue raised by the third possibility is more general.

Given that therapists need breaks and all seem determined to have them, should there be limits to the length and frequency of these? How much should the wishes or needs of consulters be taken into account? What kind of preparation is advisable and what sort of substitutes or palliatives can be arranged to tide the sufferer over the separation period?

The provision of substitutes during absences can help, although as a child who was brought up by nannies and au pairs of varying degrees of inadequacy I was never much mollified by these locums. It did act as a panacea to be told where Harriet was, sometimes to have an address or phone number where I could contact her if desperate. I rarely used this, but it was a relief to know that I could. The mere knowledge of the means to bridge the gap helped me to bear it. Being sent postcards also tided me over an absence and made me feel less abandoned. They were quite effective transitional objects.

One example of the relationship being allowed to invade life outside the consulting room was when Harriet let me visit her house. I found this profoundly therapeutic, but the orthodox would not approve. She moved address during the therapy and I had heard a lot about the beautiful new house from various mutual friends. I felt excluded from this paradise, and the sense of exclusion became agonizing. A year after the move I went through a phase of intense anxiety just before she was about to go away on a few months' holiday. For some weeks I could concentrate on nothing, enjoy nothing and cried all the time. I felt unconsolably bereft. We figured out that it had something to do with my having been sent away from London during the war, when I was three, and being separated from my parents and older brother who might quite realistically have died in an air raid. My mother told me (in response to my question after this insight) that she had not come to the station to see me off since she had been afraid of showing emotion. I had quite probably thought that this meant she didn't care.

Harriet increased our sessions to three times a week, but I was more conscious of the one hundred and sixty-five hours a week during which I did not see her. Above all I was aware of the impending two months when I would not see her at all. I felt instinctively that it would help to see her house, though I could not explain why, and reason argued that it would not help. Not without some pressure on my part, she agreed to my request. After the visit my anxiety immediately decreased. I still mourned her imminent departure, but I was freed from the acute panic and anxiety that had plagued me for weeks. I became able to work, and even relax, which is always more difficult for me.

I cannot easily account for this change. It occurred partly because I now had a concrete scene in which to visualize her when I couldn't see her. The likely explanation, which I find difficult to understand fully, is that this was related to the infant's primitive inability to believe that its mother exists when out of sight. The previous summer I had regressed badly during Harriet's absence and become unable to feed myself. After seeing her house I coped slightly better with the separation.

I think it also reassured me to find the house even more beautiful than I had imagined, and to see her obvious enjoyment of it. I concluded that she was unlikely to leave such newly-acquired beauty and return to the States, as she occasionally said she was tempted to do. Her absences could then be more readily understood as temporary, rather than permanent. My mother had frequently declared that she was so fed up with my father, and sometimes me, that she was going to go away and leave the lot of us. Every time she did go away I was terrified that she would not return. On the three occasions when I was sent away to Brownie camp I wept so much they had to send me home; presumably I was frightened that there would be no home to go back to.

Most therapists would agree that the anger involved in a break should be discussed, though it may meet with considerable denial and resistance. My experience is that it was helpful to look openly at this. I felt guilt at not just being glad the therapist was having a doubtless well-earned rest, and resentment at my minding the absence of someone who was not even part of my life when present. I found it difficult to cope with the humiliation of minding, as well as that springing from my selfishness in putting my welfare before hers (or at least, wanting to). This was complicated by resentment that Harriet was also putting her welfare before mine – just as my mother had repeatedly done. It didn't help at all to be reminded that I was just one of many; on the contrary, it underlined my lack of real importance and sense of being misunderstood and not taken seriously – again a repetition of childhood feelings. I was outraged when Harriet once said cheerfully that it hadn't mattered that she had gone away at Christmas for three weeks 'because most of the other people I see were away too'. It might have been a salutary reminder to me that I was only one of a crowd, but I had been traumatized by the absence. This exchange occurred on her return; I was trying to communicate my distress, and I was feeling too vulnerable to be able to face such a matter-of-fact statement. I think this was one of the times when Harriet's frankness bordered on tactlessness.

It did not help, either, to be told that if she was going away she was also coming back. It did not alter the message. As Nini Herman points out:

To the very insecure . . . every separation means total rejection, nothing less. The confirmation of a lifelong fear that one is never good enough, nor deserving of another's love. The proof is that they go away. They go away, this logic runs in vicious circles, because one is not good enough, clever enough or thoughtful or kind enough and so falls short of some ideal that one imagines must exist. (1985, p. 8)

Harriet never seemed to grasp this. Once when I was complaining that ten to thirteen weeks holiday a year seemed to me excessive, and that no one else I knew had such long breaks, she went into a specious rationalization about how, firstly, she had a large family scattered all over the globe, so needed time off to see them; secondly, she needed a holiday because she worked so hard, and all psychotherapists take long holidays; thirdly, she was sometimes away attending a course, and not on holiday. This hurt, mainly because she was indulging in an undignified self-justifying argument, rather than listening to my real distress. It hurt doubly because I did not really believe her affirmation that all psychotherapists take such long holidays, and this undermined my trust in her. It hurt above all because it reminded me that I had no family to go to. Moreover, she was leaving me to be with her family, just as my mother had gone away with my brother or father but only once in my whole life with me.

Harriet knew all this. Her repeated absences were a reminder to me that I did not really count. There was nothing I could do to make her stay, or take me with her. However needy or distressed I was, she would still go. Even if she had shared my feeling that this would kill me, as it came near to doing several times, she would still have gone. I even admitted that she would have been right to do so, since I was not her responsibility. Nor could I make myself nice enough for her to cease leaving me. I simply was not part of her real life, was how it felt. Although I also knew that I was a real part, I was only a part, and I resented the other parts. My resentment was probably due to my mother's having always centred her life around her work. Family and home played a minimal part in her life, and on the rare occasions when she did relax, she chose to do so in adult company, and not with her child. My brother was ten years older and counted as an adult.

The intensity of the pain was, then, due to my past, but it did also involve a real situation in the present. Moreover, loss or separation is often the factor which precipitates the person into psychotherapy. I entered therapy with Sybil because a personal relationship had ended and the therapies with Harriet and Simon both began as a result of the distress caused by multiple bereavements. Separation anxiety is a widely recognized feature of the encounter itself, and I think it has to be considered more seriously than maybe it has been. The general view is that people gradually become more able to bear separation; but I never did. On the contrary, I became less able to bear it. It reinforced, in present reality, something which had been unbearable in the past.

My own feeling, and one not likely to be popular among therapists, is that being a psychotherapist involves certain obligations. People do not just have nine-to-five problems, or distress which can be shelved for long periods, at the therapist's convenience. There is a full-time commitment, from both people. It is illogical to expect people to throw themselves unreservedly into therapy, and then switch off when it does not suit the therapist to be around. It can of course be argued that it is imperative for therapists to withdraw from this sort of intensity now and again, to recharge their batteries, and that a break may even be beneficial to some patients. I don't deny this. Yet I cannot help feeling that, when dealing with highly vulnerable people, many of whom are particularly sensitive to loss or separation, there is some irresponsibility involved in over-long or frequent absences.

One therapist (not mine), who read the manuscript of this

book, commented: 'I feel that you are stronger on the rights of patients than of therapists.' Well, of course; if we don't stand up for ourselves, who will? There are plenty of books on the rights of therapists. He continued: 'Although . . . you intellectually recognize the need of therapists to have their own space, you don't empathically recognize this need. Is this transference? Or does the therapeutic situation inhibit this kind of empathy?' The answer to the first question is simple. My parents demanded recognition of their needs but gave very little space, it seemed to me, to those of a child. The answer to the second is, I think, also yes. By encouraging the child/patient relationship therapy fosters selfish demands and an inability or refusal to acknowledge the needs of the therapist. Moreover, the set-up is designed by therapists, who are therefore able to tailor it to suit their needs. They have justifiable needs for time off, but these conflict with our needs. It may be called the consulter's therapy, but the extent to which this operates is, to say the least, variable.

Obviously there is no simple answer to the question of what does constitute excessive length or frequency, when it comes to separation. Possibly neither makes that much difference, since it is the symbolic statement made by an absence that is hurtful, rather than the actual length of the absence. Usually I could just about cope with breaks of a few weeks at a time; but I went into a deep depression lasting two years when a six-week absence was followed by a four-week break, with a mere nine weeks between them, so that there had been slightly more absence than presence in one five-month period. In this case, discussing the reasons for the second absence might have helped considerably. I also found a proposed four-month continuous absence the next year impossible to contemplate, and went into another severe depression, just as I had seemed to be emerging from the long bout of misery. However, I cannot be entirely sure that the length of absence had much to do with the depth of depression, for there were times when even a short separation was painful.

Significantly, one of the absences which affected me most strongly, though the effect was of short duration, was merely a long weekend. It occurred at a time when I was particularly distraught and regressed. Harriet had been very supportive during the crisis, then went away for five days, without our discussing the break (or indeed my thinking it mattered) and without leaving a telephone number as was her wont at such times. While she was away I again became acutely depressed, but felt I had recovered from this by the time she returned and resented having to interrupt my new-found equanimity in order to attend the session, and resurrect the despair I wanted to put behind me. As I talked about it, the misery of the past few days began to flood back. She listened but said nothing. As the silence went on I felt 'I can't bear this, I must get out of here. What am I here for? There is nothing she can or will do to help. I've got over it alone, I should have stayed alone.' Every now and then I looked at her, screaming silently 'Help!' I half got up to go, then sat down again, feeling that if I went I would never come back and my world would collapse. Harriet, who was sitting quite close, seemed to be moving further and further away. It was a bright, sunlit summer's day; the colours were sharp and clear. I knew this, and yet all I could see was a day drained of colour. Suddenly I no longer recognized Harriet; I thought someone else was masquerading as her. It was a terrifying sensation, bringing me out in goose-flesh and making it difficult to breathe. Only when she came and sat beside me, putting a hand on my shoulder, did she and the world become real again.

This non-recognition of a parent figure after a separation is a frequent feature of the childhood pattern of reaction to loss and separation as documented by Bowlby. I may have been re-experiencing some forgotten childhood trauma, but if I was it remained in the unconscious. It may alternatively have had something to do with the break being rather unexpected and coming immediately after a crisis in which the therapist had been particularly supportive.

Whatever the reason, this was the only time absence affected me this way. I sometimes found it difficult to re-establish trust or to get back into therapy, but at no other time did I become genuinely unable to recognize the therapist. It would seem, however, that separation is indeed experienced differently at different stages in the therapy, and so a person's reactions are by no means uniform. Until this point, sixteen months after the inception of therapy with Harriet, I had not minded her absences. This occurred at the beginning of my serious regression, though neither of us knew this at the time. As Casement indicates:

Even a short break in the therapy, during a regression to a more infantile dependence, is often more traumatic to a patient than a long holiday had been earlier in the therapy. Some people expect patients to be able to draw upon the fact of having coped during an earlier absence of the therapist. Clinical experience illustrates that patients are affected more by the current state of their inner reality than by their adult experience, however recent. (1985, p. 8)

My tolerance of separation did not, however, seem to increase. During one three-week holiday of Harriet's, in the last year of our therapy, I became acutely depressed and suicidal. I had tried to go away myself, but found I had become unable to get any enjoyment out of travel, and felt unbearably lonely. Before entering psychotherapy with Harriet I had often travelled alone to distant parts, and never felt lonely. I cut short the holiday and returned home. There was no postcard from Harriet waiting; this was the only time she did not send one.

The day she was due to return I became prey to acute anguish, unable to concentrate on urgent work, and cried incessantly. The next day I could bear it no more and rang her house. I was told by her husband that the plane had been delayed; he offered to give her a message that I had rung. I think that I was slightly relieved to find that her husband was occasionally left behind too. None the less, my anxiety intensified during the following hours, while I wondered whether she would ring back. When she rang, I wept down the phone and felt guilty about adding to her tiredness and jet lag, humiliated at being such a baby. However, the pain and anxiety decreased. I was able to enjoy the garden again, and to write the next day's lecture.

The depression did not, however, go away at once. It changed register. It felt less part of me, and more like something that was inflicted on me. The unbearable pain of being alive became translated into an acute and constant physical pain, which was later diagnosed as post-viral neuralgia. I felt unable to be happy, as if I were driving a car with the handbrake on. Every time I tried to move forward, something powerful held me back. I could not remember having been happy since I entered therapy with Harriet, four years previously, or how to become so again. I felt like a mouse caught in a trap. It can see all the beauty outside, and wants to run out and be part of it, but can't. I felt, as I so often had, that I would have wanted to have lived; I was passionately attached to life. But I was unable to live, as fully as I wanted to, and so felt compelled to kill myself. This acute depression went on for three more weeks, during which time all sessions with Harriet seemed abortive. I felt I was going round in vicious circles, she seemed unable to help me rephrase the despair, or surmount it. Sessions seemed to become increasingly full of silences and I felt worse after each one than before.

I kept a record of these sessions (as, indeed, of the entire therapy). The entry for one of them, typical yet crucial, runs as follows:

Yet another abortive, uncomfortable and uncomforting session with H. I said very little; so did she. Spent most of my time trying hard not to cry, with variable success. I began the session by quoting Beckett's Endgame *at her: 'You're on earth, there's no cure for that . . . all life long you wait for that to mount up to a life'* [1958, pp. 37, 65]. *I said I couldn't understand why I hadn't killed myself over the past two years, and that I concluded there* *was one part of me that wanted very much to live. She agreed. I said, 'I would so much like to have lived.' She didn't pick up the tense. I said how **untherapeutic** psychopractice was; that I needed something more analytically rigorous or, preferably, something more supportive. She agreed, but seemed at a loss to know how we could achieve this. She asked what I felt I was not getting outside sessions. I heard her; but I thought it was more important to ask what I was not getting **inside** sessions. I said nothing. I kept wanting to scream, loudly, through sheer frustration. Finally I tried to break the tension by saying 'I feel I'm screaming so loudly, in silence, that the window panes are being shattered.' She did not reply. I could express nothing of what I was feeling, it seemed, and I began to sob uncontrollably. She left the room for quite a long time to make us both coffee. I cuddled the seal* [a stuffed animal who became part of the therapy; see Chapter 6 on objects]. *I crept further and further into a corner of the chair, then made a nest of cushions on the couch and huddled into that. She returned with the coffee. I finished the Kleenex and asked for another box, hoping she would touch me when she handed it over. She didn't. She said, as so often before, that there was nothing she could do or say to help me in such misery. I wanted to say, 'Yes, there is. Come and sit beside me.' But of course I said nothing, and the sobs grew more desperate. She remarked that I shut people out. Eventually, in a small voice, feeling that I was asking a big thing, I asked, 'Do you think I shut you out?' She said, 'Yes; sometimes.' I picked up my coat and left. It was ten minutes before we need have ended.*

I felt suicidally depressed in the two days which followed, and did not go to the next session. I wrote her a note to say I didn't think it would help. Around dawn of the day when I did not attend the session I had a vivid dream; one of the few during my therapy with Harriet in which she actually figured. Usually my dreams were about her absence, or my not being able to find her. In this dream I went to see her, in a room not unlike hers, but more like those of various friends with whom I identified her. It was hung with red rugs and bark paintings, like the ones I had brought back from my travels in South and Central America. She was wearing a deep blue tunic (a colour she never wore) and as the dream progressed this turned to opal. The next day I remembered that these are the colours of Isis, the goddess associated with initiation and the unconscious, the feminine principle or anima, prototype of the Virgin Mary.

Your room at that time was white,
an attic room,
with sloping ceilings and sky lights,
hung with red tapestries
and brightly coloured bark paintings.
A room like your sisters'
like all the other rooms
in other cities where you had lived.
Opaquely delicate glass sculptures
posed on the low tables,
the smell of joss sticks lingered.
You greeted me wordlessly.
Your head in the curve of my neck
told me all I wanted to know.
We stood together without moving,
scarcely touching,
communicating silently

for a long while

of peace.

I never possessed you

so completely.

Others came in chattering,
demanding your attention,
distracting you from me,

but not from us.

They did not separate us
for there had been that moment.
Of deep blue and opal

in the soft whiteness of the room.

In the dream I found the silence of the encounter intensely fulfilling, and when Harriet suggested we should analyse it I begged her to remain silent. At one moment in the dream she said, 'But I do love you, you know that.' And I did. I awoke feeling comforted. The month-long depression lifted.

I was not able to tell her much about the dream when I saw her a week later; I felt too inhibited. But I did, after a month of hesitation, narrate it to Simon, who was concurrently my therapist. He listened very gently and respectfully, and said after a pause that he thought it was about a pre-natal state of union with my mother. It would seem to be an example of synchronicity that she wrote to me a few weeks later mentioning, for no apparent reason, how she and I had been alone together in the world for the first few hours after my birth. This had been sudden and unexpected, as I was three weeks premature and the labour was brief. It was in the middle of an air raid, and bombs were falling all around. Her intention was to convey a deep bond between us. My intuition was that she had been frightened and in pain; that she may even have wanted to kill me, before anyone knew I had existed.

The notion that the dream was an attempt to get back to the womb/room is supported by the presence of South American textiles. I had been conceived in Venezuela, which represented for my mother a pre-lapsarian state of bliss, when for thirteen years she and my father had been young, happy and rich. Just before I was born my father had a nervous breakdown, lost his job, and they returned to England, where there was a war on. Sun, tropical fruit, peace and a life dedicated mainly to pleasure, were replaced by winter, food rationing, bombs, poverty and incessant toil. Harriet had pointed out to me how depressed my parents must have been during my first year of life, and how this had probably infected me. She recommended that I should read Alice Miller's *The Drama of the Gifted Child* (1979), which demonstrates how parents can communicate their depression to a child. This rang true. For my brother, too, my arrival coincided with loss, both geographical and emotional.

He lost his country and, after ten years, his unique position in my mother's life. Maybe he also lost his father, who had apparently been something of a playmate before, but became so withdrawn that he communicated very little with anyone as far back as I can remember.

I went back to South America for the first time as an adult after I ended my therapy with Sybil. I did not consciously choose to go there in order to end the therapy, but this may have been my unconscious wish. I now felt ready to face my origins. I was happy there, although I never felt that I belonged. I went there several times, and brought back many textiles, but felt unable to return after I entered therapy with Harriet. At the time of the dream I was thinking of ending therapy with her and going to North America.

After the dream, or after Simon's interpretation of it, my suicidal despair vanished. Several very good things happened in my life at that time, which also gave me back the will to live. Significantly, the acute physical pain which had been with me for two months also went, apparently due to a course of acupuncture. However, I think the dream was crucial. It gave me back the experience of unity with both my mother and Harriet that I craved for. It showed me that my real relationship with Harriet was warm and tender, not antagonistic as it had become on the surface. It showed that what I wanted from her was not analysis or words, but the chance to experience through gesture a state beyond words. It also confirmed the odd feeling that I had had during that particular phase of depression that my depression was imposed on me from the outside, and not part of me. (My parents' reactions to my birth had been to be depressed.)

The power of the transference, and Harriet's welcome kindness, had uncovered my repressed needs for mothering, which had never been met when I was a child. I realized for the first time the extent of my emotional deprivation. In my case this was intensified by my also having become aware for the first time in this therapy of how much my ferocious independence as a paraplegic covered up the need to have help in doing things. Another need which was unmet in real life.

The problem, obviously, is that people in need can never have enough. We cannot, of course, all find a Marguerite Sèchehaye or a Ronald Laing who will take the 'children' on holiday, or live with them. But that is what most of us in therapy want, although other consulters seem to grow out of it. Indeed, the aim of analysis is supposed to be to get the analysand to accept that the analyst is not going to fulfil the wishes that he or she had as a child (a common view, lucidly expressed by Malcolm [1980, p. 58]). I felt that if I were allowed to act it out, to spend all the time I wanted with Harriet, I would probably find that she was boring, or that I simply wanted to be alone more, as was always the case with other people. Significantly, after I did have the possibility of spending a fair amount of time with Sybil, and could even have gone on holiday with her, I no longer wanted to see her more than occasionally. She became just like any other friend.

The systematic frustration in the professional encounter seems to me the most untherapeutic thing about psychotherapy. My only answer to not being able to bear Harriet's repeated absences, after I had gone through the wish to annihilate myself because this is what she did/my parents had done, was to cease psychotherapy, and go away myself.

What is it like to be missed
     when you are glad to be away?
I only know what it is like to miss you
more before you have gone than when you are away
which is hardly any different from when you are here
or when you return
which always brings your absence home to me.
I tried to go away too
     keep trying
but always take you with me.
     the absence that is you.

13 SEPARATION

Psychotherapy is probably the only close relationship entered into with the very aim that it should end. Yet how does it end? How do either of the two people concerned reach the decision to separate? How many, having decided to do so, in fact find ways of leaving the umbilical cord uncut?

The difficulties of separating definitively, particularly for a woman to separate from a female therapist, are lucidly analysed by Susie Orbach and Luise Eichenbaum in their paper 'Separation and intimacy: crucial practice issues in working with women in therapy' in *Living with the Sphinx* (Ernst and Maguire, 1987). The problems inherent in knowing when to end a therapy, and how, have been highlighted by several writers, particularly Little (1985), Herman (1985) and Hobson (1985).

The usual considerations are, as Hobson points out, in fact practical, concerning insufficient time or finances to continue, or a move to a different place. The usual assumption is that the consulter has been 'cured', or at least has improved. Hobson, interestingly enough, refrains from suggesting this. He declares instead: 'A personal relationship never ends. That is the problem raised in this book. Perhaps we should not call it "therapy"' (1985, p. 257). It would seem that he is deliberately ambiguous here. Should the exercise not be called therapy because it is, rather, an on-going relationship, or because it is not in fact therapeutic? Yet it is unlikely that Hobson, a practising therapist, although one unusually willing to explore the deficiencies inherent in the system, would maintain the second view. As someone whose main concern is to function better than before, and who has no other aim in therapy, I would however like to consider both aspects of the statement.

The number of people who, having been in therapy themselves, decide to become therapists is considerable. Imitation is after all the best form of gratitude. The exercise also tends to become fascinating to the point of addiction and it is difficult to give it up, or to relinquish a valued relationship. One way of leaving the symbiotic pair and establishing one's own independence is to become a colleague. However not everyone is suited for this, nor do they even want to be.

After four years of therapy a friend announced to me that she felt much happier about herself and her life, no longer felt depressed, and thoroughly recommended the experience, which she now felt ready to end. She indeed looked much happier. This was very encouraging, especially as I had just embarked on therapy with the same therapist. Four years later this friend was still in therapy, with the same person, but now training to be a therapist herself. I became slightly sceptical about the lasting benefits or general validity of a situation from which one could not escape, even when it had fulfilled its apparent function. Obviously my views here are coloured by sibling rivalry: there was some envy that the friend had found a way of ending without separating, indeed by becoming closer to the therapist. This neat solution did not feel right for me, because I am happy with my present career. Most of the therapists I know go on being in therapy, only they call it 'supervision'. I can see that they need to talk over problems which may arise in their professional practice and which may not have been dealt with in their own therapy. But the fact remains that therapy has not returned them to a separate existence, although it is likely that it returned them to an enhanced life.

After four and a half years of my therapy with Harriet I began to feel that there was no way I could bring myself to separate. I do not remember experiencing any difficulties the first time round, with Sybil. This does not necessarily mean that there were none, simply that if there were I do not remember them. I had decided to spend six months in another continent; this necessarily entailed ending or suspending therapy. There was a period of many months in which we could have worked through termination, but I don't think we did. As far as I remember, I decided to go, and excitement about the journey overcame other considerations. Although I do remember a number of weepy sessions before departure, I think these had more to do with misgivings about the enterprise than leaving my therapist. I did not feel the need to keep in touch with Sybil more often than by an occasional letter during the next three years. We then met again, became close friends, and it seems likely that I needed the real life relationship in which to work through unfinished business in the professional encounter. I could not possibly have done this by re-entering therapy with her.

When I felt the relationship with Harriet was becoming stagnant and even destructive I sought the counsel of Simon. The original intention had been either to transfer to him exclusively, or to work through a specific problem with him, then return to Harriet. As it turned out, I saw them both concurrently for eighteen months. On the whole this was very productive; as the two relationships were entirely different they did not overlap. I think, however, the co-existence of both meant that it was not possible for me to commit myself to the new therapy, any more than it was possible to commit myself to a real life relationship while I was bonded to Harriet. This danger of not being able to make, or keep, close relationships with others while in therapy is, I suspect, a not uncommon problem. I was also too wary of the dangers of this kind of engulfing one-sided relationship, having once experienced it, to be anything but heavily defended against Simon. My intellect told me that there was more analytical mileage in a new contract; my emotions kept me tied to the previous therapist. I again solved the problem by taking myself off to another continent (while reminding myself that there were now only two new continents left, so I could not repeat the remedy indefinitely).

Separation from Harriet was painful but friendly, and did not feel too definitive. Termination with Simon turned out to be easier than I had anticipated. It seemed to me that this was a business contract; it had outlived its usefulness, and my therapy was now to be found in life. While I was aware that this new confidence probably owed a great deal to all three therapists, I none the less felt that the real breakthrough had had more to do with increased professional recognition and new friendships, which were not being given a chance to blossom while psychopractice engaged so much of my time and emotional energy. I wanted the chance to test this. Significantly, I found that during the times when professional obligations left me no time for visits to psychotherapists I did not miss the sessions and rarely thought of the therapist. This did not, alas, obtain when it was an interruption caused by their absence, but I began to resent this dependency in a more positive way, actively cultivating new friends and interests, rather than succumbing to sterile despair. I also became increasingly determined to break out of the anguished and humiliating dependency of the transference with Harriet. We did not seem to be able to resolve it analytically; I felt that the only thing to do was to stop seeing her. This would also, it seemed, solve the problem of dreading her absences.

The pundits will almost certainly squawk about unresolved transferences, about resistance which should be tackled not evaded. I think there may be some truth in this. The fact remains that I was not prepared to stay and find out. Whenever the consulter thus decides not to pursue the consultations it would be disingenuous to declare that this represents **only** a failure on his or her part; it is also a failure of efficacity of therapy. One might as well allege that if someone dies of a hunger-strike they only have themselves to blame, without examining the situation which led them to protest in this way in the first place.

In a sense, it could be argued that this attests to the success of psychotherapy. I became more self-reliant. However, I do not myself see this as a clear-cut pattern of cause and effect. For one thing, I had always been very self-reliant. It was only during therapy with Harriet that this lifetime of independence had crumbled, **because** of the relationship with the therapist, and largely because of the element of non-fulfilment within it. I did not therefore simply grow out of dependency, but rediscovered some measure of a self I had once had, which to my mind had been as badly bruised by 'therapy' as by other relationships. A message I received very early on in life, from the quick succession of nannies and au pairs and from absent or distracted parents, was that there was no point in relying on anyone, or becoming attached to them. I had entered therapy each time because a loss or bereavement had traumatized me and reactivated this fear of attachment. Both social conditioning and personal longing for attachment had induced me to view this fearful attitude as erroneous. Yet I emerged from therapy more determined to re-establish this defence against closeness with others; I no longer saw it as based on fantasy but as reinforced by reality.

It is true that therapy had restored a sufficient sense of self in me for this gesture of independence to be possible. It would be ungenerous not to agree. I remain uncertain, however, as to the extent this was due to therapy, or due to other circumstances in life which had fostered my sense of worth. Probably it was significant that both factors were operating together. Harriet certainly gave me a lot that no one in real life had been prepared to give, in terms of warm acceptance, patience and a safe space in which to explore the torments underlying personal problems.

None the less, my experience with Harriet suggests that there are very real dangers in psychotherapy. Some of these are perhaps specific to my experience of it, and of life, but others are inherent in the exercise. The danger of addiction is, I think, considerable. It is fostered by most therapists' insistence on the need to take attendance at sessions seriously, not to arrive late or change times, and to attend more frequently at times of stress. This all presupposes that therapy is important and that significant life events have to be brought to the consulting room. Practitioners might deny this latter claim and some, at least, do not hold with it entirely. But even the more flexible ones not unnaturally believe in the importance of what they do, and collude with consulter-dependency up to a point.

Paradoxically I found that Harriet, who had perhaps unwittingly fostered my dependency, was far more willing to let me go, and do so at my own pace, than Simon, with whom 'bonding' had never really taken place, and who prided himself on being flexible. With Harriet I practised first of all reducing sessions to once a week, then being allowed to telephone an hour before the session to say whether or not I wanted to come. The hour was arranged so that it did not inconvenience the therapist, who claimed that it was equally acceptable to her to have it free for attending to correspondence or for us to meet. Occasionally she would ask me in advance whether I would mind leaving it free, but usually I could count on her availability; I could also rely on her not to give it to someone else without asking me first. The orthodox would doubtless protest that this was giving me too much control over my own therapy, and the therapist. My experience was that I badly needed this feeling of control (something I was unable to exercise over many other important domains of my life). This permission to explore the limits of my independence, with the security of a safety net there, seemed both at the time and with hindsight to have been an important factor in my becoming gradually able to leave the womb-room of the therapist, confident that I could survive alone.

Simon, generally considered by himself and others to be unorthodox, seemed to disapprove of this arrangement, and certainly reacted differently. It took me about six months of muttering that I was ready to abandon the exercise for him to remove his ear muffs sufficiently to answer, and then it was with a guarded negative. When I finally wrote saying that I wanted to put him on the back burner for three months, in order to get on with some urgent work and to see how I survived alone, he made me feel that I did not have the right to declare unilateral independence.

For reasons beyond our control we had both had to cancel more than half the planned sessions in the preceding months. Unintentionally, we had then already commenced termination. He claimed that he was willing to be more flexible, to find replacement hours if he cancelled or to give me 'therapy on demand'. In practice neither of our timetables allowed for this. He also claimed that he did not think it was good for me to be allowed to control my own therapy in this way. I felt this put me into a double-bind situation, of being told on the one hand that flexibility was permissible, and on the other that it was not. Quite possibly this pinpointed a crucial transference issue relating to my attitude to authority figures, which we acknowledged without analysing it in depth. It seemed to me that as a child, and even now, in many professional situations, I had no option but to accept other people's rules, and their definition of what 'was good for me'. Whether or not he was right I saw no reason to continue putting up with a situation I regarded as non-therapeutic, at a time when I had pressing real life problems to which I wanted to devote time. I was about to vote with my feet and leave therapy when Simon accepted my viewpoint, and we had a very productive series of discussions before I interrupted them to work abroad for a while. I say interrupted, not ended, because I do not discard the possibility that at some future date I might again feel the need to discuss problems in a more intensive way than one can do with ordinary friends. In the meantime, I would rather try out the new ego-strength on real life, and give institutionalized introspection a rest.

Another crucial factor in my own wish to terminate

therapy, which in different ways may operate for many people, is that I had had the chance to examine thoroughly all the things I found intolerable about my life. They had not become less intolerable; I had not in fact become less suicidal at times of crisis. It is true that the remissions were longer and felt more positive than during the early years of therapy, but this was much the same as in the days before entering it. Instead of coping by refusing to acknowledge there were problems (which made me much pleasanter in the eyes of others), I now failed to keep up the pretence of coping because I was overwhelmed by the genuine magnitude of some problems, which no amount of analysis could diminish. While in therapy, my previous defences had been broken down, revealed as false strategies. But I do not think that newer, more effective ways of coping took their place, as the textbooks suggest they do. I simply changed my view that I was neurotic not to cope **all** the time (although I usually did) for the view that I was actually stronger than many because I did in fact continue to function in situations which most people would find unacceptable. This restored some self-respect; I no longer felt quite so unworthy or inadequate. But it did not stop depression from engulfing me at times of crisis.

The accepted opinion would be that the demolition of false self in the interests of truth can only be good. I am not sure, from the experiencing end, of the validity of this statement to which I subscribe theoretically. My previous defences had worked; I did not dwell on my problems, but got on with living, and this was beneficial to others as well as myself. The times when the defences crumbled seemed to me just as unbearable before and after I had become aware of them as defences. The periods in between were on the whole more positive **before** I had seen through my own strategies.

However, I am still alive. I have not committed suicide, in spite of having lived almost continuously with the temptation to do so for several years; I may never do so. I have gradually come to the conclusion that there are things to be done alive which I cannot do if dead and that, for the moment, these things matter. When discussing the plays and novels of Samuel Beckett, I always remind students that it would be facile to dismiss these works as pessimistic. The characters have no illusions about the extreme misery of their situation; but they do stay there, to bear witness. They do not kill themselves. Beckett is, as I write, still alive; he is unlikely at this late age to kill himself. Creating out of his anguish has therefore been a successful form of exorcism for him.

If I had not had the chance to experience psychotherapy I would certainly have felt deprived; I would never have discovered that it was not the miraculous answer for which I had hoped. I may well have given up hope earlier, and more definitively. I learnt, very slowly and painfully, that the times when I don't want to live need not last for ever, or lead to self-destruction; they can be lived through, and are the price to pay for living so intensely most of the time. As the moth says to Archy in *Archy and Mehitabel*,

it is better to be happy for a moment and then be burned up with beauty than to live a long time and be bored all the while . . . i [sic] *do not agree with him (says Archy) myself i would rather have half the happiness and twice the longevity but at the same time i wish there was something i wanted as badly as he wanted to fry himself.* (Marquis, 1927, pp. 87–8)

While occasionally I wish I had never heard of the word psychotherapy, and at times I think the practice came near to destroying me, yet it was also very worthwhile. Yet again, psychotherapy bears analogies with being in love. I cannot say that any of my love affairs have borne results in the conventional sense of resulting in marriage or even in lasting friendships. But I cannot imagine having existed without them; they caused pain and disintegration, but also enriched my life. This is equally true of psychotherapy.

CONCLUSION

The question most people are likely to ask themselves, either before they start or on the point of ending, is: did it help? A considerable amount of research has been done on the topic, without any hard and fast conclusions being reached, because there can never be true control experiments.

Rogers firmly maintains that it does help, and that his brand of non-directive therapy helps more than others. Eysenck equally adamantly refutes the claim, although grudgingly admitting that it usually (but not always) does more good than harm. Hobson admits that it **can** do harm (1985, p. 200). Oldfield (1983) and Frischer (1977) go further in exploring the views of consulters and analysands themselves. The reader emerges with the impression that on the whole people benefit, but in a diffuse way, and the degree of satisfaction is variable. Accounts of dramatic improvements made by people who are often borderline psychotics, rather than averagely neurotic, are usually written by therapists and are therefore selected from among their many cases, not all of which may have been so successful, and the case histories could be suspected of having a self-justificatory element about them.

The evidence of other people is, then, variable. It would certainly be presumptuous to say that psychotherapy does not help many people. I am sure that short-term counselling for specific problems usually does help. The dangers are more likely to concern long-term or in-depth therapy of a more analytic nature. From my own experience, backed up by observation of friends, I would suggest that the dangers are threefold: firstly, that the breaking down of defences during therapy temporarily makes the person unable to cope with life; secondly, that there is a distortion of reality (which becomes seen as only the unreality of the consulting room) and thirdly, that addiction to the practice makes it very difficult to terminate. It is also vital that support from other people outside the therapy should be available. I am not at all convinced that those who are very much alone in the world can be expected to weather the crises engendered by psychotherapy itself, although these are precisely the people who most need it.

However, psychotherapy does exist, whether or not it functions effectively. The question is not whether to ignore it, but how to conduct it so that it really is therapeutic, and does not exacerbate problems, or merely fail to relieve them. The problem, as I have formulated it, is not whether one should embark on psychotherapy in the first place, since it seems to me evident that there is a need for people who feel overwhelmed by their problems or simply dissatisfied with their lives to examine the root cause of this distress and not to cover it up with drugs. Psychopractice is not always therapeutic, but it can and should be.

The starting-point for this critical examination of the procedures governing psychotherapy was to explore why it should be 'difficult for two people to meet, in a natural and ordinary way to discuss the problems of one of them' (Lomas, 1973, p. 19). It sounds very simple, stated like that. It turns out to be very much more complicated in practice. Some of this is due to the inherent difficulties of combining a professional framework with a personal relationship. Some of the problems arise because the traditional concepts governing the professional framework are often interpreted too rigidly, and inhibit the expression of the personal relationship.

I found that the more I read about psychotherapy, the more I got annoyed by some of the practices most analysts and therapists purported to advocate. These misgivings were often reinforced by discussions with friends in therapy or the scanty books mentioning the attitude of the consumer. Yet my own experience of psychotherapy, as well as my theoretical convictions, suggested that there was room for far more flexibility in practice, and that this did not prove harmful. I wanted to show how it felt to be on the receiving end, both of conventions and their relaxation. If at times my attitude has been inconclusive, it is because it is not always possible to know, even with hindsight, whether a particular procedure was the best at the time, or even 'good enough'. It will be quite easy for the sceptics to say that I was deluding myself about the benefits of experiences which might be regarded as gratification, therefore reprehensible. None the less, although it is not always simple to judge the wisdom of an attitude, there is no doubt in my mind as to what felt helpful or harmful; and these effects do not always correlate with the textbooks' views.

The positive effects came about less through greater self-knowledge than through the gradual development of a warm and trusting relationship. (This correlation of positive outcome with positive feelings towards the therapist is attested by Oldfield, Frischer, Rogers and Strupp, Fox and Lessler.) Conversely, such negative effects as there were related to my feeling of betrayal when the therapist proved less than totally reliable.

None of my therapists were complete traditionalists, although their flexibility varied. But having experienced diverse degrees of inscrutability, I am quite sure that the truly therapeutic effects of each encounter were in direct ratio to the warmth, and above all authenticity, of the therapist. This does not necessarily mean that the therapist should involve him or herself in the exchanges as a real person; Sybil showed me that someone can inspire confidence as being honest and genuine, without revealing anything of herself. Yet my personal need was to believe in the other person's reality, before I could believe in my own. I am not suggesting that everyone would have found it as reassuring as I did to know that these were real people, with identities and views of their own, some of which they were prepared to share. But while it is axiomatic that everyone in therapy is likely to benefit from a sense of genuine caring and interest, it is too readily assumed that this can be adequately conveyed by an impassive professional.

As long as I experienced the therapist as an enigmatic and non-communicative stranger, apparently devoid of feelings and normal human responses, I compensated for every moment of unguarded confidence by a period of reticence or devious game-playing, designed to maintain the distance she seemed to want – and having the effect of blocking any progress in therapy for a while. The more I felt secure in the feeling of being accepted as me, not necessarily liked, but responded to as an individual, the more I felt able to explore this self, and its more unsavoury aspects. This acknowledgement by the therapist of my reality was accompanied by the recognition of the reality of our interaction, as opposed to transference fantasies, without denying the presence of transference **attitudes**. Significantly, the element of reality in the relationship was different in each therapy, and the degree of frankness and security with which I explored problems was directly correlated with this; openness on the part of the therapist encouraged a similar attitude in me.

There are also the good moments to be shared. Therapy is not all pain and despair. It makes it much easier to explore delicate areas with someone you trust and like; it is easier to trust and like an equal with whom you have shared jokes, normal exchanges in which both people participate, positive as well as negative feelings. Trust is not readily going to be bestowed on a relative stranger, nor yet an enigmatic individual whose view of us is a matter of pure conjecture.

The quality of the relationship seems to me unquestionably the most valuable part of the experience. It provides the security and motivation indispensable for the more cognitive work in the therapy, and for survival during the really testing moments.

I am not sure if the agony involved in my therapy with Harriet was inevitable, much less therapeutic. But there is no way I would have come through it without a solid bond that had been built up and tested over time. The formation of this bond was in itself an enriching experience, and an important factor in it was my sense of Harriet as a real person, different from my fantasies and so uncontaminated by them. I still feel that only those with a fair amount of emotional resilience, and support in the outside world, between sessions, should embark on such a perilous enterprise. Even if the majority benefit, the dangers are considerable. Having survived, I feel the value of the continued presence of a witness to the period of disaster; someone who can therefore fully appreciate the happiness involved merely in being released from it. There is a very real feeling of sharing in this, which would lose its integrity if we had only shared either positive exploration or trauma.

Psychotherapy is a shared experience; it is a painful exploration two people undergo together. One of the two is more experienced, and needs to remain detached to some extent from the suffering; but this does not imply retaining the aloofness of a superior and less vulnerable being. How is it possible to believe that such a paragon can really understand, or that they will not despise you for your weakness?

The more it was conveyed to me that I was intrinsically a human being with equal rights, merely suffering from the temporary and remediable inequality of being less good at coping, the more I became confident that there might be some hope that I was not condemned to a lifelong inability to cope, but could become equal with other people.

The stress in psychotherapeutic theory and practice needs, I think, to shift from the idea that this is a treatment meted out by a specialist to a sick person, who has no right to question it, to the attitude that this is a co-operative venture between two equals, with the same goal of effectively enhancing the life of the consulter, and freeing him or her from the temporary bond created with the therapist. Stanislas Grof writes:

It should be made clear that in its very nature the psychotherapeutic process is not the treatment of a disease, but an adventure of self-exploration and self-discovery. Thus, from the beginning to the end, the client is the main protagonist, with full responsibility; – the therapist functions as a facilitator. (1985, p. 375)

The value of psychotherapy cannot, of course, be determined piecemeal, with reference to isolated episodes. These only gain significance as part of a developing relationship. Nor can the real benefits, in terms of change, be assessed without a time lapse. There are obviously some instantaneous benefits to be felt during the therapy itself. There may be relief from certain symptoms, gain of cognitive insights and the opportunity to talk on a regular basis with someone about problems that often cannot be discussed with others; with someone who, moreover, is invariably patient, understanding and non-condemning. These benefits are somewhat undermined, however, by only being available in a strictly circumscribed framework, limited to specific hours which are subject to the apparently arbitrary withdrawal through the therapist's holidays and other absences. There are also deleterious effects (generally considered to be temporary), attendant on the breaking down of previous defences and the dependency on the therapist. But the real benefits would seem to become manifest slowly, in the continued growth after the actual therapy has ceased. As Schneiderman says: 'What happens during a psychoanalysis is grasped most truly when the analysis is over' (1983, p. 126).

An analogy may be drawn with the educational process. The real value of what people have learnt in school or at university does not seem to me to be measurable in terms of examination results; nor is it apparent the moment they leave the establishment of learning. Their encounters with others, with ideas and experiences during their time as students gradually filter through into their attitudes towards life and form an ever-expanding consciousness, which has inevitably been modified (and, one hopes, enriched) by their more formal education. So it is with therapy.

CONCLUSION

In much the same way as reading Proust was not just a literary experience, but opened up an entire new vision of the world for me, psychotherapy was not just a talking cure, but opened my eyes and ears to the life inside me and around me. In the end it restored colour and movement to life, though it drained both for a long time.

NOTES

INTRODUCTION

1. For a fuller discussion of this, see Smail (1978, pp. 13–14 and Chapter 3, 'Research in psychotherapy', pp. 45–63).

2. A walk-in day centre, situated in the community and available to all members of the public, who make their own approach. It provides counselling services varying from one meeting to regular sessions with trained staff, not all of whom are psychiatrists or psychotherapists.

3. This phenomenon is mentioned by Turkle (1978) and is the central subject of Tytell (1982); see also Bowie (1987) and Wright (1985).

1/EXPECTATIONS

1. For the concept of the 'corrective emotional experience' or the idea that a good therapeutic experience can undo previous damage, see Alexander (1946; 1957). There is a lucid and interesting discussion of various analysts' attitudes to this in Malcolm (1980, pp. 118 ff.).

2/CHOICE OF THERAPIST

1. For a more detailed presentation of this, see the responses to a questionnaire analysed in *Spinal Injuries in Women* (Women's Editorial Board S.I.A., ed., Spinal Injuries Association and Women's Press, forthcoming).

4/TRANSFERENCE OR UNREALITY

1. For an example of this need for validation of one's views and the denial of it through counter-transference, see Margaret Little's account (1985) of her own analysis with Winnicott.

5/THE THERAPIST AS REAL PERSON

1. Fromm-Reichmann (1950, p. 46) adamantly rebuts the idea that people would really want any non-professional relation with the therapist. Horney (1946, p. 203) mentions the special nature of friendship in psychotherapy, and its limits.

2. Ernst and Maguire (1987, p. 103) discuss the use of the coffee-making equipment in the Women's Therapy Centre. Barnett (1973) considers it important for coffee, as well as help, to be available round the clock, and this attitude is also to be found in R.D. Laing. Little (1985) mentions how Winnicott always offered coffee to her at the end of a session.

9/INTERPRETATION

1. See J.B. Miller (1973), Mitchell (1974), Irigaray (1974; 1977) and Kristeva (1983). See also the pioneering work of Karen Horney (1967).

12/ABSENCE AND LOSS

1. For a categorical statement on this, see Fromm-Reichmann (1950, p. 46).

BIBLIOGRAPHY

All books are published in London unless otherwise indicated.

Alexander, F. (1946) *Psychoanalytic Therapy*. New York: Ronald Press.

—— (1957) *Psychoanalysis and Psychotherapy*. Allen & Unwin.

Arieti, S. and Bemporad, J. (1978) *Severe and Mild Depression*. New York: Basic.

Artaud, A. (1913–48) *Oeuvres complètes*, 13 vols. Paris: Gallimard, vol. 13.

Axline, V.M. (1964) *Dibs: In Search of Self*. Gollancz, 1966; Pelican, 1971.

Balint, M. (1968) *The Basic Fault*. Tavistock.

Barnes, M. and Berke, J. (1973) *Mary Barnes: Two Accounts of a Journey into Madness*. Harmondsworth: Penguin.

Barnett, M. (1973) *People Not Psychiatry*. Allen & Unwin.

Bateson, G. (1972) *Steps to an Ecology of Mind*. Paladin, 1973.

Beckett, S. (1958) *Endgame*. Faber.

Bowie, M. (1987) *Freud, Proust and Lacan: Theory as Fiction*. Cambridge: Cambridge University Press.

Bowlby, J. (1969) *Attachment*, in *Attachment and Loss*, 3 vols. Hogarth and Pelican, 1971. vol. 1.

—— (1973) *Separation*, in *Attachment and Loss*, 3 vols. Hogarth and Pelican, 1975. vol. 2.

—— (1979) *The Making and Breaking of Affectional Bonds*. Tavistock.

Brenner, D. (1982) *The Effective Psychotherapist*. Oxford: Pergamon.

Cardinal, M. (1975) *Les Mots pour le dire*. Paris: Grasset. Pat Goodheart, trans. *The Words To Say It*. Picador, 1983.

—— (1977) *Autrement dit*. Paris: Grasset.

Carentuto, A. (1979) *The Spiral Way: A Woman's Healing Journey*.
  John Shepley, trans. Toronto: Inner City Books, 1986.
Casement, P. (1985) *On Learning from the Patient*. Tavistock.
Cooper, D. (1970) *Psychiatry and Anti-Psychiatry*. Paladin.
—— (1971) *The Death of the Family*. Allen Lane and Pelican, 1972.
Cox, M. (1978) *Structuring the Therapeutic Process*. Oxford: Pergamon.
Dollard, J. and Miller, N.E. (1950) *Personality and Psychotherapy*.
  New York: Yale University Institute of Human Relations.
Dolto, F. (1971) *Le Cas Dominique*. Paris: Editions du Seuil.
Doubrovsky, S. (1977) *Fils*. Paris: Galilée.
—— (1982) *Un amour de soi*. Paris: Hachette.
Ernst, S. and Goodison, L.(1981) *In Our Own Hands*. Women's
  Press.
Ernst, S. and Maguire, M., eds (1987) *Living with the Sphinx: Papers
  from the Women's Therapy Centre*. Women's Press.
Esterson, A. (1970) *The Leaves of Spring*. Tavistock and Pelican,
  1972.
Ferenczi, S. (1950) *Further Contributions to the Theory and Technique of
  Psychoanalysis*. Hogarth.
Ferguson, S. (1973) *A Guard Within*. Chatto & Windus and
  Harmondsworth: Penguin, 1976.
Fingarette, H. (1963) *The Self in Transformation*. New York: Basic.
Fraser, R. (1984) *In Search of a Past: The Manor House at Amnersfield,
  1933–45*. Verso.
Freud, S. (1912) 'Recommendations to physicians practising
  psychoanalysis', in James Strachey, ed. *The Standard Edition of the
  Complete Psychological Works of Sigmund Freud*, 24 vols. Hogarth
  1953–73. vol. 12, pp. 109–20.
—— (1914) 'Remembering, repeating and working through'. *S.E.*
  12, pp. 145–56.
—— (1915) 'Observations on transference love'. *S.E.* 12, pp. 157–71.
—— (1917) *Introductory Lectures on Psychoanalysis. S.E.* 16.
—— (1944) 'Psychoanalysis: Freudian school'. *Encyclopaedia
  Britannica*, pp. 672–4.
Frischer, D. (1977) *Les Analysés parlent*. Paris: Stock.
Fromm-Reichmann, F. (1950) *The Principles of Intensive
  Psychotherapy*. Chicago: University of Chicago Press.
Gellner, E. (1985) *The Psychoanalytic Movement*. Paladin.
Giovacchini, P., ed. (1972) *Tactics and Techniques in Psychoanalytic*

Therapy. Hogarth, Institute of Psycho-Analysis and New York: Aronson, 1975.

Green, H. (1967) *I Never Promised You a Rose Garden*. Pan and New York: Gollancz.

Grof, S. (1985) *Beyond the Brain*. Albany, NY: State University of New York Press.

Guntrip, H. (1975) 'My experience of analysis with Fairbairn and Winnicott', *Int. J. Psycho-Anal.* 2: 145–56.

Halmos, P. (1965) *The Faith of the Counsellors*. Constable.

Hayley, J. (1963) *Strategies of Psychotherapy*. New York: Grune & Stratton.

Herman, N. (1985) *My Kleinian Home*. Quartet.

—— (1987) *Why Psychotherapy?* Free Association Books.

Hildum, D.C. and Brown, R.W. (1956) 'Verbal reinforcement and interviewer bias', *Journal of Abnormal and Social Psychology* 53: 108–11.

Hobson, R.F. (1985) *Forms of Feeling: The Heart of Psychotherapy*. Tavistock.

Horney, K. (1939) *New Ways in Psychoanalysis*. New York: Norton and Norton paperbacks, 1966.

—— (1942) *Self-Analysis*. Routledge & Kegan Paul, 1962.

—— (1946) ed., *Are You Considering Psychoanalysis?* New York: Norton and Norton paperbacks, 1962.

—— (1950) *Neurosis and Human Growth*. New York: Norton, 1980.

—— (1967) *Feminine Psychology*. New York: Norton, 1983.

Huizinga, J. (1949) *Homo Ludens*. Routledge & Kegan Paul.

Irigaray, L. (1974) *Speculum de l'autre femme*. Paris: Editions de Minuit. Gillian C. Gill, trans. *The Speculum of the Other Woman*. Ithaca, NY: Cornell University Press, 1985.

—— (1977) *Ce Sexe qui n'en est pas un*. Paris: Editions de Minuit. Catherine Porter, trans. *This Sex Which Is Not One*. Ithaca, NY: Cornell University Press, 1985.

Jung, C.G. (1921) 'The therapeutic value of abreaction', in H. Read, M. Fordham, G. Adler and W. McGuire, eds *The Collected Works of C.G. Jung*, 20 vols. Routledge & Kegan Paul, 1953. vol. 16, pp. 129–38.

—— (1929) 'The aims of psychotherapy'. *C.W.* 16, pp. 36–52.

Klauber, J. (1986) *Difficulties in the Analytic Encounter*. Free Association Books and Maresfield Library.

Klein, M. (1957) *Envy and Gratitude: A Study of Unconscious Sources.* Hogarth and Institute of Psycho-Analysis, 1980.

Knight, L. (1986) *Talking to a Stranger: A Consumer's Guide to Therapy.* Fontana.

Kohut, H. (1977) *The Restoration of the Self.* New York: International Universities Press.

Kopp, S. (1979) *An End to Innocence.* Macmillan and New York: Bantam Books, 1981.

Kristeva, J. (1983) *Histoires d'amour.* Paris: Denoël.

—— (1987) *Soleil noir: dépression et mélancolie.* Paris: Gallimard.

Lacan, J. (1949 and 1966) *Ecrits I & II.* Paris: Editions du Seuil. Alan Sheridan, trans. *Ecrits: A Selection.* Tavistock, 1977.

Laing, R. (1960) *The Divided Self.* Tavistock and Harmondsworth: Penguin, 1965.

—— (1961) *Self and Others.* Tavistock and Pelican, 1971.

—— (1967) *The Politics of Experience and the Bird of Paradise.* Harmondsworth: Penguin.

—— (1971) *The Politics of the Family.* Tavistock and Pelican, 1976.

Little, M.I. (1985) 'Winnicott: a personal record', *Free Associations* 3: 9–42.

—— (1986) *Toward Basic Unity: Transference Neurosis and Transference Psychosis.* Free Association Books and Maresfield Library.

Lomas, P., ed. (1967) *The Predicament of the Family.* Hogarth.

—— (1973) *True and False Experience.* Allen Lane.

—— (1981) *The Case for a Personal Psychotherapy.* Oxford University Press.

Malcolm, J. (1980) *Psychoanalysis: The Impossible Profession.* Picador and New York: Knopf, 1982.

Marquis, D. (1927) *Archy and Mehitabel.* New York: Doubleday and Faber, 1968.

Mayer, J.E and Timms, N. (1970) *The Client Speaks.* Routledge & Kegan Paul.

Miller, A. (1979) *The Drama of the Gifted Child.* R. Ward, trans. Faber, 1983. Reissued as *The Drama of Being a Child.* Virago, 1987.

Miller, J. Baker. (1973) *Psychoanalysis and Women.* Harmondsworth: Penguin.

Milner, M. (1934) (pseud. Joanna Field) *A Life of One's Own.* Chatto & Windus and Penguin, 1952; Virago, 1987.

—— (1950) *On Not Being Able to Paint*. Heinemann.

—— (1952) 'Aspects of symbolism in comprehension of the not-self', *Int. J. Psycho-Anal.* 33: 181–95.

—— (1969) *The Hands of the Living God: An Account of a Psychoanalytic Treatment*. Hogarth Press, Institute of Psycho-Analysis.

Mitchell, J. (1974) *Psychoanalysis and Feminism*. Harmondsworth: Penguin.

Nielsen, N. (1960) 'Value judgements in psychoanalysis', *Int. J. Psycho-Anal.* 41: 425–39.

Nin, A. (1966) *Journals*, vol. 1, *1931–4*. Quartet, 1973.

Oldfield, S. (1983) *The Counselling Relationship*. Routledge & Kegan Paul.

Perlman, H.H. (1979) *Relationship: The Heart of Helping People*. Chicago: University of Chicago Press.

Plath, S. (1963) *The Bell Jar*. Faber, 1966.

Pratt, J.W. and Mason, A. (1981) *The Caring Touch*. Heyden.

Racker, H. (1968) *Transference and Counter-Transference*. Hogarth, Institute of Psycho-Analysis.

The Radical Therapist Inc. (1974) *The Radical Therapist*. Harmondsworth: Penguin.

Reed, D. (1976) *Anna*. Harmondsworth: Penguin, 1977.

Reik, T. (1936) *Surprise and the Psychoanalyst*. Routledge & Kegan Paul.

Rogers, C. (1951) *Client-Centered Therapy*. Constable.

—— (1961) *On Becoming a Person: A Therapist's View of Psychotherapy*. Constable.

—— (1969) *Encounter Groups*. Allen Lane and Pelican, 1973.

—— (1980) *A Way of Being*. Boston: Houghton Mifflin.

Rossner, J. (1983) *August*. New York: Warner.

Rousseau-Dujardin, J. (1980) *Couché par écrit*. Paris: Galilée.

Rycroft, C., ed. (1966) *Psychoanalysis Observed*. Constable and Pelican, 1968.

—— (1985) *Psychoanalysis and Beyond*. Chatto & Windus and Hogarth.

Sandler, J., Dare, C. and Holder, A. (1973) *The Patient and the Analyst: The Basis of the Psychoanalytic Process*. Allen & Unwin.

Schatzmann, M. (1980) *The Story of Ruth*. Harmondsworth: Penguin.

Schneiderman, S. (1983) *Lacan: The Death of an Intellectual Hero*.

Cambridge, MA: Harvard University Press.

Schreiber, F.R. (1973) *Sybil*. Harmondsworth: Penguin, 1974.

Searles, H. (1979) *Counter-Transference and Related Subjects*. New York: International Universities Press.

Sèchehaye, M.A. (1950) *Journal d'une schizophrène*. Paris: Presses Universitaires Françaises.

Shaffer, P. (1973) *Equus*. Harmondsworth: Penguin, 1977.

Skynner, R. and Cleese, J. (1983) *Families and How to Survive Them*. Methuen.

Smail, D.J. (1978) *Psychotherapy: A Personal Approach*. Dent.

—— (1987) *Taking Care: An Alternative to Therapy*. Dent.

Steinzor, B. (1968) *The Healing Partnership*. Secker & Warburg.

Storr, A. (1979) *The Art of Psychotherapy*. Secker & Warburg and Heinemann.

Strupp, H., Fox, P. and Lessler, V. (1969) *Patients View Their Psychotherapy*. Baltimore, MD: University of Johns Hopkins Press.

Sullivan, H.S. (1953) *The Interpersonal Theory of Psychoanalysis*. New York: Norton.

Sutherland, S. (1976) *Breakdown*. Weidenfeld & Nicolson.

Suttie, I. (1935) *The Origins of Love and Hate*. Routledge & Kegan Paul.

Symington, N. (1986) *The Analytic Experience: Lectures from the Tavistock*. Free Association Books.

Szasz, T. (1963) 'The concept of transference', *Int. J. Psycho-Anal.* 44: 432–43.

—— (1965) *The Ethics of Psychoanalysis*. Routledge & Kegan Paul, 1974.

—— (1973) *The Second Sin*. Routledge & Kegan Paul, 1974.

Turkle, S. (1978) *Psychoanalytic Politics: Freud's French Revolution*. New York: Basic and Deutsch, 1979.

Thompson, C. (1964) *Interpersonal Psychoanalysis: Selected Papers*, M. Green, ed. New York: Basic.

Tytell, P. (1982) *La Plume sur le divan*. Paris: Aubier-Montaigne.

Walrond-Skinner, S. (1986) *Dictionary of Psychotherapy*. Routledge & Kegan Paul.

Watkins, J.G. (1978) *The Therapeutic Self*. New York: Human Sciences.

Welwood, J., ed. (1983) *Awakening the Heart: East–West Approaches* to *Psychotherapy and the Healing Relationship*. Boulder, CO: New Science Literature, Shambala and Routledge & Kegan Paul.

Weyergans, F. (1973) *Le Pitre*. Paris: Gallimard.

Wiley, J., ed. (1966) *Psychotherapy and the Psychology of Behavior Change*. New York: Goldstein, Seckrest, Heller.

Winnicott, D.W. (1953) 'Transitional objects and transitional phenomena', *Int. J. Psycho-Anal.* 34: 77–89.

—— (1958) *Collected Papers: Through Paediatrics to Psychoanalysis*. Tavistock.

—— (1965) *The Maturational Processes and the Facilitating Environment*. Hogarth and Institute of Psycho-Analysis.

—— (1971) *Playing and Reality*. Tavistock and Pelican, 1974.

—— (1972) 'Fragment of an analysis' in Giovacchini, ed. (1972) pp. 445–693.

—— (1977) *The Piggle*. Harmondsworth: Penguin.

Wright, E. (1985) *Psychoanalytic Criticism*. Methuen.

INDEX

190, 191, 204–5; on validity of
patient's viewpoint 169, 204–5
love as 'agape' not 'eros' 206

Malcolm, J. 22, 25, 32, 45, 61, 64,
229, 246n.
Mayer, J.E. and Timms, N. 4–5, 16
Milner, M. 9, 144
Minnesota Multiphasic Personality
Inventory 4
mother: absences of 215, 217, 219,
220; and birth 227; as false image
80, 91; gifts from 136–7; and
greed 172–3; identification of
therapist with 87, 92, 94–5, 98;
lack of affection from 194, 207;
and her need to be mothered 123,
201; relationship with 36, 42, 44;
silences of 182; in transference
87–90, 214

National Health Service 34, 57, 65,
193, 212
Nerval, G. 177
non-directive psychotherapy 13, 27,
83, 114, 164
non-verbal communication 81–3, 86,
115–16, 134–5, 137, 185, 193,
228

Oedipal interpretations 73, 78, 166–7
Oldfield, S., see Isis Centre
Orbach, S. 42, 230

patient, see 'consulter'
penis-envy, see feminist concept of
Primal Scream therapy 12
problem-solving therapy 25–6, 50
projection 81, 87, 100, 104–5, 125,
159; theory of 73–8
Proust, M. 52, 245
psychiatrists: and human warmth

195–6; and negative transference
77; practical help from 96; and
unconditional positive regard
113–14
psychotherapy, definition of 12–14,
21

Racker, H. 99, 165–7, 179
radical therapy 5, 54
Rapaport, D. 22
regression 30, 101, 128, 182, 217,
222–3
research on effectiveness of
psychotherapy 3–6, 22, 25, 26–8,
239
resistance 60, 62–3, 147, 165, 169
Rogers, C.: and alternative to
transference 100–1; on
client-centred therapy 27–8, 55–6
(see also client-centred therapy);
on laughter in therapy 141; and
non-directive statements 164; on
testing of results 3–4, 5, 22, 28,
239; and therapist's silence 186;
on unconditional positive regard
111–12, 114–15

Samaritans: availability on phone 57,
212; flexibility of 57; help from
88, 96, 196–7; home visits by 213;
and provision of coffee 106 (see
also coffee)
Schneiderman, S. 5, 10, 13–14, 51–2,
58–9, 174, 244
Sèchehaye, M.A. 9, 229
self-disclosure by therapist:
experienced as helpful 74, 79, 86,
101–2, 216–17; of feelings
119–21, 122–4, 128–30; of
information 121, 124–7, 211–12;
veto against 73–6
sessions: frequency of, conflicting
with needs 54–5; providing
insight 36–7; providing intensity

This first edition of
CONSUMING PSYCHOTHERAPY
was finished in March 1988.

It was set in 10/13pt Plantin
on a Linotron 202 and
printed on a Miller TP41 offset-litho press
onto Supreme antique wove 80g/m^2/vol. 18. paper.

The book was commissioned by Robert M. Young,
edited by Ann Scott,
copy-edited by Derek Derbyshire,
designed by Carlos Sapochnik,
and produced by Selina O'Grady
and David Williams for
Free Association Books.